Fight
Like a Girl
...and Win

Fight
Like a Girl
...and Win

◄ Defense Decisions for Women ►

Lori Hartman Gervasi

ST. MARTIN'S GRIFFIN
New York

www.stmartins.com

Library of Congress Cataloging-in-Publication Data

Gervasi, Lori Hartman.
    Fight like a girl—and win : defense decisions for women /
Lori Hartman Gervasi.—1st ed.
      p. cm.
    Includes bibliographical references.
    ISBN-13: 978-0-312-35772-6
    ISBN-10: 0-312-35772-9
      1. Women—Crime against—Prevention. 2. Women—
Violence against—Prevention. 3. Self-defense for women.
4. Safety education.
    HV6250.4.W65 G516 2007
    613.6'6082—dc22

                          2007017216

First Edition: September 2007

10 9 8 7 6 5 4 3 2 1

Author's Note

All of the names have been changed. This book is for informational purposes only. It should not be deemed advice for any particular individual or situation. Circumstances that may call for self-defense vary as to the setting and the capabilities of the attacker and the defender, and the laws on permissible self-defense vary from jurisdiction to jurisdiction. As a result, neither the publisher nor the author shall be liable for any injuries arising to the reader or others from the use of any of the self-defense techniques described in this book. Further, Web sites may have changed or disappeared between when this book was written and when it is read. The fact that an organization or Web site is referred to as a citation and/or a potential source of further information does not mean that the author or the publisher endorses the information the organization or Web site may provide or recommendations it may make.

For the good guys:

Frank, Tyler, and Lucas

No weapon turned against you shall succeed.

—ISAIAH 54:17

Contents

PART II
Mental Decisions

PART III
Physical Decisions

Acknowledgments

This book has come about because of the efforts of some wonderful people. With much gratitude, I offer them my deepest thanks.

To my literary agent, Stephany Evans of the Imprint Agency, Inc., thank you for putting your trust in me and for believing in this book from the beginning.

This experience has been one of enrichment, productivity, and great joy due to the diligent efforts of my editor, Regina Scarpa. Thank you, Gina, for your insights, talents, and excellent capabilities. Your role in this project has meant everything to me.

I am very grateful to each member on the staff of professionals at St. Martin's Press who contributed his or her skills in order to produce this book. My appreciation extends to Matthew Shear, Colleen Schwartz, Frances Sayers, Peggy Lindgren, and to others who helped with the book, including Heather Florence. And a special thank-you to Diane Reverand for her efforts on my behalf.

I am indebted to Laura Taylor and all that she brought to this project. Thank you for sharing your experience as a multi-published author and for your generous contributions as my freelance editor, instructor, and friend. My gratitude goes out to those affiliated with the Santa Barbara Writers Conference, including founders Barnaby and Mary Conrad, director Marcia Meier, and instructors Cork Millner and Marla Miller.

My high regard and gratefulness extend to Sensei Chris Pellitteri for his rigorous training sessions and knowledgeable instruction of the martial arts. Your support and encouragement have been a gift. Thank you, Sensei Raymond Hoyt, for introducing me to karate and for your insightful teachings along the way. Sensei Martin Dickey, without your discussions about women's personal security issues, these defense decisions would never have been elaborated upon. I thank each one of my fellow karate students, especially my friend Sensei Ronda Navarette, for the numerous hours we shared training, practicing, studying, and mutually appreciating the martial arts.

My heartfelt gratitude goes to Edie and Pete Happe. Thank you for touching my heart and for sharing Roberta's story with all of us.

I am blessed to have terrific friends who were willing to listen, read, critique, research, inspire, share, and offer their talents on my behalf. Thank you, Tamara Jones, Kelli Power, Pam Galli, Dana Gerken, Nancy White, Laurie Gordon, Maureen Dresner, Carroll Skelton, Pam Keehn, Shelley Patterson, and Julie Nauroth. I'm also grateful to Greg and Michelle Ellis, Yvonne Iruke, Stephanie Brady, and Shelly Gervasi. Thank you for your creative talents, Annabel Lopez, John Gordon, and James Duffin II. I appreciate the help I received from Sheriff's Deputies Joseph and Loreen Rosalez. And much thanks to Jennifer Gay Summers, whose friendship I cherish and whose writing I admire.

To my father, Robert Hartman, thank you for your inspiration and the gift of a fighting spirit. To my mother, Yvonne Hartman, you are a true expert in the things that matter most—listening, loving, and being there. I extend gratitude to my sister, Cindie Masui, and her family, Glenn, Megan, and Jennifer, whose encouragement for this book has been unwavering.

To my amazing husband, Frank, and our wonderful sons, Tyler and Lucas, thank you for all of your love and support. You are the best.

I am so obliged to each woman who was willing to reveal her personal experiences on behalf of this project. May your stories keep others safe.

Fight
Like a Girl
...and Win

Introduction

On the playground of my elementary school, the fistfights used to break out over things like a push, a dirty look, an angry word, or someone's attempt to cheat at dodgeball. Usually, a few boys instigated the scuffle, but before long every kid in the school would gather to witness the two of them as they duked it out. One time I heard someone heckle from the sidelines, "You fight like a couple of girls!" That comment was quite possibly the most damaging blow of the whole day. A direct hit to the nose couldn't have done more destruction.

It's been a long time since I've witnessed one of those schoolyard battles, but that remark still resonates in my mind. I now know that fighting like a girl is anything but negative. Quite the contrary, it is a massive, potent power that I've come to admire and embrace in my own life. I also recognize that power in others. I've seen the unique ways in which women are naturally able to fend for themselves. But women require knowledge and encouragement in this area. We need to be reminded of our innate talents for survival. We need to dive deep within ourselves and summon to the surface the subtle truths we've always known but have never before utilized. We need to learn more, decide more, and put more of our abilities into position on the front line of our own self-defense.

We have to decide that we won't be vulnerable and defenseless, and we need to choose to fight for our lives.

To fight like a girl is to wage a war by using our innate female skills. Our personal arsenals are stocked with qualities such as quick thinking, decisiveness, intelligence, and finesse in dealing with people. We use our minds. We analyze. We carefully observe and draw conclusions. We size things up. We think on our feet. We prepare. We use intuition to our advantage. We manipulate and compel. We talk a mean streak. Heck, we *have* a mean streak. We get those gut feelings. Deep down inside, we know when something is about to go down. We just do. We outwit our opponents. We go ballistic. We know who we are.

This is a book about preparing for the worst. Thankfully, most of you will never experience in the real world the threats described in the following pages. Some of you will adopt the advice you find here, apply it to your lives, and watch it go to work for you immediately, often in mysterious ways. Others will ward off would-be attackers without even realizing you've done so. Unfortunately, statistics indicate that every two and a half minutes, someone is raped or sexually assaulted in this country. Some of you will encounter attacks, violent or otherwise, and after reading this book, you will have the vital tools you need to deal with those assaults in a fast, decisive, and fully defensive manner. It is impossible to know which group you may fall into one day, so it's a good thing that you're reading this book.

Preparing for the worst doesn't mean living in fear, being paranoid, or dwelling on the dreadful things that could happen to us. The concept is simple and straightforward—we take the time now, in a quiet moment on an uneventful day, to consider an unpleasant situation, knowing that someday, in the midst of danger, our bodies will know exactly what to do.

For years I have been on an empowering journey preparing to fight like a girl. After graduating from UCLA's Television/Film School, I began employment as a journalist at television stations in

Los Angeles, and I enjoyed an eleven-year career working mostly as a newswriter and producer. I also appeared on air as a weather-caster and as a cohost for *Jack LaLanne and You*. I married and gave birth to a son. When my second son was born, I quit working in order to be a full-time mom.

It was then that I enrolled in a karate class. I was hooked from that first training session. I began to practice diligently at home in between class sessions. As time passed my husband transformed our garage into my own private dojo (karate studio) with carpet on the floor, a heavy bag, a huge mirror, and all of my weapons hanging on the wall. Every morning for several years, I spent two or three hours in my dojo while the rest of the family was still asleep.

I studied a style of karate called Traditional American Karate, which is a linear "hard" karate style (with blocks, chops, punches, and kicks) based on conventional methods such as Okinawan Shorin-Ryu, Japanese Shotokan, and others. It took me seven and a half years to progress to the black belt level. I performed various drills and exercises. I studied dozens of katas. I padded up and sparred with other students on the mat. I learned to use weapons such as the bo (a tall wooden staff), the escrima (a pair of light-weight sticks), the sai (a pair of pronged, twenty-inch-long spears), the swords, the nunchaku (usually pronounced "nunchucks," which is one set of double wooden sticks connected by a cord), and others. I broke bricks and wood with my hands and forearms. My favorite part of class was when we worked on self-defense techniques. One person (the uke) would attack while the other person (the tori) would defend. Then we'd switch roles. We studied hundreds of self-defense techniques at our dojo in this manner.

Webster's describes self-defense as "the right to defend oneself with whatever force is reasonably necessary against actual or threatened violence." What does this mean for you and me? How does it apply to women who are just trying to get around safely in the world these days?

It's up to you. You need to do whatever it takes, using whatever force is reasonably necessary.

In the martial arts world, there are various ways that instructors break down the concept of self-defense. Teachers often invent their own insightful definitions to share in the dojo. Some call self-defense an attitude or a lifestyle. They might describe the quiet warrior approach to life that holds a mysterious power of keeping attackers away.

Two of my instructors broke it down to these main components. One taught that self-defense was 90 percent *common sense*. Another described self-defense as 90 percent *awareness*.

Each of these definitions is truly correct, providing an excellent route to achieving increased personal safety. But if you combine these two elements, common sense and awareness, you can take your security measures to new heights and bring about your greatest potential for invulnerability yet. When called to the front line of your defense system, this combination becomes your most efficient ally. Common sense allows you to evaluate situations with intelligence and clarity, discerning what is reasonably necessary in danger. Awareness gives you a mindful perception and intuition beyond your normal senses.

Now let's do the math. Ninety percent is huge, definitely the majority, but unfortunately it's not the whole banana. It's not enough to save our lives every time. There is still that remaining 10 percent that needs to be dealt with. The 10 percent zone is where the sheer craziness goes down, when the absolute unexpected occurs, when the bad guy pops out of the bushes or shows up at your doorstep and manages to push his way into your entry hall. The 10 percent zone is where, no matter what you were doing right in your life to be prepared, safe, smart, aware, and assertive, *something happened anyway.*

Once in a while, my sensei (karate instructor) would grow very quiet before imparting the following tidbit of profound knowledge: "Sometimes," he would say, looking deep into his students' eyes, "sometimes, you're just screwed." Okay, so it's not exactly a quote that Zen masters would jot down for later haiku, bow over, or clink a teacup to. But boy, does it smack of realism and truth. Sometimes you are just totally screwed! If a bullet is flying out of the barrel of a gun from ten feet away and heading straight for your nose, guess what? You're screwed! If six guys ambush you on the street, knock you senseless with a baseball bat, and drag you off into their car, you are most definitely screwed. This is the harsh reality of self-defense and that unpredictable, sometimes inescapable 10 percent zone. You can't possibly be safe 100 percent of the time. None of us ever will be.

That's exactly why we'll be learning to fight like a girl every second of every day. Before you're screwed. Before the guy with the loaded gun gets within ten feet of your nose. Before the six guys even think about choosing you as their victim. Before things get ugly.

This book does not contain pictures of people in frozen fighting positions with stances, punches, kicks, and takedowns. If I gave you the definition of a roundhouse kick, described its force and how it should be initiated and carried out, then showed pictures displaying this kick, much time and practice would still be required to perform a good one, especially without the benefit of an instructor's guidance. We're talking years here. You would need to practice your roundhouse kick alone several thousand times in order to strike properly with your foot. Then you would need to practice with an opponent another several thousand times in order to study the effects of distance and timing. You would try to hit a specific target with the kick a few thousand times more. As your practices continued, you would discover where the energy for an effective roundhouse kick originates, from your flow of force (your ki), which is deep inside you. You would need decades to perfect your roundhouse kick as all students of karate do. Right now, in various parts of the world, there are ninety-year-old masters of the martial arts still working on the kicks they learned in the earliest days of their journey. No matter how skilled they are, their practice on the basics continues forever. Despite the magnificence of their kick's execution, their goal of perfection is never to be attained.

You and I are on a different journey. Yes, this journey will require muscle and movement. It will take power, speed, and action, but I'm confident that you will learn never to let your opponent get far enough in his planned assault to get close to you. As one of my senseis put it, "If you ever find yourself in a full-blown fight, there's a good chance you made a mistake in the very recent past. You seriously blew it ten minutes ago or two minutes ago or twenty seconds ago. You missed a clue. Something got by you. Someone got through."

After reading this book, you may feel compelled to develop your physical preparedness more fully. For this, I highly recommend a self-defense course or a martial arts school. There you can start at the beginning and work on the marvelous techniques we'll only be able to touch on here. Studying karate has been one of the greatest highlights of my life. Not only is it a complete blast, it is empowering stuff, great exercise, and a wonderful path for self-improvement. In many ways, karate has changed me inside and out. It's given me intensity, strength, focus, and confidence. It's heightened my curiosity and improved my mind.

With almost 2.5 million women victimized in personal crimes each year, you may not feel as if you have ten or fifteen years to invest in a martial arts school. Perhaps you're planning a move to the city or going off to college or just trying to safely navigate the parking garage after dark. You need a plan of action right now. With this book you can begin to jump-start your personal security program, regain your individual space, take control in threatening situations, and effectively govern your own body always. But you need to get organized. You need a battle plan. You need to make some decisions about your life and your safety. You need to start fighting like a girl. This journey begins with your mind.

PART I

Get Your Guard Up

In ancient times skillful warriors first made
themselves invincible, and then watched
for vulnerability in their opponents.

SUN TZU,
THE ART OF WAR

◄ 1 ►

THE FIGHTER WITHIN
Set Your Boundaries

Fortune favors the audacious.

ERASMUS

I am a fighter. I have a fighting spirit. This realization came to me after I'd been a student of karate for quite some time, while applying the ideals, techniques, and disciplines of the martial arts to my life.

One day my father and I were visiting when he asked how my training was going.

"Great!"

"Well, you were always the fighter, weren't you?" He smiled, acting as if that were a good thing.

We laughed together although I wasn't sure which memory he was recalling. Was it when I leveled the biggest boy in the school after he'd been harassing me? The time I grabbed some punk by the collar of his shirt and slammed him against the railing of a dock because he'd spit on me? Or was it the incident during which I went after a man with a pair of scissors because he'd stolen fifty dollars from me?

Yes, I am a fighter.

And I have boundaries. My line of defense is a border around me, colored in deep black. Inside that line, it's *my* rules. When someone tries to cross this line, it's obvious: I see it, I feel it, and I'm well aware that it's time to get busy. I'll do anything to secure that line. I'll move. I'll get completely out of the situation. I'll take off running if the need arises. I'll shout. I'll get everyone's attention. I'll immediately let him know that he's stepping past a boundary line, that he's off-limits, treading into sacred territory—*my* territory. Yes, I have boundaries. Nobody stalks me without my response. Nobody invades my personal space. Nobody touches me. Nobody persists or pushes me when I've dismissed them or said, "No, thank you." Nobody makes off-color remarks or speaks in a way that makes me uncomfortable. If they try, I'm on the move and out of there. My boundaries keep me safe. Because I know exactly where they are, I have never doubted myself or hesitated when the moment has come to start swinging.

My inner fighter is often visually manifested. Others perceive it as confidence, discipline, boldness, or something weird or wacky that they can't quite put their finger on. This fighting spirit has the potential to change the dynamics in a room filled with people. I've noticed that there are some who become uncomfortable around it while others bask in the glow.

Most of us would prefer not to think about the bad things in life, about anything sick or evil happening to us or to one of our children. We would rather not contemplate the thousands of monsters lurking in our world. But no matter what we choose to think, the truth is that predators are everywhere—they walk freely among us. Then, one day, it's too late. A woman who never thought about threats or attacks discovers her mind has gone blank, her lungs are deprived of oxygen, and her body has stopped moving. Quite simply, she just doesn't know what to do. She's paralyzed.

Every day I allow the monsters to emerge from the back of my mind.

I see one who comes after me with fierce determination. Because

I'm a woman, and smaller than him, he wants to prey on what he believes are my vulnerabilities. He wants to slap me silly, torture me, and kill me. He wants to drag me off into the brush and leave me for dead. He wants all of my possessions. He wants me to pay for his pathetic life, or for all the women who did him wrong, or for the love he never received at home. He wants to punish me for the sins of total strangers. He expects me to do penance for things I will never begin to know or understand about him. He doesn't know me, but he intends to leave me maimed or so psychologically damaged that I will never reclaim myself or my life. My husband would be left with a basket case for a wife. My kids would never again recognize their mother. But the monster doesn't care. He has urges. He needs a victim. He needs a woman, any woman. He doesn't care who she is. But I do.

I've worked on the moment mentally and physically. When my girlfriends were hanging out and going out for dinner, I was moving in a sequence, thinking of this moment. When my family was watching television, I was visualizing this scene.

When the day arrives, my biggest advantage is that the monster is unaware that I've seen him coming for years.

Something is wrong. Someone has crossed that line—the one that defines *my* space. There is a quick movement, the softest sound, an inappropriate word, an overt action. Something doesn't compute. Something doesn't belong here in this fragment of my life right now. My head whips around. My eyes are open. My ears perk up. I'm all-seeing, all-knowing. I am breathing. I am a force. Immediately, I embrace the presence of adrenaline and fear. All at once, I feel a relentless desire to win, a deep love for life, the clear knowledge of my decisions, and the power of my abilities. These qualities are my greatest allies. I've already moved, and he's only just advancing on me. I've already made noise. It is the guttural sound of a vicious dog. I block out his commands. I don't listen or respond to monsters. I am in control. I am active and in the game. His superior strength fails to stop me—I don't have time to stop. His weapon, his size, the attack itself, and the shock of it all: none of these gives the monster the control he so desperately wants. He is incapable of controlling anything, even his screwed-up life. That's why he's here in the first place.

I'm in control. And, thank God, I'm totally out of control. I'm completely nuts. And that's exactly where I need to be in order to survive.

Everything I've ever learned comes to me in a brilliant flash. I recall the weapons I possess, body parts, and objects that are stashed on me and around me. There are several. They are perfectly wicked things, each one able to maim, or even kill, in a smooth, sweeping blow. I feel only my energy, the intensity of the goal, and the depth of strength necessary to win this battle. I consider the fighter within me. She is huge now. She is a massive explosion, the biggest thing I've ever known.

The truth of it is this: when it comes down to the monster who confronts me in the middle of this horrific moment, I am the more brutal animal.

I'm the monster now.

I am a fighter. Are you?

In order to set your boundaries, you'll have to go deep inside yourself to the fighter within. Here are ways to accomplish this:

- Realize who you are and the strength you possess.
- Think continually about your well-being.
- Access your ability to perceive threats.
- Always be aware of your environment and your option to change locations.

- Regard yourself as an individual of mobility, energy, and determination.
- Be on the watch for suspicious activity and impending danger.
- Look for predators in every situation.
- Don't allow yourself to be the target of verbal intimidation.
- Never endure a physical threat against your body.
- Stay on guard, on top of your safety concerns, and one step ahead of the bad guy.
- When things are going wrong, go somewhere else, and go fast.
- Decide to call upon the fighter within.

◄ 2 ►

GIVE YOURSELF
PERMISSION

**There are only two powers in the world:
the sword and the mind. In the long run, the
sword is always defeated by the mind.**

NAPOLEON

Picture this: a cross between Kirk Douglas in *Spartacus* and the guy on the Mr. Clean bottle minus the earring. That was my dad thirty-five years ago when he gave me the gift of a fighting spirit.

My father served in the Naval Reserves and the Army. While working Army counterintelligence in Japan at the end of the Korean War, he studied judo, received a black belt, and went on to travel with a Japanese judo exhibition team. When he returned to Southern California, he worked as an officer for the Burbank Police Department. Later, he joined the California Highway Patrol. By the time he retired from the CHP, he was one of the chiefs in the state. Every day I watched that man strap on a gun and head out to work. On Saturdays, he woke up everyone in the house with patriotic marching band music blasting from the stereo. He exercised daily by jogging and lifting weights. To this day, he remains one of the most disciplined and physically fit individuals I've ever known.

When I was young and my dad and I passed in the hallway at home, he'd stop, spread out his feet, tense up his stomach, and order me to punch him. "Hit me!" he'd growl with his arms to his sides, providing an open target. I'd usually stop just for a moment to throw a punch or two. "Harder!" he'd say. Or, "Ah, come on! Hit me like you mean it!" I thought this kind of thing was happening between fathers and daughters throughout the whole country until my girlfriends happened to witness a few of these encounters and I saw the confusion on their faces. After a while, it became clear that Dad was doing this not only for my benefit, but to flaunt his rock-hard stomach muscles. Nonetheless, it got me punching.

The true impact of this punching ritual wasn't fully realized until years later, when I developed the desire for self-protection. The fact that Dad absolutely demanded that I slug him on a regular basis was all the permission I would ever need to turn around and actually use that skill on anyone who posed a threat to me. If I could punch my dad like that, I could certainly punch some slimeball coming across my personal boundary line, invading my space, and breaking a couple of my rules.

For many women, permission to hit, kick, or fight does not come naturally. But it is crucial. Permission is the powerful starting point, the door swinging wide open for the many decisions that follow. Permission is what allows us the absolute freedom to engage in a fight in order to save ourselves. No woman should hesitate to give this personal consent to herself, her friends, or her loved ones.

The day arrived when it was time for me to put my punch to the test. I'd never had a problem sticking up for myself against bullies, but this time I was truly scared. It was the sixth grade, and it wasn't just any bully. It was the biggest boy in the entire school who was pushing me around. Every day during P.E., he would throw me on the ground, trip me, or kick me. It's possible he was teasing me just to get my attention, but his size and strength made this kind of play extremely rough and frightening. I hadn't tried to defend myself, because he was so darn huge. Even all the boys were afraid of him. But I knew I had to put a stop to this constant abuse, so I went home and talked it over with my dad. He listened quietly to my problem and then responded, "Lori, I've watched you sock that tetherball out in the backyard every afternoon for a few years straight. You can really hit that thing with power! So here's what you do. When that boy bothers you the next time, you wait for him to turn his back. With that same tetherball punch [which I now know is a hammer fist], you strike him as hard as you can right to the middle of his back. He won't bother you after that."

The very next day, that boy pushed me to the ground. He immediately turned his back on me and started to walk away. I picked myself up, chased him down, got close enough to strike, and then I slammed him with my fist hammer-style in the middle of his back like there was no tomorrow. I remember thinking, "I'd better make this good, or he's really going to come after me!" Then, to my utter amazement, I watched the biggest kid in school go face-down like a ton of bricks. I'd knocked the wind completely out of him. That's when I turned and ran for my life. Dad was right. That guy never bothered me again. In fact, he didn't even make eye contact with me for about five years.

This is a typical guy story. Almost every man has one like it in his memory bank—the day he finally stuck up for his rights and gave some bully the well-deserved black eye. Boys are often quite young when they are given permission, even detailed instruction on exactly how to defend themselves. It's not quite as common for a girl to physically defend herself against the school-yard bully alone. Often the girl will tell her parents or report the incident to a teacher or principal. Subsequently, the adults resolve the matter for her. At the end of the school day, the girl has learned a dangerous lesson, one that can cripple her defenses and bring about serious, or perhaps even fatal, consequences later in life: when it comes to personal safety, get help from someone else.

Before I studied karate, there were several times during which I found myself in threatening situations with men. In every case, because I'd already given myself permission, I chose to act in wildly aggressive ways in order to put a stop to the man's actions. Since studying karate, I've never actually had to employ a kick, a punch, a controlling hold, a takedown, or any other tactic against another person in self-defense. My sensei said this is common. "Once you study the martial arts, you often find you will never have to use them." No doubt he was speaking of the physical application. I use lessons learned in the martial arts almost every day, keeping potentially threatening situations in check, so they won't advance to the level of a physical fight. The attitude of confident preparedness, the heightened awareness, and the demeanor—all are powerful tools. But so is the obvious determination of a woman who's given herself permission to save her own life at any cost.

These days, self-protection is essential, but few women have been brought up to give it due consideration. It's likely they don't know what on earth they would do with a bad guy on their heels or in their faces. Maybe their fathers didn't give them permission to sock anybody in the stomach or perform the tetherball punch to someone's back. Maybe no one was around to validate their strengths and abilities or to praise their power in this world. Maybe fighting was looked down upon for nice young ladies in their home.

If no one has ever given you permission to embrace your power, you're just going to have to do it yourself.

You will need to give yourself permission to throw a few punches. You will need to allow yourself to fight no matter who is abusing you. You must decide that you are authorized to do whatever it takes to maintain your safety, whether it's abruptly changing locations, running away, insulting a threatening man, or even inflicting physical harm. You must consent to being in control of your own body. Always.

As we embark on this journey together, go ahead and give yourself all the permission you'll ever need to be completely inspired about your personal security. And now give yourself permission to become enraged about the crimes that occur against women. You just might need some of that anger working on your behalf at some point in the future.

KNOW YOUR ENEMY
The Statistics

In order to achieve victory you must place
yourself in your opponent's skin. If you don't
understand yourself, you will lose 100 percent
of the time. If you understand yourself,
you will win 50 percent of the time. If you
understand yourself and your opponent,
you will win 100 percent of the time.

TSUTOMU OHSHIMA,
FOUNDER OF SHOTOKAN KARATE OF AMERICA

In karate class we were instructed to visualize our imaginary opponent. We had to *see* that guy coming after us. As we moved through the sequence of a kata—a form consisting of predetermined combat movements—our eyes were continually directed toward our invisible attacker. We'd often snap our heads around to focus on our opponent as we prepared to counterattack. We stared him down in the middle of absolute nothingness. It was our imaginary opponent who motivated us when exhaustion or discouragement set in. At times we felt like pausing to collect ourselves or to start a technique over from the beginning. But this was never permitted. Even a brief pause was equal to giving up. When it comes to defending ourselves, we can never give up. There are no "do overs" in real fights. You can't say to the bad guy, "Wait a minute, I think I can punch you harder than that." Or, "Turn this way so I can get a better shot at your groin." No matter what, we instantly refocused, reclaimed the moment, and resumed our fight. After all, our imaginary opponent was ready and waiting. We had to go take that guy out.

It's crucial for us to understand our opponents and ourselves in order to win fights, so we need to start to identify this bad guy and who we are in relation to him. With the use of crime statistics, we can catch glimpses of the enemy. We can see how he operates and whom he chooses to victimize. While evaluating these factors, it's important to read between the lines. Pay attention, especially if you recognize yourself or your habits in the data regarding victims. Then watch closely as two distinct images emerge. One is the face of a victim; the other is that of her attacker.

- Statistics show that the hour of the day is a major factor in the type of crime committed against us. In 2005, most violence occurred during the day, between the hours of 6:00 A.M. and 6:00 P.M., but two-thirds of rapes and sexual assaults took place between 6:00 P.M. and 6:00 A.M.

Think about your schedule and the safety measures you employ during the day and at night. Do you take precautions after dark (double-bolt your door, activate the security alarm, lock the windows, and so on), which you don't implement during the day? One of my karate instructors, who was also a law enforcement officer, warned, "Don't let the daylight fool you. Four o'clock in the afternoon is 'golden hour' for criminals targeting victims in suburbs and family neighborhoods. Doors are often unlocked, and kids are running in and out of the house."

- The FBI's 2004 *Crime in the United States* report showed the highest percentage of rapes occurring in the months of March, May, June, July, August, and October.

Warm weather might be part of the reason for the increase of rapes in these months, since women open their windows and doors, providing easy access for attackers. Also, attackers realize there are fewer layers of clothing to rip off victims in the summertime. Do you keep your guard up during the lazy days of summer? Or is your only protection against an intruder a screen door or window?

My mind was forever changed about open windows during the hottest days of a Los Angeles summer in 1985. This was Night Stalker time, when a sadistic, Satan-worshipping home invader named Richard Ramirez molested, raped, mutilated, and murdered dozens of victims. As a television news journalist at the time, I was bombarded with his story, overloaded with the gruesome details, and constantly reminded that his usual mode of entry was through an open or unlocked window. So call it home sweet home, but where you live and spend your time is of major significance to the crimes you could encounter someday.

- The FBI reports more than two million unlawful entries to commit a felony or theft annually. Violent attackers often hit close to home, striking at the respondent's or victim's place of residence almost 15 percent of the time, and near the residence in more than 10 percent of the cases. Other common sites were streets, schools, a friend's home, and parking garages.

Think about the various environments you experience on a regular basis. Is your home as safe as it should be? Are your door and window locks secure? Do you have efficient lighting outdoors? What measures could you employ to increase your security in public places or communal areas? Try implementing a few simple changes. Make a habit of carrying your cell phone whenever you're away from home. Practice heightened awareness by looking around regularly, even checking behind you. Notice the people nearby. Put distance between yourself and any suspicious characters.

- When it comes to rape and sexual assault, more than 36 percent take place at the victim's home, while almost 24 percent take place in the home of a friend, neighbor, or relative. Rapes by intimates (people known to the victim) often take place at or near the victim's home or at a friend's or relative's home. Rapes by strangers often occur in public places, such as streets and schools, but they also take place in homes.

Are you "at ease" or "on guard" when going about your daily routine at home? It's best to be ready for anything, especially in those familiar places where an attacker might think you're relaxed and most vulnerable. When you're out of the house, remember to make personal safety a top priority.

Now consider how you work and play.

- In 2005, more than 16 percent of violent crimes in the United States occurred on the job. According to the Justice Department, the occupations most vulnerable to attacks are police and correctional officers, medical and mental health workers, taxicab drivers, private security workers, teachers, retail sales employees, and bartenders.

Who are you forced to deal with on the job? Does your profession put you in the company of unstable or unsavory individuals? Do you work in isolation? In what ways might you avoid dangerous situations with individuals in the workplace? Are you the lone woman secretary in a warehouse full of men? Or are you a real estate agent obligated to show abandoned homes and buildings to strangers? Everyone from a lecherous boss to a deranged coworker, the latter behaving as though he might "go postal" one day, should be considered a potential threat.

Time away from work is even more dangerous, according to the statistics.

- Leisure activity by victims away from home accounted for 22 percent of violent attacks and 29 percent of rapes and sexual assaults. Activities at home brought about more than 21 percent of violent acts and almost 25 percent of rapes and sexual assaults.

What do you do for recreation? How safe is that environment, and who's keeping company with you? While it's true that being alone is sometimes dangerous, being in the wrong place or around the wrong people can be worse. If you travel for leisure, be sure to stay alert, well informed, and prepared. If you exercise in your free time, try participating with others at the gym. Or join a walking or running group. The bar and nightclub scene is another vulnerable spot for women. It's best to go in groups, to keep an eye on one another, and to limit alcohol intake. Also, be ready with cell phones, knowledge of exit routes, and plans for transportation home.

Think about your ethnic background. According to the experts, most violence remains intraracial among victims and offenders. This is to say, blacks commit crimes against blacks, whites against whites, and so on.

- The Violence Policy Center reports that African-American women are murdered at a rate almost three times higher than white women. More than 48 percent of the rape and sexual assault offenders in 2005 were black men, and almost 33 percent were white. American Indian and Alaskan Native women are more likely to report they were raped than women of other races. Hispanic women are less likely than non-Hispanics to report a rape in their lifetimes.

How does your race factor into your chances for attack? Have you been living under the assumption that an assault would most likely come from an offender of a different race? Be watchful of everyone, including those of your own color and nationality.

To you, it's a mode of transportation. To the thief, it's his goal for the day—to threaten you and make off with your car.

- The Justice Department reports thirty-eight thousand carjackings per year. Ninety-three percent take place in cities and suburbs, 68 percent happen at night; 74 percent of the time weapons are used, and more than half the time multiple attackers work as a team.

So keep your eye on the road or, better yet, on that guy approaching your vehicle. Are you on guard when you're sitting behind the wheel? Are you ready and willing to bolt on foot or use your car as a weapon?

Girl-watching might seem to be a national pastime in the United States, but have you noticed the man who's been watching you or the degree of interest or intensity he is exhibiting as he observes you?

- The National Center for Victims of Crime reports that one in twelve women will be stalked during her lifetime. Of these victims, 77 percent know their stalkers. On college campuses, it's much worse. According to a Justice Department report entitled *The Sexual Victimization of College Women,* 13 percent of female students report being stalked at school. Eighty percent of the victims know their stalkers. Fifty-nine percent of stalked females are victimized by an intimate partner.

Tracy Bahm, the director of the National Center for Victims of Crime's Stalking Resource Center, says, "Most stalkers do not just go away. They stalk for a reason. Either they are planning to commit a further crime . . . like sexual assault, [an]other serious physical assault, or murder; or they are trying to provoke a reaction from the victim." Can you differentiate between admiring glances and serious stalking? Is someone you know the type of man who is capable of stalking you? As you visualize your imaginary opponent, remember that he could be the guy who first observes you before following you home.

Sex crime statistics prompt us to wonder if we should stay out in the open all day long or barricade ourselves in our homes, and to question if we aren't safer with complete strangers than with the people we know and love.

- The FBI reports a forcible rape in this country every five minutes. For more than two decades, experts have either quoted or debated a *Ms.* magazine study estimating that one in four women will be raped in her lifetime. Current statistics estimate that one in six American women has already been the victim of rape or attempted rape. And sadly, the figures become even more horrific with further study. A survey showed that 54 percent of rape and attempted rape victims are under eighteen years of age, while almost 22 percent of those are under the age of twelve.

Considering your gender and age, what are your chances for attack? Sexual assault crimes happen far too often for us to be casual about our security measures. All women need to be prepared.

Now take a closer look at your imaginary opponent. Over and over again, the statistics point to the people we know as our potential attackers.

- More than five million cases of intimate partner violence are carried out against U.S. women yearly. Females are most likely to be attacked by a relative, friend, or acquaintance. Seventy-three percent of rape and sexual assault victims are attacked by non-strangers. In 38 percent of those, the offender is described as a friend, while in 28 percent of those cases, it is an intimate. Of rapes that occur on college campuses, nine out of ten are committed by an individual known to the victim.

After a while the statistics make it hard to differentiate your imaginary opponent from some of the guys with whom you are friends: the man who lives next door, your former boyfriend, or your dad's best friend. But as a sheriff's deputy told me, "Violence is violence. Whether it's a husband beating his wife to death in the kitchen, an ex-lover raping his old girlfriend the day after their breakup, or the total stranger jumping out of the bushes, violence is always still violence."

So how feisty are you? There are encouraging numbers when it comes to self-defense.

- Victims were able to help themselves by using protective measures against violent attackers in more than 64 percent of incidents in 2005. Victims of rape and sexual assault fought back and avoided injury or greater injury in 38 percent of cases. They managed to scare off their attackers over 30 percent of the time, and they escaped in 23 percent of cases.

Assuming these women weren't built like Amazons, trained as professional killers, or swinging machetes at the time of their attacks, this is definitely good news.

Another interesting note. Weapon usage varies by crime.

- Firearms are used in 70 percent of murders. Robberies are more likely to involve an armed assailant (someone with a gun, knife, or blunt object), while rape and sexual assaults are the least likely to have a weapon involved. In 2005, rape and sexual assault victims were confronted by unarmed attackers in 85 percent of the incidents. Knives and firearms were each used 3 percent of the time.

Weapons are so intimidating, the very sight of them can bring almost anyone into instant and total submission. Many bad guys use weapons as "power tools" in order to seize and maintain control. However, there are criminals who will kill you at the drop of a hat. At the time of an attack, it's anyone's guess as to whether the guy will use the weapon to dominate and direct you or to murder you. For the victim there are huge risks either way—whether she complies with his demands or fights to free herself.

In cases of intimate crimes like date or acquaintance rape, weapons are hardly necessary. The rapist is counting on the fact that your relationship, courtship, or friendship allows him closer access to you than a stranger would achieve under similar circumstances. He knows he doesn't need a weapon in order to get into the same room or car as his victim. After all, she's his date, or his friend at the party, or the girl with whom he jogs, or his study partner. Later, in the final moments preceding the rape, he often just uses sheer muscle to overpower her.

In light of all this, take a fresh look at your imaginary opponent. Is he beginning to take shape right before your eyes? Imagine the enemy being someone you know, a person you consider a casual friend, or someone you even care about. Or maybe your attacker *is* a stranger. He could be one of the sexual predators on the street, or he might be a carjacker closing in on you some evening in the suburbs. The thought of a stranger catching you unaware is sickening, isn't it?

Take a moment and picture these scenarios: if a stranger assaulted you, it's likely he'd strike in a public place. If your attacker were an acquaintance, he'd probably try to corner you in or around your home. Go ahead, visualize those places.

From these statistics, the picture of a victim begins to form as well. Yes, she could be anyone in the world. Healthy, sick, weak, strong, big, small, handicapped, young, old, married, single, black, white, rich, poor, nice, mean, rude, shy, educated, or not. If you are a woman, you face a degree of peril unique to your gender. One out of four women raped or sexually assaulted translates into one of the women in the golf foursome at the club, one of the coeds heading off to the dorms, and one of the women in the booth at the restaurant becoming a victim. But there are factors that increase the risk.

The greatest risk factor for rape is to be female, but another high-risk characteristic is to be young. A bad guy is willing to bet that the younger the woman, the easier the target. Heck, she's practically a kid, perhaps out on her own for the first time, with less life experience and little practice dealing with men. Attention from the opposite sex is still new ground for discovery. This happens to be exactly what the rapist is looking for: a hesitant, rather confused target with a lack of firsthand knowledge of men. A young woman can be mighty distracted in the years prior to adulthood. Her mind is on anything and everything except turning around and kicking some guy's teeth down his throat.

Now, add a year or two to our victim's age and put her on a university campus or at a singles club. Pour alcohol down everybody's throats and the experts say the chances of being attacked increase further. In the meantime, every drink she consumes decreases the odds that she can successfully fight off an attacker. Numerous studies warn that if she's hanging out with college fraternity boys or athletes, her vulnerability to sexual attack is even greater. And if she happens to find herself keeping company with a hedonistic creep who has a sexually promiscuous past that includes violence but excludes religiosity, who boasts of hostility toward women but suffers from low self-worth, and whose friends condone aggressive sexual conquests, well, watch out. Better yet, run. Fast.

At least, that's what the statistics say.

Of course, there's always the possibility that the bad guy will be unique and one of a kind. He could totally evade the statistical norms. Now here's something the experts fail to itemize: all attackers *surprise* their victims 100 percent of the time.

If you are ever attacked, you are going to be surprised. It can be one of your assailant's greatest blows against you. The shock of the surprise can feel like a swift kick to your gut. It can knock the wind out of you, turn your knees to jelly, and debilitate you. But here's a piece of good news: surprise works both ways. As you will read in upcoming chapters, we can use surprise anytime to fight like a girl against an attacker.

◄ 4 ►

MEN VERSUS WOMEN

**Men of all ages and in all parts of the world
are more violent than women.**

GAVIN DE BECKER,
THE GIFT OF FEAR

The bad guy is a man.

When it comes to assaults against women, more often than not men are committing the crimes. This fact is proven by the statistics, confirmed by the experts, and discussed by women themselves when they confess their greatest fears.

Year after year, the Bureau of Justice Statistics reports that violence against women is predominantly male violence. Studies and surveys confirm these findings. Research on crimes against women and their attackers has been conducted for decades. Volumes have been written on the male gender with detailed examination of its psyche, biology, and physiology. Analysts could contemplate the aggressive nature of testosterone or the curious characteristics of the Y chromosome until the end of time.

Meanwhile, a woman may watch the evening news, observe the latest wave of violence to hit the television, view the suspect's mug shot, and wonder, "Why? Why is it always some man?" or, "What on earth is wrong with these creeps?" But to waste her energies on questions like these would be ridiculous for the female fighter. What is, simply is. But you can prepare.

If you, on some horrific day, should ever face a brutal attacker, the odds are pretty overwhelming that you will be dealing with a man. Yes, there are exceptions to the rule. Female criminals and con artists rip off people every day. There are female thieves, kidnappers, molesters, murderers, and serial killers. You name it and there's a woman who's done it, and possibly with more barbarism and heartlessness than most of us could even imagine.

But whom do you truly fear? Does the thought of some woman coming after you on a dark night cause you to be terrified? Think back to that imaginary opponent you created in the last chapter. Was the ugly monster you visualized a female? Probably not. Deep down inside, every woman intuitively knows that her biggest threat of physical violence is going to come from a man.

But women have another enemy to contend with, and you may be surprised to learn who this additional adversary is. It's us! By thinking and behaving in certain ways, we cause our own personal security systems to break down on a regular basis. This doesn't mean we should accept the responsibility for men's crimes against us, but we do need to face facts and clear up the misconceptions we have about ourselves.

THE TROUBLE WITH WOMEN

Women often rely on false security measures.

We fool ourselves into thinking that a lock on the door or a walk through the parking lot with a friend equals "safety." Quite often that's the extent of our personal defense plan. Our beliefs about our "nice" neighborhoods full of "decent" people and our "trustworthy" acquaintances give us no reason to worry, let alone think much about matters of safety or preparedness. Besides, aren't our fathers, boyfriends, or husbands supposed to protect us?

Women underestimate their power.

We have countless strengths and abilities that we hardly ever draw upon or give ourselves credit for possessing. We wonder what good our puny efforts would ever accomplish. We don't know how to direct our focus and concentration on moves or abilities that we might need to put into action during a time of potentially critical danger. This isn't the way we were brought up or trained to think. As a result, our personal power is sacrificed.

Women exhibit what they're taught: feminine characteristics and qualities.

Most of us are encouraged to behave like ladies. Throughout our lives we're taught to be submissive, soft, gentle, and kind. Unfortunately, we often end up practicing these attributes so diligently that it leads to our detriment. Because these female traits are deeply embedded in our society and thriving in our communities, workplaces, and homes, we know that acting differently could be weird or strange. We fear that we'll seem too harsh or that we'll even seem masculine. We wonder if it's possible to maintain our feminine characteristics and yet possess the kind of strength and power that sends a forceful message to the world and its attackers.

Women are not usually trained or experienced physical fighters.

While there are a few women who grow up being pounded in the head by their big brothers, the majority of females don't have a clue about how it feels to face a physical opponent. Most of us haven't had the opportunity to pad up and step into the ring for serious, concentrated, hand-to-hand combat. Because of this, many females find it difficult to believe they can actually fight back with any effectiveness. This lack of belief zaps a woman's courage and freezes her physically. The result: she is left utterly defenseless.

Women lack muscle compared to the brawn of men.

We know trouble when we see it, and here is where the odds are heavily stacked against us. It's pretty clear to most women that we are the weaker sex when brute strength and muscle mass are considered. Because our frames are smaller and our bones less sizable and dense, it's hard to believe we could ever stand a chance in a battle with a man. Wouldn't they overpower us in a matter of seconds?

Women tend to be thorough thinkers and emotionally caring and nurturing creatures.

Many of us would rather take the time to be 100 percent certain of a man's suspicious or violent intentions before ever causing embarrassment to ourselves or pain, insult, and humiliation to him. We ponder the situation as it's unfolding rather than instinctively acting on our own behalf and asking questions later. We wait to make sure we're not jumping to conclusions at the expense of another human being's feelings, although he may appear rude, untrustworthy, suspicious, or even dangerous.

Women watch and wait in situations of danger, and then it's too late.

Our skills as spectators are quite remarkable, to such an extent that our lives can often be put in jeopardy. Since most women haven't made all of their defense decisions or practiced instant mobility, they find themselves standing still, simply watching as a crime against them unfolds. And since an attack is always a unique experience, full of surprise and confusion, it's never boring to observe, and the temptation to see what might happen next is enormous. Often, the most action we'll put into these situations is to hope for a good outcome for ourselves. This lack of a response, or lack of a *swift* response, or our absolute stillness places the attacker in the driver's seat, controlling everything. Meanwhile, we shift into the passenger's seat or the backseat and, at worst, into the role of victim.

> **Women believe they do not have the time in their busy schedules to understand and adopt an effective defense plan.**

All that's needed are a couple of hours to mentally and physically educate ourselves on these important issues. The truth is, most of us are so busy, we do not take the time to do so. With our full calendars and daily demands, we wonder what woman has the luxury to set aside time to prepare for something that may very well never happen to her. We believe this preparation is tougher on our schedules than it really is.

> **Women haven't made the necessary lifesaving decisions.**

There are many things we can do to stay safe, but rarely do we stop to consider, explore, or practice the application of these options. Self-defense and fighting in general often remain great mysteries to women. We haven't been prompted to crack the code by thinking truthfully about ourselves and the situations we could someday face. Our safety choices have not been contemplated, nor have we finalized the details of our personal security plans. Translation: we don't know precisely what we would or could do in certain perilous predicaments.

The fact that we are sabotaged by our own misconceptions is bad enough. Now, add men to the equation, along with all their physical powers and abilities. When it comes to protecting ourselves, we really have our work cut out for us.

THE TROUBLE WITH MEN

Men know how to fight.

For the most part, males are natural warriors. This is partly
due to the many inherent characteristics they possess: size,
strength, well-developed muscle mass, physical agility, and often a vast and varied sports history that builds on all of the
above. It's also because they get plenty of practice. Their bodies
act like fighters and move like fighters throughout much of their
lives. As toddlers they scuffle with their friends and punch it
out regularly with their siblings. They play G.I. Joe, spy, karate
ninja, and action-packed video games. When a boy becomes a
teenager, he goes out for football or the wrestling team. Then,
one day, Dad takes him out back to teach him a few self-defense
moves. He puts Junior in a pair of boxing gloves and instructs
him on how to throw a left jab followed by a right cross. It's no
wonder that men have been the ones fighting the wars and protecting the village from invaders throughout the world since
time began. Fighting is in their blood, in their brawn, and in
their bones. And yes, they are very good at it.

Men are strong and can easily inflict pain.

Ladies, just in case you've never been sucker-punched out of
nowhere by some guy, here's a big heads up—fighting hurts!
I discovered this the first night I sparred against a fellow karate
student. I was a brand-new, white-belt novice with absolutely
no clue as to what I was doing. The instructor paired me up
with a huge, strong man with several years' experience under
his brown, soon-to-be black, belt. What ensued was a twenty-
minute sparring match that felt like an eternity. It was a very
humbling experience, to say the least. I remember driving home
that night with my knuckles bleeding, my head pounding, and
my whole body aching and traumatized. A couple of days later,

I had so many black-and-blue marks, my husband questioned the wisdom of my desire to learn karate. Men can possess a shocking amount of strength, but unless that strength has been used against us, we don't always understand or appreciate its force. Our enemy is not puny or pitiful, but one of massive power.

Men are still getting away with murder.

It's amazing to consider some of the actions toward women that continue to occur in our so-called sophisticated culture. Because we display our feminine characteristics (by trying to be nice, polite, ladylike, and understanding, or just hoping we're not disliked by anybody), we often find ourselves the victims of what I call "little assaults" from men. "Little assaults" are the subtle, "innocent," or "accidental" touching that women often endure from strangers in public places. They can also occur in more intimate settings from non-strangers. Such improper advances can be verbal or physical. They include ordeals of sexual harassment on the job. Men who "flash" or expose themselves to women, though never touching them, are committing "little assaults." Even a comment that is intended to keep a woman "down" or "in her place" qualifies as a "little assault." These minor infractions can make a woman wonder if she's some uptight lunatic who's imagining things to be worse than they really are. Most of these don't cause serious harm, but make no mistake, "little assaults" can damage women in a very big way.

THE TROUBLE WHEN MEN FIGHT

When men fight each other, it's ugly. But when a man fights (or attacks) a woman, there's often a jump in the intensity of the situation. While men are sometimes willing to throw punches with other men for a variety of reasons, including competition, ego, or masculine behavior, they won't usually think of doing so with a female opponent. With other men, they fight on the street, in the bar, at a party, on the ball field, or at school. One guy thinks the other guy gave him a weird or threatening look. Someone thinks another guy is ogling his girlfriend. This guy owes that guy money. That guy deliberately shoved him during the game. These men can start out as friends. Or end up as friends.

Their physical altercations can be playful or just plain bizarre, such as one I remember happening years ago.

An old boyfriend of mine named Brad had a big fight on the shoulder of a major freeway in Northern California with some knucklehead that cut us off. Brad gave him a look and the guy forced us off the road and challenged Brad to a fight. Brad got out of the car, the guy took a swing, and Brad proceeded to beat the stuffing out of him in record time. When I finally gave Brad a look that said, "Don't you think he's had enough?" the back of the guy's head had been bashed into his trunk for about the tenth time and his eyes were rolling completely back. So Brad pulled that guy up to his feet, picked up the watch that had fallen off the guy's wrist, and gave it back to him. Then, to my absolute astonishment, they shook hands and even smiled at each other before going their separate ways.

Not always, but sometimes, that is how men fight.

THE TROUBLE WHEN MEN FIGHT WOMEN

When it comes to a man physically fighting a woman, there are three things she can be absolutely sure of:

It is serious.

The bad guy is never scuffling with a woman to prove his manhood or to save face. He doesn't want to fight her over a freeway lane change and smile at her afterward. He doesn't want to shake her hand, either. Something is up, and the stakes are high.

This is not a game or a competition. Any hint of an impending assault is serious business for the female victim. She must critically regard any fight with a man as something that could easily become a life-and-death matter.

He has a goal.

His goal might be to snag her purse or steal her car. He may want to frighten her and assert his control over her. He may want to drag her off somewhere to rape and kill her. His motives may be obvious, as in the case of a purse snatcher, and she might be able to quickly hand over her bag and get away. Or his motives may be unknown, as in the case of a man physically jumping her or trying to force her to go somewhere in a car.

As women, we have goals, too. These goals can be summed up with three D's: decide, distance, and defend. We must always choose to distance ourselves from a threatening person, but if it's too late to move away, we must decide to defend ourselves and make our escape immediately.

She just ran out of time.

There is absolutely no time to figure out this guy's agenda. It doesn't matter how serious he is or what his goal might be. It doesn't matter what he wants or what he thinks he's going do to her. The important thing is her immediate response.

During the course of the attack, the victim has no time for anything except swift defensive action that will lead to her freedom. She must react promptly and effectively in order to get away as fast as she can. Later in this book, we'll learn numerous methods of escape, many of which can be used before the bad guy gets within close proximity of his victim.

THE TROUBLE WITH HOW MEN ATTACK WOMEN

Before a woman becomes fully involved in a fight with a bad guy, she has to be approached and attacked by him. The assailant can choose one of hundreds of physical strikes on his victim in the middle of that fight. But if you turn it sideways and break it down, there are only a few methods this guy will use when he's in the process of coming to get her. Two of these are sly and subtle. At the onset, a woman might find them hard to recognize or believe as actual attacks. The third is about as inconspicuous as a bulldozer.

These are the most common ways men attack women:

Men sneak up on women.

Women can be stalked for ten years or three seconds. The action is the same. Some guy is watching you, studying your routine, and following you. He knows when you see him and when you don't. Perhaps you never notice him at all. He waits for your most vulnerable moment.

Patti was an attractive teenager, and for an entire decade she was stalked by a man whose identity remains a mystery to this day. He used a constant barrage of obscene phone calls, nasty notes, threatening graffiti, and crude gifts in order to keep Patti terrified on a continual basis. Her parents were nervous wrecks. The stalker was an expert at sneaking around. He knew her schedule at work, school, and home. He knew where she lived, the identity of her friends, which school locker she used, and he often called to harass Patti on the phone. The police and the FBI never found this pervert.

Though her stalker never physically assaulted Patti, he certainly had the ability to do so. He was a pro at the sneak-up tactic, and he managed to keep Patti's entire family emotionally on edge for more than ten years. Then one day it was over, and he was never heard from again.

A few years later in a completely different city, Patti *was* attacked by someone that the police determined was a completely different man. This one stalked her for only a moment while he planned his assault. He turned out to be an alleged rapist with no idea that this particular victim had lived ready for such an attack for ten years. Patti was mentally prepared, in terrific physical shape, and not afraid to battle for her life. She brutally fought off her assailant and escaped unharmed.

Men cozy up to women.

A guy goes out of his way to create reasons and opportunities to be with you. He tries to be your friend, perhaps even moments after meeting you. He bends over backward to be a really nice guy. He might be your coworker or the door-to-door salesman. He insists on doing favors for you that appear chivalrous but are, in fact, all part of the cozy-up routine. He appears to be extremely nice or trying so hard that, at times, you almost feel sorry for him. You also feel unable to put a firm stop to whatever he is doing.

Mona was a woman in her twenties who worked as a secretary in a large advertising agency. A high-level male coworker invited her for a drink after work one day to discuss her career goals. He reminded Mona how well connected he was in the business, and offered to help her as she searched for a more prominent position. After a glass of wine, the man stopped discussing Mona's career and began asking lewd questions about her naked body and her sex life. He urged her to give him the intimate details about her relationship with her boyfriend. Caught off guard, Mona wondered if the wine had gone straight to his head. As soon as she showed her displeasure with his choice of topics, the man quickly switched back and began talking about professional matters. He told her he planned to recommend her work to a friend of his the very next day. Mona relaxed again and decided he probably hadn't meant anything by his earlier remarks. Then he suddenly probed her again with sexual questions, all the while complimenting her on both her appearance and her excellent work on the job. Mona's feeling of unease came flooding back, so she left the restaurant, watching her back the whole way to the car. The next day, she reported the incident to their boss, and the male coworker was advised to stay away from her for the rest of his time on the job.

Mona wised-up to this guy's attempt to cozy up to her. She nipped it in the bud and quickly removed herself from an uncomfortable situation.

Men ambush women.

This can be either a total surprise attack from nowhere or the moment the sneaky stalker or the cozy-up guy reveals his true intentions. An ambush scenario is when a man tackles you and throws you to the ground. Or he comes at you already swinging. Or he lunges out from behind the corner with a gun. What might have begun as a sneak-up or a cozy-up type of attack has now given way to a full-blown assault with intense physical fighting.

Nicole was jogging, as she did every day through her residential neighborhood. Suddenly, just a few doors away from her apartment, she was pounced upon by an attacker from behind. He sent her tumbling face-first onto the sidewalk and ended up on top of her. Then he began to beat her head with a rock. Stunned but still able to move, Nicole kept trying to shake him off her and to get back on her feet. Though her attacker stayed on her and continued striking her with the rock, Nicole never gave up on her attempt to wrestle and squirm her way out of the ordeal. She refused to stop moving despite the pain of the rock repeatedly slamming her skull. Amazingly enough, she was able to break free when a sudden surge of adrenaline pushed her up to a standing position. As soon as he saw she was ready to defend herself, her attacker fled.

Paramedics took Nicole to the hospital with a fractured skull and orbital bone. A week later, police believe that this same man struck again, and he managed to rape a woman after she drove home late one night. A month went by and the man allegedly attacked a third time, targeting another jogger on her morning run. This woman shot him with pepper spray, and he took off. The police still haven't caught this violent criminal.

Nicole's incident was a classic ambush attack. It was fast-moving, rough, and violent. This is usually the case—one minute he's over there, and the next minute he's on top of you. A victim can barely catch her breath, let alone fight him with optimum strength.

A combination of the three tactics.

The bad guy will often stalk his victim before approaching her in a seemingly friendly way. Then at some point, he will use sheer force to overpower and assault her.

Barbara worked for a production company that was shooting a music video out of town. She and her colleagues were staying in various rooms at the same hotel. After a full day followed by a meeting in the conference room, she headed for the elevator, intending to spend the rest of the evening alone in her hotel room. Unbeknownst to her, one of Barbara's male coworkers spotted her and began to follow her down the hall toward the elevator. Jumping quickly to hold the door for her, he made a few friendly comments about the shoot they were working on. But when the doors shut, his tone changed completely. He immediately stepped forward, pushed her violently against the wall, and held her there. Then he began kissing her on the lips while groping some of her body parts.

This man's attack consisted of all three elements. He stalked her when he watched her walk to the elevator (the sneak up). He befriended her with pleasant conversation and gentlemanly manners (the cozy up). When he struck, it was hard and fast, taking her completely by surprise (the ambush). Though reeling from the shock of being slammed into the elevator wall, Barbara was able to react immediately. Using both hands against his chest, she pushed the man away from her as hard as she could. She berated him for his actions and demanded that he get off the elevator at the next floor. Within weeks, she had a new job.

When fighting like a girl, we are always preparing ourselves for a fight with a man. If, by some statistical freak of nature, our attacker should turn out to be a woman, so be it. Either way, you'll be ready.

◄ 5 ►

THE BIG FEARS

Fear is nature's warning signal to get busy.

HENRY CHARLES LINK,
PSYCHOLOGIST AND
INSPIRATIONAL PHILOSOPHER

S o what are you so afraid of?

Being abducted. My fear is that I'll be forced into a car and taken to some deserted place. I'm mostly afraid of being tortured by some creep at that next location. I'd just as soon die.

—*Colleen, forty-four years old, personnel administrator*

ABDUCTIONS AND SECOND LOCATIONS

A kidnapping is a horrific crime to imagine, and being trapped in a car with some maniac is equally terrifying. But to be transported to another, more secluded place is your worst nightmare yet.

Security experts always agree on this one—the second location is where the really horrible stuff goes down. In fact, it's been estimated that 95 percent of the victims transported to a second location do not survive. Like animals dragging their prey to the brush or into their dens, these attackers are forcing their victims to some private place for a reason—in order to take their time with them, to be as violent as they want with them. It is at this second location that the real torture begins. For human victims this torment can continue for hours, even days or months. At some point, a final kill is often the result.

> *It's stalking that scares me. The way some women are watched and followed then suddenly attacked. I'm always looking behind me. My husband thinks I'm crazy I look around so much. He says I'm completely paranoid.*
> —*Claire, forty-five years old, flight attendant*

THE ACT OF STALKING

Stalking is a serious crime in this country. It is illegal in all fifty states and a felony on the first offense in fifteen of them. Most stalkers are men, and most women know who their stalkers are.

"Stalking is far more prevalent and dangerous than most people realize," says Tracy Bahm, the director of the Stalking Resource Center at the National Center for Victims of Crime. "Victims report having to take drastic steps to escape the stalking and feel safe—including moving, changing jobs, changing their identity, undergoing counseling, arming themselves, and more."

> *I have a fear that's very much a reality to me. Each night after work I have to walk through a subterranean parking lot, usually all by myself. Most of the time, I work later than the other women in my office so I have no one to walk with. I take an elevator down two flights into what is usually an empty parking lot. There's hardly anyone around. I know how vulnerable I am there. But what can I do about it? It's my job.*   —*Jill, thirty-six years old, physician's assistant*

CRIME HOT SPOTS

This fear is certainly not an unreasonable one. In our statistics chapter, we discovered that women are often attacked in parking garages. If you think about it, women carry purses, books, briefcases, or shopping bags as they make their way through these garages. They're trying to find their vehicles as well as their keys, which are sometimes buried in the bottom of their handbags. Every car in the garage provides an excellent hiding spot for the bad guy.

Other areas prove dangerous as well, places such as streets, school classrooms and college campuses, grocery stores' outdoor parking lots, stairwells and hallways of hotels, or any locale void of people such as a vacant building or an alley,

But it's wise to remember that women are often attacked by someone they know. This means an assault by a friend, boyfriend, ex-husband or ex-boyfriend, coworker, neighbor, or relative is as much a possibility as an attack from a stranger in a parking garage.

Home invasions are what scare me most. A cop told me the guys who do that stuff are vicious. They come in swinging and shooting. There's always high-level violence that occurs. They kill the men. Tie people up. Rape all the women. It's animal stuff. I would lose my mind if that ever went down. Or I'd just die on the spot.

—Shelly, forty-four years old, homemaker

THREATS AT HOME

There are two kinds of burglars dying to get into your house: the ones who don't want to run into you, and the ones who think your presence will make things easier for them.

While most burglars attempt to rob houses when they're unoccupied, home invasion criminals intentionally target occupied homes, usually at night or on weekends. They do this to gain entrance while residents are inside moving about and the security alarm is not activated.

Home invaders often come in like madmen. Some bring guns or restraints such as duct tape, rope, and handcuffs. Intense violence may occur in the first couple of minutes in order to get all of the family members scared, intimidated, and willing to cooperate. The biggest threat for victims is that the home invaders' violence could escalate to include sexual assault or even murder.

> *I like to think that I'd fight off an attacker, but the truth of it is if he has a weapon, I'd freeze. It's knives that scare me most. If he's coming after you with a knife, how would you ever escape without getting all cut up?*
> *—Maryanne, forty-two years old, retail salesclerk*

WEAPONS OF CHOICE

Weapons are downright scary. Who can compete against a bullet, a blade, or a club? Surveys show that the presence of a weapon during a violent crime is related to the type of crime committed. For example, robbery victims often find themselves face-to-face with an armed attacker (48 percent of incidents), while rape and sexual assault victims are less likely (7 percent of cases).

Some women who've faced attackers with weapons later admit having been overpowered by the belief that they were going to be stabbed or shot at any second. Others report that the weapon became their catalyst and the reason they were able to fight. They claim it became secondary to the imminent danger they faced and the knowledge of what they had to do. All they could think about was fighting for their lives in order to escape.

> *I'm scared of being drugged up with some substance. A guy could just jump out of nowhere and stab you with*

a hypodermic needle. Then, that's it. You're done, com-
pletely under his power, losing all consciousness and con-
trol. That's what I fear. Having no control.
—*Janine, twenty-four years old, administrative assistant*

DRUG DANGERS

The criminal who uses drugs to control and violate his victim is one sick individual. But so is another kind of attacker, the one who watches a woman willingly ingest drugs before he pounces on her.

More common than incidents where perpetrators use hypodermic needles are cases where "club drugs" and "date rape drugs" are used for rape, sexual assault, and other violating crimes. The National Institute on Drug Abuse reports shocking increases in the popularity of some hazardous club drugs, such as MDMA (ecstasy), GHB (liquid ecstasy), Rohypnol (roofie), ketamine, and methamphetamine.

If a woman chooses to experiment with such narcotics at a rave party or club, she is taking huge chances with her life and safety. An attacker can simply wait until she is too drug-induced to protect herself, then make his move. Or, in the case of date rape drugs, he'll slip a narcotic (such as a "roofie") into the drink of an unsuspecting woman and watch as she is quickly transported into a hypnotic, sedative state.

I've always believed that men are robbed or killed and
women are raped. Because it seems the most likely thing
to happen to me—a woman—I fear rape.
—*Kathy, thirty-seven years old, family counselor*

RAPE FACTS

Rapists seek out "the rapeable." They don't necessarily go after the women they find attractive or the ones who dress suggestively.

Their victims can include the old, the young, the innocent, and the vulnerable.

Women don't usually "cry rape." This crime remains the most underreported offense in the country, with almost 62 percent of rapes and sexual assaults never being recounted to police. This brings about a double whammy of destruction for society. Rape cases are more numerous than we might imagine, while the perpetrators are still "out there," repeating the crime against additional victims.

I was raped more than ten years ago. My counselor told me rape victims have a greater chance of being raped again by someone else later in life than other women do. So what does that mean? That I'm unknowingly sending out signals that I'm a victim or something? That thought really disturbs me.

—Ronda, thirty-five years old, saleswoman

THE SEQUEL TO SEXUAL ASSAULT

The name for this scenario is rape revictimization, and it occurs when a woman is sexually assaulted or molested as a child, then subsequently raped as an adult.

There are various factors that bring about such reoccurring assaults, but a major risk component is post-traumatic stress disorder because the victim feels vulnerable. Often that vulnerability is apparent to others, particularly to the rapist in search of a victim. Statisitics show that women with childhood histories that include sexual abuse are almost five times more likely to be raped as adults.

The Sum of All Fears

So are you ready to wrap your head around the real scary stuff? When it gets right down to it, our biggest fears as woman should be these:

- Neglecting continual reality checks in situations involving men.
- Failing to observe what is going down anytime, anywhere.
- Missing the opportunity to react immediately to danger.
- Neglecting to communicate exactly who we are.
- Remaining in a situation when we're concerned about a man's actions or attitude toward us or toward women in general.
- Ignoring a comment or clue that could jeopardize our safety.
- Overlooking our human right to protect ourselves at any cost.
- Shirking from the daily responsibility we have to boost our security, build our self-esteem, and embrace our self-worth.
- Not watching our backs (and everything else along with it).
- Not stopping long enough to learn how to throw a punch, kick out a knee, or swing a golf club at our opponent's head.
- Losing control through drugs, alcohol, abusive situations, or unhealthy relationships.
- Stifling our strong sides.
- Acting dumb, easy, or loose in order to attract the attention of men.
- Being dumb, easy, or loose in the first place.

- Failing to assert ourselves.
- Passing up the chance to create and enforce a personal security plan for our lives.
- Not seeing the threat before it's too late.
- Not deciding ahead of time exactly who we are and what we're willing to put up with.
- Not fighting like a girl.

◄ 6 ►

DEGREES OF DEFENSE

**When the going gets tough,
the tough get going.**

JOSEPH P. KENNEDY

What's a girl to do?

Picture the following scenario: you are shopping in your local grocery store one day and a man comes down the aisle and suddenly heads straight toward you. When he is positioned right beside you, he reaches out and grabs your forearm. It's not a rough or painful grab, but it is a grab nonetheless.

How should you respond?

1. Jam your thumb into his eye socket, knee him in the testicles, grab him by the hair, and slam his face into a shelf, sweep his leg, take him to the ground, and choke him until he's unconscious.
2. Scream at the top of your lungs for security while hurling canned goods directly at his face.
3. Point your finger at his nose and instruct him to get out of your space.
4. Immediately and firmly step back and away from him

while pulling your arm free. Move so that he's no longer in your space. Get to the other side of the shopping cart, so that it forms a barrier between the two of you. Watch him carefully. If the threat remains or intensifies, get out of there. Run if you have to. Leave your cart and all the groceries you just collected for the last hour and start moving completely away, but don't turn your back on him. If necessary, report his actions to store security.

Despite the ridiculous exaggeration and complete overkill described in our little scenario, hang in there with me for a moment. Now, it's quite possible this guy has a perfectly good reason for touching your forearm. Obviously, he wants something. Perhaps it's just your attention he's after. Maybe he has a question for you. He might mistakenly believe he knows you from somewhere, and it could have been acceptable for him to touch you. Perhaps he's having a heart attack and desperately needs your help. He may want to ask you where the pickle aisle is located, because he's spotted a jar of his favorite pickles in your cart.

But let's hope that a perfect stranger placing a hand on you is sending all your warning lights into a flashing frenzy somewhere in your mind. By touching you—a woman he does not know—this shopper has done something that, quite frankly, just isn't done. Innocent or not, he's just pushed across your line of defense a few degrees, and now it's your turn for a response.

As we begin to explore these options, we discover there are virtually limitless ways in which to respond. And many of them won't cause extreme harm like numbers one and two would. It's great to know if a stranger places his hand on your forearm in the grocery store someday, you don't have to rupture his testicles or knock a tooth down his throat or yank an eyeball out of its socket in order to make him stop.

But you don't need to stand there doing nothing and waiting for his next move, either.

The best choice is number four. It's firm, yet fluid and alive. It puts you back in the driver's seat. It gets you moving and buys you distance. Keep in mind that you got active about the situation right away. You moved to safety. You didn't wait for him to let go or release you or convince you that it was okay for him to touch you like that. You didn't pause for his explanation. You didn't bother waiting to see what he was up to. You gained your freedom with a quick, simple movement.

You didn't have to smack anybody around or hurt anybody's feelings. You could've done the whole darn thing with a smile on your face and still have been just as effective. You simply went from one area of personal space where you felt controlled by some strange guy to another space, a few feet away with a cart in between. In your new personal space, that guy lost his chance for control. The simple act of moving away from him put you back in control.

But let's heat up our situation by a few degrees of intensity. Let's say that same joker grabs your forearm and hangs on, refusing to let go. Now, you have a more serious problem. You need more force, right? How about if he latches on and begins dragging you out of the store to his car where three hoodlums are waiting to toss you in the trunk and drive you off to the boonies and bury you in a shallow desert grave? You'd better increase your force by a thousand degrees. What if he pulls you to the floor? What if he doesn't let go of your forearm? What would you do if he releases you, but then follows you throughout the store harassing you?

Okay, now try this on for size. Perhaps that guy uses the same amount of force we mentioned the first time, a simple grab to the forearm. It may even be something you would describe as a light grab. But now, let's change the location and the time. It's late at night. You are walking alone on a street to your car. A man approaches from behind. You sense him coming, so you keep hurrying forward. Suddenly he rushes right up, reaches out, and grabs your forearm. What's your response, and what degree of force would you use to carry it out?

Everyone in this country has the right to use self-defense. We can legally protect ourselves from danger and harm. Remember *Webster*'s definition: "whatever force is reasonably necessary." The tricky thing is that each attack has its own unique set of circumstances, making it virtually impossible to have a definite and detailed strategy for success every single time. Besides that, what are the chances we'll be *reasonable* in the middle of incredible danger? How on earth, in a split second, do we correctly measure the threat against us and then counterattack with the right moves and the proper amount of force?

Throughout the rest of this book, you'll be thinking as never before and making dozens of decisions to sharpen your personal security measures. You'll learn to recognize danger and identify threats. But first, it's important to learn what measures you can take to protect yourself legally and rightfully, anywhere, anytime.

In any attack, there are always two questions that need to be answered intuitively, intelligently, and faster than the speed of light:

1. What is the level of force being used against me?
2. How much force is necessary to defend myself and escape?

The technique in the crowded, well-lit supermarket isn't going to cut the mustard in the dark hallway of your home. What works against his controlling hold won't do squat when you're shoved against a brick wall in the deserted alleyway. What might be effective in a verbal confrontation won't amount to a hill of beans when some creep has thrown you to the floor.

Fighting like a girl is not rocket science. It's as natural as seeing things as they are and then making them into what they should be.

LEVELS OF FORCE

**What counts is not necessarily the size
of the dog in the fight—it's the
size of the fight in the dog.**

DWIGHT D. EISENHOWER

How low will you go?

Attacks have elevations. Each one contains a specific level of force. It can remain at one level, or it can rise and fall to other elevations.

These elevations vary in pain, intensity, and danger. Some attackers go straight to the highest level and instantly kill their victims. Others aim lower, seeking to maim the victim. They may leave their victims alive and breathing, but injured physically, mentally, and, in some cases, both. There are harmless situations with elevations so low that physical fighting can often be avoided altogether. Then there are true battles that rage at the highest peak of danger.

It all begins at some level or elevation. The bad guy introduces the level. We respond by immediately recognizing that level and then matching it with our own counterattack intensity. In order to survive a fight and escape from our enemy, we must rise to the level of force being introduced by our opponent, and then sometimes go higher and harder. It will never do a woman a bit of good to respond at a lower degree of force. Her strength will be no match for his intensity.

In a verbal confrontation, the higher and harder way is to let it go, to keep quiet, or to leave. But in the physical confrontations, it is the aggressive fighter with the more rigorous will to survive who will elevate herself, defend her ground, and ultimately win.

Below are the Four Levels of Force. They are your best clues for determining the degree of peril you could face against an attacker. Recognizing force levels allows you instant, critical information on the amount of power being used by your assailant. And they give a clear indication of the needed response.

The Four Levels of Force

1. Verbal Argument
2. Controlling Moves
3. The Physical Fight
4. Lethal Attack, Rape, or Abduction

The key idea is this: to be both legally appropriate and victorious in a physical attack, you must instantly realize the force level your attacker is utilizing. Then you must physically meet him at that same force level with your own self-defense. Sometimes, in order to survive his muscle mass and brute strength, you must go a step higher and harder.

Your goal is always the same: to put a stop to his assault, to end the confrontation, and to escape with the least amount of injury to you. Your goal is not to hurt him or kill him. You are not showing him a thing or two, teaching him a lesson, or taking revenge for the horrendous blow he has just delivered or the crime he has attempted. Your role is never that of the vigilante. Instead, you are to be the survivor and the escape artist. You must always be the one who got away.

This overall objective never changes. No matter how hard he tries or what techniques he manages to throw at you, you have one single purpose of dire urgency: to make a safe escape with little or no injury inflicted upon you.

1. VERBAL ARGUMENT

Some lunatic is losing his mind right in front of you. He's completely coming unglued in your face, screaming and shouting. You're thinking that if his tirade continues he could possibly end up using you as a punching bag.

When words are flying but there is no physical contact, your best bet is to defuse the situation by not arguing back. *To engage is to enrage,* and if this happens to occur with a stranger, you'll find yourself immediately involved with a person whose actions and behavior are absolutely impossible to predict. When it comes to a quarrel or a heated debate, putting up and shutting up is always the best plan.

Times like these are great opportunities to apply *passive defense.* Keep your eyes open and your mind alert. Continue breathing deeply and steadily. Go ahead and apologize if you think that will cool him off a bit, even if you're not wrong. If you cannot bring yourself to apologize to this fool, say something like "Hey, it's cool . . . no problem." Always regard patience and self-control as two of your most valuable weapons of warfare. Don't be ignorant, though. If the situation is truly volatile, you must open your intuitive wisdom in order to see it, feel it, and fully realize it. Be sure to remain on high alert. Continue to be aware. Stay focused and energized, ready to flee or pounce should the need arise. Keep your sight directed on the area around his throat and upper chest while allowing yourself to see all of him with your peripheral vision. Be prepared for any sudden movements on his part, something the martial artists call "telegraphing." That's when you see his shoulder suddenly jerk or twitch, or the collar of his shirt begin to move, and you know a punch or a grab is now in the offing. Or his hip shifts, and you know a kick has been initiated and is now heading your way. Telegraphing is your opponent's clear indication that he's now on the physical attack. He might as well be yelling, "Okay, lady, here it comes."

But if he is just screaming and hollering, remain on the lookout for his possible physical escalation. Let him see you intensely studying him and the situation. Get your hands above your belt, higher than waist level, in case you need them for blocking your face, throat, or chest. Protect your space by moving back and away from him if necessary. Keep breathing. Be quiet and make your move to immediately flee the entire situation.

2. CONTROLLING MOVES

Someone has taken captive one or more of your body parts. With varying degrees of discomfort, that person is using his hold on that body part to dominate you, move you, keep you in place, manipulate you, or direct your actions. You don't necessarily feel hurt or injured by this person, but you do feel controlled.

Nobody is allowed to control your movements. Period. End of story.

There are only a few obvious exceptions to this very basic, unwritten law of self-defense. These include such things as a child being trained or disciplined by a parent, a criminal being manipulated by a policeman in order to be handcuffed or restrained, or a disabled person being directed by a caretaker. Unless there is a legitimate reason, no one has the right to control your body or its actions.

Controlling holds are considered serious maneuvers. They give instant power to the controller. This is where he gains the upper hand. Controlling moves and holds won't kill you unless he happens to be pressing his fingers against your throat or keeping your head underwater, which lethally pumps up his hold on you to a Force Level Four. However, anytime a person is dominating your mobility, you have a sobering problem on your hands.

The second someone begins to manage and manipulate your movements or direct your actions, you can bet he's using a controlling move. He can push you through the doorway or pull you by the lapel of your shirt. He can be twisting your wrist and arm up behind your back while guiding you in a certain direction. He can be hanging on to your clothing or purse. He can be leading you somewhere by applying pressure to your wrist.

One of the crazy truths about control holds is that the pain factor is partially regulated by the victim. When we comply with the bad guy's demands or directions, there is relatively little pain. When we resist, the pain increases. This is why people often allow themselves to be controlled. It simply doesn't hurt as much.

The second any controlling move is placed on you, it's time to turn the tables and regain control. After all, you never know what situation this slimeball is planning to direct you into. In the case of arm, hand, or wrist holds, you can release yourself by yanking your arm, hand, or wrist away and out of his grasp. To do this, simply take the arm, hand, or wrist he's controlling and arc your hand out of it swiftly and forcefully toward the direction of his thumb. His thumb is always the weaker side of his hand. If you find it difficult or impossible to free yourself in this manner, because of his superior strength, go ahead and let him have that arm, hand, or wrist. Then try using one of the many other available weapons on your body to force him to release you. For example, with your other hand, make a fist and punch his lights out. Or crack his nose with a palm heel strike (using the pad of your inner hand with fingers pulled back) straight up and against his face. Scratch his eyes with your fingernails. Your feet and legs are free, right? So put them to use. Kick his knee out, knee him in the groin, rake your boot down his shin, or stomp on his foot with your stiletto heel. If you hit any of the above targets, there's a good chance he'll react by releasing your hand. At the very least, you'll have him distracted by pain and thinking about something other than your hand and holding on to it so tightly.

Remember the key idea in the beginning of this chapter? Recognize his level of force, then if necessary go higher and harder. To be effective against a man's controlling move, a woman must often rise to the next level of force. In this case, it would be the third category, a Physical Fight. That means you'll need to add some good physical fighting counterattacks.

Powerful Moves for Getting Physical and Escaping His Control

- A rapid backfist to the nose.
- A shuto—or karate chop—using the stiff outside edge of your hand aimed at the carotid artery in his neck.
- A hard hammer fist (think of the tetherball strike) to his temple.
- A swift elbow strike to his stomach or rib cage.
- A punch with the fist to his solar plexus (the sensitive area in his upper belly, just below the sternum, which contains many nerves).
- A kick with the ball or pad of your foot to his knee or abdomen.
- A forearm planted into his face, directed at the jaw or nose.

Remember to follow up those counterattacks with as many additional moves as you need. (Have ten on hand at all times! Practice them regularly!) Aim for different targets on his body as quickly as possible in order to keep him from knowing where the next attack is going to hit. In other words, he's not going to let you pop him in the nose ten times in a row. By about the third time, he'll have figured you out, and he'll start blocking that area more effectively. So pop him in the nose once or twice and then knee him in the groin. Distract him by forcing him to think about both his nose and groin. Then plant a knuckle in his temple. Deliver a crushing kick onto his knee. Pull him by the hair until he's on the ground. Drop all your weight on his solar plexus with your elbow. Stomp on his face. Jump on his rib cage. Pretty soon, the hand or wrist he once controlled will probably be forgotten.

For pushing and pulling controlling moves, think "go with the flow," but always go with strength and purpose. For example, if he's pushing you backward, go ahead and move in that direction, but get there quicker than he ever intended so that you pull him off balance. If he's pulling you to the side, use your weight to get there first, forcing him to be off center and unsteady. Use his moves and his momentum against him. Once he's unstable, you'll find it's easier to break free and counterattack. When released from his hold, fight only as much as necessary and then get away as fast as you can.

3. THE PHYSICAL FIGHT

A brawl has broken out. You are a target and participant.
Kicks and punches are flying fast and furious, and they're
coming straight for you. This is now a full-blown fight.

The good thing about the previous force level, Controlling Moves, was that you had a fraction of time on your hands. When you find yourself being held against your will, you usually have at least a second or two to digest what's going on, plan your release, and counterattack. You may think, "He's holding me by the shirt collar, so I'll grab his long hair and pull hard enough to yank it straight out of his scalp!" As you're grabbing his hair, you're thinking, "Now that I'm yanking his hair out by the roots, I'm taking him nose down and straight onto my rising kneecap." And so on.

But when the attacker escalates to the Physical Fight, time is now working against us with record speed. Bruce Lee wasn't kidding when he wrote, "The punches will not wait for you," in *Jeet Kune Do: Bruce Lee's Commentaries on the Martial Way*. When someone's clenched fist is heading toward your face, you have very little time. If a kick is coming straight at your stomach, you have only a couple of seconds before impact. This means you'll need to move quickly.

The good news regarding this Physical Fight category is that it's not the most common way for men to attack women. A woman will tend to be controlled, ambushed, sexually assaulted, or lethally attacked rather than come up against some guy who suddenly decides to haul off and sucker punch her without any warning. It does happen, though, especially when an attack situation isn't going the way the bad guy planned and he wants to punch her silly for a while or knock her out in order to control her more efficiently. When this is happening, she'll need to react fast.

By far, the best plan to survive and avoid a punch or a kick is this two-step defense technique.

Slip a punch or escape a kick by following these simple directions:

- See it coming.
- Move out of the way.

Easy as pie, right? You don't need to do a body slam against his punch with all your might. You don't have to knock down his techniques with your face. Just watch and realize what's happening and very quickly move! Veer off the course of that punch or kick aimed at you. You can make any kind of move you wish in order to get yourself out of the way. You can step, transition, dive, skip, roll, cartwheel, leapfrog, tap-dance, or anything else that removes you from the range of that punch or kick.

Some Techniques for Avoiding a Punch or Kick

- By blocking firmly with your hand or forearm, you are providing yourself some added security that will protect your face, neck, throat, or abdomen.
- By stepping *toward* him, either to the *inside* (near his chest) or the *outside* (near his shoulder), you are moving off the line of his incoming punch or kick.
- As his momentum continues on that straight line, you are now positioned either *inside* or *outside* and out of the way, avoiding his punch or kick.
- Having moved in close to him, you are now in position to render a solid counterattack.
- When his punch or kick hits nothing but air, he'll most likely be off balance, and that's a perfect time to counter from your close-up position.
- After you deliver solid counterattack strikes, get away quickly.

But hey, always feel free to cut to the chase by jumping out of the way and running for dear life! Running is a perfectly legitimate self-defense technique; in fact, it's one of the best forms of action available to you.

4. LETHAL ATTACK, RAPE, OR ABDUCTION

Someone is ripping your pants off and prying your legs apart. He is grabbing you and forcing you into a car. He is strangling you with his bare hands. He is attacking you in your home. He is tackling you from behind and throwing you to the ground in the dark. He is using a dangerous or deadly weapon. Perhaps he's telling you exactly what he plans to do to you. "I'm going to rape you." "I'm going to kill you." "I'm going to cut you up in little pieces and eat you for dinner." Whatever. This is when your very life is about to be cut short if you do not retaliate by rising to a Force Level Four. Then go higher and harder, which means going completely "nuts." You are now at the highest elevation, in the most important fight of your life—for your life.

First of all, nothing matters but this very moment. If you made a few mistakes and landed yourself in this awful mess, that's okay, because you're about to get out of it. Maybe you missed some clues. You went out with the wrong guy. You trusted some idiot. The warning bells sounded like gongs in your head, and still you came to this area in the dark or jogged alone by the lake or stepped into an elevator with that guy who gave you the creeps. Or maybe you just got surprised. No matter how badly you blew it or how life suddenly threw you a curve, the time has come to pull out all the stops.

Your opponent may have cozied up, snuck up, or ambushed you. Perhaps he argued, controlled, and fought his way up to this high elevation. Whatever the case, a Force Level Four attack means it's time to go "nuts." Turn yourself into an animal. Show this monster that attacking you was the biggest mistake of his life.

The Most Serious Self-defense Counterattack Moves Are Acceptable When . . .

- an attacker is attempting to kill, kidnap, or rape you, or to maim or mutilate some part of your body.
- someone is abducting your child or an individual under your supervision.
- the perpetrator is assaulting you with a serious weapon of violence, such as a firearm, knife, or heavy blunt object.
- an offender is committing a "home invasion" by breaking into your house with a lethal weapon in hand.
- the aggressor is handcuffing you to a car door, the bedpost, the stair banister, or the pipes in the basement.
- the bad guy is coming at you with a rope and duct tape, an ax, a baseball bat, ice pick, poison, or a syringe.
- your attacker is trying to cut off your air supply by choking you or strangling you.
- an assailant is attempting to burn you or set you on fire or drown you by holding your head underwater.
- a bad guy is attacking you in some other barbaric manner, giving you no choice but to conclude that his imposing threat is a life-and-death matter.

To fight back at this dangerous elevation, it's important that you have some knowledge under your belt. You must have imagined certain scenarios and made specific decisions about your life. You'll also need a huge dose of confidence to know that you are doing the right thing in a particular life-threatening situation, one with its own set of unique circumstances. That's why it's vital for you to scrutinize and understand the Four Levels of Force.

Many law enforcement officers believe that women fail to properly protect themselves because they do not react fast enough or at the level of force necessary. Quite often, females are not certain what is happening to them or how to respond. They do not fight back fiercely enough, primarily because they are not clear about what's going on or what the bad guy is attempting to do to them. Of course, by the time they figure it out, it's too late.

If you are looking for absolutes, here's one thing you can be certain of: you'll never have absolute proof that the bad guy intended to kill you until you are dead. But starting today, you will know that anything resembling a Force Level Four, Lethal Attack, Rape, or Abduction, deserves a fatal, going "nuts," fight-of-your-life, immediate response.

A key word to remember at a Force Level Four is *explosion*. We'll learn exactly how to explode in chapter 27, "Decide to Go 'Nuts.'" Think about the stories of women who've used massive surges of adrenaline to lift cars off their loved ones. It's almost impossible to believe that anyone could be infused with such extraordinary power, but that's exactly what you have to expect and demand of yourself if you are ever attacked at this level. Use every lethal move and technique you know until this jerk is disabled.

If you find yourself the victim of a Force Level Four assault, there are three areas to direct your most vigorous counterattack intensity.

- **The Eyes.** It's one thing to scratch some bad guy's eyes, but at a Force Level Four, you might have to be willing to do more. With all of your energy work a hand free, or both hands if possible, then get serious about damaging his eye or even putting his eye out. Remember, though, you've got to be in some horribly grave danger. When your life is at stake, you also need to be ready and willing to stick your finger in the bad guy's eye socket at least two inches deep and then yank that thing out.

- **The Groin.** When it comes to the groin, you are aiming for the testicles. Kick them all the way up into his bladder if you have to. Though painful when struck, the penis is not the best place to target when striking the groin. If you have an open shot, go *up* and *under*, aiming directly at those testicles.

- **The Throat.** If your attacker takes you to a Force Level Four, the throat is another excellent target. But remember to go "nuts" and punch your fist straight through his Adam's apple. If he has long hair, pull his head back with it so you've got a nice clean shot at his throat. Don't just hit him, *crush* his trachea. Flatten that thing. Stab him with something through the throat. A ballpoint pen. A rattail comb. A fingernail file. A dinner fork. A chopstick. Practically anything will work.

If you manage to effectively attack the bad guy's eyes, groin, or throat at a Level Four response, your chances of escape increase dramatically. If the bad guy loses an eye or becomes visually impaired or uncomfortable because of an eye injury, there's a pretty good chance that the fight's over. It's really hard to fight if you can't see. If his ruptured testicles have him vomiting in the street, he's probably no longer capable of trying to kill you. If his trachea has collapsed and he can't draw air into his lungs, he's not going to be interested in you anymore. Now is the time for you to flee.

There are numerous effective targets planted all over the bad guy's body. You have options up the wazoo. If you cannot get a clear shot at his eyes, groin, or throat, just keep battling until you win. Break, maim, or damage anything and everything you can get your hands on. Crack bones, bruise or crush organs, but don't bother with his muscles. Hitting some guy in the biceps or the hamstrings won't do anything except hurt your hand.

While Force Level Four attacks do happen, and unfortunately all too often, our biggest goal in fighting like a girl remains this: to live with such effective personal security in place that the threat of physical harm never reaches this point. Think back to the very start of this book and the karate instructor who told me, "If you ever find yourself in a full-blown fight, there's a good chance you made a mistake in the very recent past. You seriously blew it ten minutes ago or two minutes ago or twenty seconds ago. You missed a clue. Something got by you. Someone got through." With the exception of a total surprise attack, we should always identify danger before it starts going down. And we should always act on our impulses when a situation causes us concern or discomfort.

So how do we do that? By stopping right now to make all our life-and-death decisions.

It's time to figure out where we stand on everything. Let's do it now.

◄ 8 ►

DECISIONS

**Courage and decision are essential factors
to success in fighting.**

Bruce Lee,
*Jeet Kune Do: Bruce Lee's Commentaries
on the Martial Way*

The choice is yours.

Making decisions about personal security will give you a great advantage in this world. You'll need it, too, because in any fight, the attacker always has huge advantages right from the start. I call these the pick-and-choose options. The bad guy may not be a genius, but he's well aware of his choices in a fight scenario. He picks the day and time of his attack. He chooses you as his victim. He decides on the location where he will initiate the assault and the type of violence he will use against you. He will wait for the exact conditions he desires in order to begin his assault.

As the physical confrontation gets under way, the attacker still has choices, and the two biggest ones are fairly obvious. He can either continue advancing on you until he's exhausted every possibility of achieving whatever goal he has in mind. Or he can simply disengage. At any time during the conflict, the bad guy can decide he's just not having fun anymore. Or suddenly, he's not so sure about this harebrained scheme of his. And you can help him with this decision by making him uncomfortable. Perhaps your finger could shoot straight into his eye socket and dig in about two inches. Or your knee could swing up and forward, connecting swiftly with his testicles as you jerk him toward you by his shoulders. Then go ahead, scrape your boot all the way down his shinbone. Shove the tip of your umbrella up his nose. Rake or stab a pen in his eye. This is the kind of discomfort that will encourage him to think about disengaging. He may need this type of assistance to arrive at the conclusion that you're a little too feisty for his planned assault.

At any moment throughout the course of the attack, this loser can make the choice to stop attacking you. He can quit and call it a day. He can go home, fix a sandwich, and turn on the television. He has that choice.

You, on the other hand, don't.

While most of us would agree that women have tons of choices in life these days, we never have more than one in the confines of a violent battle—and that is to survive, to live, to be the last one standing at the end of the day.

Right now, though, you have multiple choices and numerous options to begin thinking about in order to keep yourself continually safe. These are ones designed to give you the upper hand.

If fighting for your life is the biggest test you face at some point in the future, consider the rest of this book to be your study guide. This one differs from the usual study guide you'd likely pick up at a college bookstore or receive from a professor. That's because it's unique to you and to every other woman willing to study its concepts and apply them to her life. It is specifically designed for each individual female. It is flexible, yet decisive. It raises questions just as easily as it answers them. It suggests boundaries, but it also permits freedom of choice.

You are the author, participant, and heroine of your decisive destiny. You are definitely in charge. But only of yourself. Everyone else is on her own. The only person who can make the right decisions for your personal circumstances is you. Your best friend can't. Your mom can't. Your husband can't. And I wouldn't dare to try.

What you do in the middle of some huge, horrendous test against physical violence at some point in the immediate or distant future must be decided now. It must become second nature. It's got to be self-programmed in your mind, body, and soul. Don't think you can evade this topic because it's so darn unpleasant and then expect to come through like a winner when the bad guy has you cornered. Address it now, in a quiet moment, on an uneventful day. Begin trusting yourself. Trust your mind to learn and your body to respond. Trust that if danger comes, you will know exactly what to do.

Just as a student pores over chapters and lecture notes, so should you focus your concentration on matters that are so vital to your personal success and well-being. Some martial arts masters call this focus *kime,* or "the tightening of your mind." They describe it as the process of directing one's full attention on a particular subject or goal.

To "tighten our minds" on our personal security offers numerous rewards, including inner strength, confidence, and a deeper knowledge of exactly who we are as women. This preparation has the power to win future fights, but until then, it will boost self-reliance and build inner strength. To "tighten our minds" settles the score in advance. It provides assurance that what we might need to do in our own self-defense someday has already, on some level, been taken care of.

When your life's greatest test is thrown at you, the choices you make today need to be on automatic. Your body needs to be moving before you've even told it what to do. If the bell has rung, and the test is in front of you, you've just run out of time. You won't have time to figure yourself out. You won't have time to measure how much trouble you're willing to take from some jerk who happened to choose you out of everybody else on the planet to be his

next victim. You won't have time to remember what you thought
you knew, let alone contemplate decisions about your life.

When time is up on testing day, you've got to be already gaining
on him—gaining speed, distance, and protection through "tightening your mind" today.

Let's gain the upper hand over this invaluable area of our lives.
Let's decide now.

There are two groups of decisions, mental and physical.

The mental decisions include any thought-provoking, moral, or
ethical questions that you need to resolve now. They include defensive reasoning and techniques for extreme preparation. The biggest
mental decision is whether you are psychologically prepared to
fight, or possibly seriously injure another person, for the purpose of
self-defense. The mental decisions you will read about will help
you resolve this and other issues such as who's really responsible
for your personal security, how you will create strategies for optimum safety, and how you can increase your awareness. The mental
decisions will allow you to think logically while also maintaining
your relentless fighting spirit. They will inform and confirm. They
will psyche you up to the mental challenge of a fight.

The physical decisions will put your body in motion. They involve action, space, self-control, strength, awareness, and every
physical aspect of the fight you will first try to avoid but, if push
comes to shove (so to speak), will survive and win. These physical
decisions are designed to get you moving and, while you're at it,
swinging, protecting, guarding, running, jumping, and targeting.
They will inspire you to get in shape and to stay active. They will
pump up your body, put it in a fighting stance, and crank it into
motion. The physical decisions will provide the muscle to back up
what you've previously determined in the mental decisions.

Decide as much as you can today, tomorrow, and the next day.
Perhaps you'll write down how you feel about this process to

reflect on at a later date. Maybe you'll begin talking about these decisions with your friends. Think over your choices periodically. Make changes as necessary. Beef them up. Remember them. Tighten your mind around them.

This is how girls fight.

PART II
Mental Decisions

Decisions determine destiny.

FREDERICK SPEAKMAN

9

DECIDE TO BELIEVE
IN YOUR FIGHT

**A man's fortune must first be
changed from within.**

CHINESE PROVERB

Fight from the inside out.

It's not enough to have your body engaged in battle. Everything within you must be fighting, too. This means that your heart, soul, conscience, intelligence, and guts must be committed to the cause.

To be effective against attackers, we must first be certain of what we believe about ourselves, the lives we are attempting to preserve, and about others. The only way to have that lethal, "going nuts" response against an attacking rapist or a murderer is to thoroughly explore it in our heads in advance. On that fateful day, we will need to be 100 percent behind our actions, and that means settling a few critical issues beforehand.

In chapter 7, we learned about the Levels of Force and discovered ways to physically defend ourselves in the most serious assaults. If you didn't do it then, start deciding now if you are the kind of person who, when threatened, could injure another human being. Decide if you are really prepared to make someone suffer, bleed, choke, or writhe with pain. Could you cause permanent physical damage to another person and live with yourself afterward? Exactly how horrible would his crime have to be to make you respond with potentially deadly force? How bad would things have to get? What would it take to put you in a position to fight with everything you possess? Would you ever take someone's life? Now is the time to consider these questions.

It's common to hear a woman say, "Hey, if some guy was going to mess me up for life by raping me or if he was trying to kill me, I'd fight for my life. I'd kill him if I had to!" This comment sounds like a decisive, confident response, but in her quiet moments, has she really thought about this?

To kill someone, anyone, even the horrible monster preying on her, would not only be one of the toughest things she's ever done physically, it would also be the ugliest deed of her existence. Death is final. The memory of such an act would remain in her mind and reside forever in her soul. It would permanently impact her life and possibly haunt and confuse her. Ultimately, it would become a part of her.

Because of its gravity, this decision deserves your utmost consideration. Life is a precious, irreplaceable gift. Criminals might have forgotten this fact, but you cannot. To take a life or to cause serious harm and injury to another human constitutes drastic actions. You would never be the same.

But you would be alive.

Another woman may see things differently. "No matter how awful it all was, I could never cause a person's death. I just don't believe in it. I don't think killing is ever the right thing for anyone else, so how could I justify doing it myself? I guess I'd just have to go on with my life after he was done with me. Or if he ended up being a killer, I suppose I'd end up dead."

For whatever reason, you might decide that you could never lethally counterattack another human being, even in a critical life-and-death assault. As long as you realize this, you can prepare yourself for some other means of survival. But you must under-stand your choice now in order to calculate sufficient alternatives. Perhaps you could see yourself fighting brutally, but stopping short of that final, fatal blow. Maybe you could fight hard enough to es-cape. Ideally, this is what we are always striving for—a counterat-tack strong enough to stop our assailant in his tracks and render him defenseless so that we can take off running. Remember the goal is never to kill anyone. The goal is to escape from the bad guys and remain safe.

There is another kind of woman out there, and she is the one that scares me the most. She says, "I don't know for sure what I'd do in a brutal attack. I take each day as it comes. Who could possi-bly decide now exactly what they'd do in a future situation? Be-sides, I don't like thinking about that depressing stuff."

The time to figure out whether you could really hit, kick, hurt, or kill someone in life-or-death self-defense is not after the guy's taken aim at your head with a crowbar. The time is now.

Danielle told me the story about the night she was raped at knife-point. It was summertime, a beautiful evening, she remembers. Danielle and a girlfriend were hanging out with some boys they'd just met at a party.

"Hey," one of the boys suggested, "you wanna go look at the stars?" He finished a beer and grabbed his keys.

At the time, Danielle thought that question was one of the most ro-mantic things a boy had ever said to her. "Okay, that sounds like fun."

There were four of them in the car. Danielle and her girlfriend, and the two boys they'd just met. The guy driving turned toward a mountain road, cruised into a remote area, and parked. The four of them were talking and laughing as they headed up a grassy hill-side. For stargazing, or so the girls thought.

On the hill, one of the boys revealed a knife he'd been hiding in his pocket.

"We'll go over there," he whispered and grabbed Danielle's arm, pointing the knife at the trees before placing the blade next to her ribs.

Danielle recalls feeling hopeless and numb, and yet, for some inexplicable reason, extremely calm as her attacker proceeded to rape her. At that moment, she made the mental decision to cooperate and comply with her rapist's demands. She remained quiet and still throughout the attack. She figured she would somehow endure the rape, and she had a strong hunch he would keep her alive afterward.

After the rape, the group walked down the grassy hillside under the stars and back to the boy's car. Danielle and her friend got inside and sat silently as they were driven back to town. Had it been only an hour ago that Danielle actually thought this night might prove to be fun, even romantic? The girls were dropped off at Danielle's car shortly afterward.

Today, Danielle has moved past the ordeal. She lives with no regrets. Her conscious decision to go along with her attacker's plan might very well have kept her alive that night. What would have happened if she'd fought for her life? Could she have been stabbed? Would she have been killed out there on that hill under the stars?

Complying with a rapist's demands is never a sure path to survival. There are many rapists who will kill their victims after the act, so cooperating with a rapist is not a definite ticket to freedom later. But sometimes things do work out that way. The rape ends, the man lets her go free, the woman survives, seeks counseling, and goes on to live a productive, peaceful life.

Danielle is now an accomplished professional with a successful career. She is also an experienced martial artist. Her relationships with men are happy and healthy. She is mentally and psychologically sound. To someone else, her story might seem like one of defeat, but the personal decision she made still feels like a victory to her. That night on the hillside, she made her best choice.

She used every bit of strength, bravery, and endurance to somehow find her way out of a nightmare, and she succeeded. If you think about it, that's self-defense, too, perhaps in its most courageous form. It may not be your style or mine, but for Danielle, it worked.

In deciding what you believe and where you stand on these issues, you'll need to measure the value of all the things in your life.

For many women, a threat against her life, a rape, torture, serious physical violation, or abduction is worth fighting for or killing for. The same usually applies when protecting the people she loves. If some bad guy is grabbing her child out of her arms or right off the front sidewalk, she will go after the bad guy and she will be out for blood. If a bad guy is trying to kill her husband, she's going to be lethal about her response. If a man is dragging her off into a dark alley or a clump of shrubs or over to his car, she'd better be fighting for her life and willing to die trying.

But there are also situations involving all kinds of other people. Would you fight like a crazy maniac for your neighbor's kid? Maybe he's a little brat and you can barely stand him, but would you fight anyway? How about a total stranger who is attacked without provocation on the street? Would you risk your life to help him? Would you think twice, wondering if it was some kind of a trick or setup? If that were the case, what kinds of clues would you look for? Is a human life worth defending at any cost? Would you just have to get involved? What if your small children were in tow? Would you stop to help?

While you're placing value on all the important things in your life, consider also the less significant. Right here and now, make the decision to let go of all the stuff you can live without. Some days it may seem as if you wouldn't survive five minutes without your purse, because it feels like your whole life's in there: money, credit cards, phone book, and a calendar with all your appointments and travel dates. It would be hard to relinquish it to some sleazy bad guy. For one thing, there's always the threat that he may want to victimize you further. He might help himself to your personal information such as your address and burglarize your home after becoming familiar with your schedule or calendar. With your credit cards and checks, he can steal your identity or make a mess of your personal finances. If it's obvious he's a purse-snatching little punk and you think you can take him down, go for it. But if he's got a dangerous weapon, give him the darn purse and straighten out the mess later. Get on the phone immediately to block any chaos he tries to bring to your life.

Make this same decision about all your cars, jewelry, sentimental items, and money; all that material stuff is replaceable. Okay, you may never get Grandma's emerald ring back, but someday you can buy another piece of jewelry because you will be alive and able to do so. Just decide right now to give it all away if the situation dictates that response from you. If some guy's got a gun pointed at you and he wants your purse, hand it over and run as fast as you can to escape him. Don't even think twice. Let the bad guys have all the things you can buy with money. While we know many bad guys use guns only as "power tools," there are plenty of others who are trigger-happy idiots. They'll kill you for your hamburger if they are in the mood.

Usually "what's worth fighting for" translates into "what's worth dying for."

These are not easy decisions. They require deep thought and, often, the rules of a higher law. Take the Bible, for instance. Even there you can find examples that go both ways. There are God-ordained battles in the Old Testament that make the wars of our current century sound almost tame in comparison. But in the New Testament, Jesus withstood beatings and tortures with no physical or verbal response whatsoever. So, what's it going to be for you? Are you a turn-the-other-cheek woman or an-eye-for-an-eye type of gal? You're going to have to decide. Now. Picture your attacker's level of force, imagine his crime, see yourself, envision your life now and in the future, and then decide.

If core beliefs or religious convictions prevent you from fighting like a lethal maniac, that's perfectly fine. These are, after all, your decisions. But figure it out now, and then find another way. The best "other" way is to outsmart the enemy, fight like a girl, and keep the bad guys as far away from you as possible. If that sounds difficult, just proceed with the rest of your decisions. With each determination, watch as a foundation of security forms beneath you, builds strength around you, and moves into position to encompass you like the walls of a huge fortress.

On a recent trip to China, my family and I had the thrilling experience of climbing that country's most famous tourist attraction—the Great Wall. This structure epitomizes the idea of "extreme defense" as it stretches more than six thousand kilometers from east to west across the mountains of northern China. Construction of the wall began in the seventh century B.C. as a way for the Chinese to keep the enemies "out" and "over there." For several centuries, the Empire flourished within the security of this amazing wall.

But the Chinese didn't stop there. As our group traveled through Beijing and the surrounding countryside, we discovered there were walls all over the place. Hotels, gardens, shops, restaurants, neighborhoods, parks, ancient locations, tombs—thousands of these sites were enclosed by walls.

For the female fighter, such walls are important to keep in mind as we begin moving toward optimum personal security. In deciding what you believe, you figure out what you'd fight for and you begin building a fortification of your own, one that will keep you safely inside while others remain "out" and "over there." With this kind of "extreme defense" in place, lethal counterattacks should never be necessary.

Every woman has her limits. She knows what and whom she's willing to fight for. So, put a price on it. If it doesn't breathe, hand it over. If you can't live without it, put up your fight.

Self-defense is dirty business, but somebody's got to do it.

Defense Dos and Don'ts

- Do meditate carefully on your core beliefs.
- Do measure the threat to the valued things in your life.
- Don't use any self-defense you'll regret later.
- Don't risk a lethal attack to save some replaceable, inanimate object.

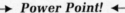

→ Power Point! ←

You and those you love are the things worth fighting for.

10

DECIDE YOU ARE YOUR OWN BODYGUARD

Do not rely completely on any other human being, however dear. We meet all of life's greatest tests alone.

AGNES MACPHAIL,
CANADIAN POLITICIAN AND
CHAMPION OF HUMAN RIGHTS

Y ou are in this alone.

Unless you're a political bigwig or some famous movie star with a full-time security staff, I'm going to assume that you don't have anyone watching your back. Not too many of us do. So it's a wonder that we say such things as "I feel secure in my neighborhood, because everybody's always watching out for one another." Or, "My home is totally safe. After all, I've got a policeman living next door and a sheriff's deputy across the street!" Or, "I don't need to worry about my security. My husband's a gun collector, and we've got an entire arsenal upstairs in the safe."

It can be extremely beneficial to have eagle-eyed neighbors. There are advantages to having law enforcement officers living nearby. There's nothing wrong with the safe packing heat. But unless those neighbors don't ever blink or go to the bathroom, or unless that policeman is doing round-the-clock security detail on *you,* and unless you've got your husband's guns strapped to your waistband as part of your everyday attire, you really can't count on them very much. If you are relying on those types of preventative measures for your personal security, you may find yourself caught empty-handed or extremely vulnerable when all the neighbors are at work.

When fighting like a girl, you are the Lone Ranger. Never mind how safe you feel with your spouse. It doesn't matter how big and burly your boyfriend or husband is. You can't possibly rely on him all the time. The same goes for your older brother, the police squad at the local station house a block away, the Navy Seal living on the next street, your security alarm system, your vicious Rottweiler, or that gun in the safe.

There is no one and nothing ready at all times to protect you better than you.

Not all men "get it" when it comes to our self-defense and safety concerns. Because their fears are far different from women's, men aren't always perceiving threats as we are. Your husband may not be as concerned or aware as you are in a particular security situation. You might be walking down the street, holding hands with your husband. He may be in hog heaven because his favorite model car happens to be cruising down the street. But you don't really give a rip about cars. What's got your attention right now is some dude heading straight your way with a rather intense look on his face. In fact, he's making a beeline for you. Suddenly he's jerking the slack out of the shoulder strap of your purse. Meantime, your husband has stopped to look back and get the full view of that car cruising past. The guy rips the purse free from you and takes off. Your husband missed the entire event.

We are surrounded by opportunities to rely on seemingly strong people and decent, reliable safeguards. But to depend on them completely is nothing but lax personal security. These measures should never allow you to lower your guard. Your husband may not protect you. He may not even be paying attention! Your big, strong boyfriend might be next door when the bad guy strikes. You may not have time to get your gun out of the safe, let alone load it. The Rottweiler might be getting his monthly flea bath at the dog spa. The last thing you want to do is build your trust on false security measures that will leave you unprotected and vulnerable for attack.

Years ago I learned a valuable lesson about false protection.

My husband and I had purchased a security alarm for our home. One night we went to bed, having forgotten to double-bolt a door downstairs. When the wind kicked up later, it caused that door to vibrate and set off our new alarm.

I'd been a student of karate for about a year and was a bit overzealous, so I instantly jumped out of bed ninja-style. With funky hand signs and barely a whisper, I told my husband, "Let's go."

I will never forget his listless response. He barely rolled over, but I did hear him say loudly, "Well, what are you waiting for? Just go turn it off." (I should have known better. I've always described my husband as extremely laid-back and not the easiest guy to rouse when sleeping.)

Now, keep in mind, neither of us really knew for sure what was going on at the time. We certainly weren't aware of the fact that the door hadn't been double-bolted when we went to bed. And suddenly waking up from a sound sleep, we hadn't quite figured out that the wind had kicked up, either. There didn't seem to be an obvious reason that the alarm was blaring.

"What if somebody's really in here?" I whispered again, barely audible.

"Well, you're the one who knows karate" was his response as he settled back into his most comfortable sleeping position.

Okay, so it was a false alarm, and Frank had probably guessed it from the start. The wind, the vibration, and the motion detector: all these things had set off our brand-new security alarm system. But needless to say, that wasn't the only thing set off that night. The next morning, I told my husband to yank that alarm out of the wall, get a refund, and buy a big, toothy German shepherd instead. At least a dog would have rolled over in what could've been a real-life emergency!

Back in karate class, I relayed my story to the group. "This is a very common experience," my instructor remarked. "You were doing what is typical for so many of us, relying on false security measures. You counted on two things to come to your rescue that night: your husband, but he was too busy trying to get some sleep, and your security alarm, but that's just a piece of metal with wires stuffed inside the wall of your home."

A security alarm will deter intruders. It will make loud noises. It may trigger a police reaction several minutes later. But it does not have the power to save your life. What will save you when it's clanging like a cowbell in the middle of the night is *your response* to it. When you can get yourself armed within three seconds after it starts ringing, then you'll be in business. If your husband happens to join in the fight, great, but you are still on your own. If the dogs wake up and start attacking, perfect, but you are still on your own. If poison darts begin ejecting from the walls, wonderful, but yes, you are still on your own.

Motion lights. Security alarms. Weapons. Dogs. I say bring it on. Bring it all on. Line them up one after the other so the bad guy has to creep through an obstacle course to get to you. Turn your home into a fortress. Beef up your car like a tank. Stash weapons all over your body if you feel the need. But always be ready to save your own butt empty-handed.

It's interesting to note that *karate* or actually *karate-do* means "the way of the empty hand." There is a reason for the name. Throughout time, karate fighters have not traditionally armed themselves with weapons or any other man-made security devices. They enter the battle with only their willing bodies and trained minds. They arrive empty-handed to defense situations. This may not be our first choice of how we'd like to fight someday, but it could be our only option, if the safe's locked, or the dog's outside, or the husband's out of town. (Or sleeping!)

Incidentally, because we are often empty-handed and all alone fending for ourselves, it's wise to acknowledge the number of victimized women who scream for help during attacks to no avail. I've heard from countless women who describe experiences of fighting for their lives with people right near them, in cars or homes close by, beyond walkways, on the other side of the doors and windows. But these victims didn't get help from anyone. Half the time, no one even called 911.

Ladies, what is that about?

Yes, in preparing to fight like a girl, we must first accept that we are alone. But as a society of empowered women, it would be the next best thing to hope that we are in this together. If you see someone in danger, do something. Call 911. Scream as loudly as you can. Please, don't allow another woman to go down for the count without an effort on your part to help her.

The burden of personal security is all ours. And it's yours. It's always going to be dumped right in your lap. Saving your life is your problem, your right, and your responsibility. The rescue squad is not coming. Backup has not been requested or dispatched.

Nobody can dig you out of this one but you.

Defense Dos and Don'ts

- Do take your personal security into your own hands.
- Don't rely too much on other people in order to stay safe.
- Do understand that the men in your life are not always there to protect you.

→ *Power Point!* ←

It's up to you and you alone.

11

DECIDE IT CAN HAPPEN TO YOU

People don't ever seem to realize that doing what's right is no guarantee against misfortune.

WILLIAM MCFEE,
WRITER

S tuff happens.

When life's dangerous dramas occur, there's always the woman who asks, "Why me?" She wonders, "How could this have happened to me?" Or, "There I was, minding my own business. Why did this guy have to pick me?" Or, "I had no clue what to do. Heck, I couldn't even believe it was happening!"

Believe it.

Believe it now, and believe it if you ever find that you've been chosen as somebody's next victim. Things have a way of going down in this world. When they do, it can even happen to you. Don't ever fool yourself into thinking that you are somehow exempt from the monsters. These guys are everywhere in our modern society. They're in the workplace, on the streets of your neighborhood, and at the local schools. They show up in the nice areas of town as well as the not-so-nice. They go to church. They wear expensive suits. They get haircuts. They look harmless.

Flip on the evening news, and you'll be quickly introduced to the new monster of the moment. Just when you think you've already heard the worst, some sick psycho will redefine the word *evil* for you. Then, all of his old coworkers and neighbors will give twenty-second sound bites on what a great guy they thought the monster was. "He was very quiet," they always seem to say. Or, "He kept to himself."

No one is immune. That doesn't mean you should live your life dwelling on the hopeless state of mankind. Neither should you reside in some constant state of fear or paranoia. If you run around scared to death of everybody all day long, you'll never recognize genuine fear or the moment when the real bad guy shows up. But if you take a deep breath and heighten your alertness in terms of how you look at others and study situations, you will begin to notice the warning signals.

The last thing you want to do is wake up in the middle of an attack only to wonder how this awful nightmare could have happened to a nice gal like you. Don't waste one precious second on that nonsense. Never stop to dwell on the fact that you are a person who didn't deserve to be assaulted, robbed, or raped.

This decision puts you in the real world, where bad things happen to good people all the time.

Consider Mary, who was traveling on the freeway. Suddenly her car was rear-ended by the driver behind her. Aware that she needed the other driver's insurance information and phone number, Mary pulled over and stepped out of her car.

The other motorist got out of his car and walked up to her, but he wasn't carrying his license or insurance card. Without warning, he hauled off and punched Mary in the face. She dropped onto the gravel in a semiconscious state.

When Mary regained consciousness, the motorist was gone.

Nancy's story is similar.

She and her aunt were attending a relative's wedding in another city. After the day's festivities, they went back to their beautiful hotel at the beach. In the elevator, Nancy pushed the button for the fourth floor while a man who was also riding pushed the button for floor number three. He exited the elevator at the third floor.

When the doors opened on the fourth floor, Nancy and her aunt exited and started down the hall. At her aunt's hotel room door, Nancy tried the key for her just as they heard someone coming down the hall. It was the same man they'd ridden in the elevator with, but now he was on the fourth floor instead of the third. Nancy turned back to the door, thinking about how temperamental hotel room keys were. As the man passed them in the hall, he got right behind Nancy, quickly reached up her dress, grabbed her crotch, and took off running.

Hotel security called police officers to the scene who defined the assault as sexual battery in their report.

Anything can happen to anyone at any time. If you can accept this, you will always be ready. Remember the statement by my sensei a few chapters back, "Sometimes, you're just screwed." Good people are sometimes placed in dangerous situations by unscrupulous characters. It's a fact of life.

This is why when it comes to fights, there are no apologies, no excuses, no guilt trips, and no scapegoats. You just clear your head, tighten your mind, and defend yourself to the best of your ability. If you're going to waste energy by wondering what went wrong, or by feeling sorry or responsible for someone's crimes against you or what you had to do for counterattack defenses, just write yourself off as a victim and be done with it.

Anything you think you might be sorry for or guilty about later should be dealt with today.

One of the great things about making all our decisions now is that we take care of anything that resembles guilt or regret long before the incident. If you are setting aside time today to plan and contemplate your decisions in a cautious, responsible manner, then you should never doubt your actions later in a situation of self-defense. In the middle of an attack, today's decisions will be your ticket to freedom. They will allow you to move and react with more confidence and clarity. Ultimately, they will save your life.

Sometimes, in an attempt to figure out "why" or to make sense of it all, a woman will bear some of the guilt and responsibility for the crime committed against her. "Maybe I brought this upon myself," or, "Maybe I shouldn't have ever talked to that guy in the first place," she will say as she tries to answer the question "Why?"

In cases of date and acquaintance rapes, self-condemnation by the victims is almost as rampant as the crime itself. Young women blame themselves for going out with a particular guy who later turned on them. They fault themselves for saying "No" ninety-five times instead of one hundred. They hold themselves responsible for what they were wearing or what they were drinking, for what they said or didn't say, and for everything else but the full moon.

Yes, you need to conduct yourself in a safe, secure manner at all times. Yes, it's better to watch how much you drink and what you wear if you plan on having successful experiences and relationships. Yes, you need to make all your decisions, and yes, you need to be smart. But never forget that a rape or sexual assault is *his* problem. Don't ever let him make it yours. Don't waste one ounce of time second-guessing your actions or placing blame on yourself. This is a situation you can't fix for him. And you'll never fix it for yourself by feeling guilty.

In the martial arts, there are things to be sorry for. Injuries in particular. It just goes with the territory.

At our school, students and instructors sometimes showed up for class with black eyes, broken ribs and noses, teeth knocked out, and various joints wrapped in bandages. At one point, I thought my nose was broken from a sparring match. I practiced for months and tested for a couple of days for my black belt exam with a couple of broken ribs. I wanted so badly to make excuses for myself, to tell my instructor that my ribs were killing me, in case he would decide that my techniques were lacking ability. But I kept silent. I was, and still am, aware that there were no excuses or apologies in self-defense. It was understood that in any fight we were bound to get hurt, so fighting while injured would only better prepare us for real life.

If one student took down another on the mat, and it looked as if he had just hurt him, he couldn't ever say, "Oops, sorry about that." The focus had to remain on the fight, on winning, and on rendering the opponent defenseless. Let's face it, in the real world you'd never help a bad guy to his feet after you decked him, make sure he was okay, or give him a ride to the emergency room. That same rule applied in class.

This didn't mean you'd deliberately try to hurt your uke (your self-defense partner). In fact, before beginning to fight, partners always bowed to each other as an oath of respect. It was a sign of our silent, solemn promise to never deliberately cause pain or injury. If someone was injured, the apology had to wait until class was over and students left the dojo.

During the actual fight, only a forceful determination could prevail.

If you want to blame yourself for anything, here's something to consider. Apologize for how ugly you're going to get someday, because you're going to be atrocious. Mad cow, distemper, PMS, and just plain ready to rip someone's head off all rolled into one nasty ball of girl fight. Snot dripping from your nostrils. Spit flying. Even your mother won't recognize you, or if she does, she won't admit it. You're going to be crazy and furious, much uglier than a nice gal like you should ever be. That's okay. This is no beauty contest. It's self-defense, and it's about the ugliest your pretty little self is ever going to get.

If someday the worst happens, and it happens to you, and self-defense is your only way out, and you happen to get some bad guy on the ground only to land the perfect kick straight into his testicles, so be it. No wondering what went wrong. No guilt. No apologies. Another kick maybe. But not a sorry moment. Strikes to the ribs and kidneys perhaps. But no downtime to make sure the guy's still breathing or to figure out why he came after you in the first place. Instead, just haul your ugly, testicle-kicking self out of there. For a decisive woman like you, blame is not your concern.

Get downright ugly. Get the job done. Then get over it.

Defense Dos and Don'ts

- Do understand that those around you could suddenly turn on you.
- Do think things through today to alleviate guilt later.
- Don't ever take the blame for some bad guy's crime.

→ *Power Point!* ←

Good or bad, anything can happen. Get real, then get fighting.

12

DECIDE YOUR CHANCES AS AS GOOD AS ANYBODY'S

The "fog of war" works both ways.
The enemy is as much in the dark
as you are. BE BOLD!!!!!

GEORGE S. PATTON, JR.

We are all in the same boat.

Many women think they don't know enough about fighting to ever seriously try it. They lack confidence simply because they haven't been professionally trained or well rehearsed. This belief cripples their defenses, and it can often neutralize their entire personal security system.

But victory is always up for grabs.

What a relief it is to discover that training does not always equal success in a fight, and likewise, lack of experience doesn't mean instant defeat. It's always anybody's fight.

At some point in my training, each of my karate instructors said that if they were attacked on the street, most of their martial arts techniques would fly right out the window. They admitted they would get right down to basic survival fighting, the kind you or I might use in a crisis. This is because, on the street, the

martial artist can't really fight with the form and finesse he practices regularly. He can't deliver a sequence of moves with the execution he'd prefer while practicing in the dojo. Perhaps the street
fight would place the action up against a car or next to a brick
wall. The martial artist would need to adapt and maneuver
around these (or better yet, use them for some nifty head banging
and other moves). Perhaps the punch he just slammed into his
opponent's abdomen sent the bad guy crumbling forward on top
of him instead of knocking him backward. At that point, it could
be a win for either fighter. For a woman, it might deteriorate into
a big hairy catfight with all the fingernail scratching, hair pulling,
and biting you can imagine. Men might pull out the cowboy
punches and hit each other over the head with beer bottles.
Whatever works.

Just because there are people out there who fight, box, kickbox,
and train in the martial arts regularly, it doesn't mean that *you*
can't fight. If someone you know has taken a couple of weekend
self-defense seminars, that doesn't mean you aren't going to be able
to defend yourself as well as she might. If you can, by all means,
take the boxing or kickboxing course, enroll in a martial arts class,
or take the weekend seminar on self-defense for women. If anything, it will give you the confidence to know that you are able to
do numerous things if attacked.

But if you never take such a class, you are not necessarily miles
behind the pack. There are plenty of women who've successfully
fought off attackers with no training whatsoever. These are women
who have never been instructed on fighting techniques. They have
not read books on self-defense. But when the bad guys showed up,
these female victims were able to go ballistic. And if you can go
ballistic, you might not need a heck of a lot of physical fighting
training. Women do this all the time, and they are able to emerge
safely from dangerous situations.

On the other hand, I've heard of seasoned black belt karate students being beaten and even killed by criminals. In fighting, there

are not a lot of certainties, but who you are, what you know, and what you decide to do are some of the sure things.

When I think of the odds being stacked against us, I am reminded of Soya. This ninety-three-year-old Lithuanian goat farmer's wife is living proof that our chances are as good as anyone else's. I found her story in the newspaper and felt genuine regret that I'd never given goat milking a try.

One day when Soya opened the door of her farmhouse in Lithuania, two young men came in and shoved her roughly to the ground. From there, she reached up and grabbed one of the men by the testicles. Then she squeezed with what she later described as "all of my force as hard as I could." The man started screaming like a wounded animal. The neighbors heard the racket, got involved, and called the police. Still, Soja wouldn't let go. Even as the other thug tried everything he could to free his partner, he couldn't shake the ninety-three-year-old woman off him.

Soja later claimed that what saved her that day was the iron grip she had developed from all of her years of goat milking.

For many women, the concept of fighting remains a mystery. They can't shake their preconceived notion that men are the ones who excel at combat. If a woman's attacker is a man—which we know from the statistics that he most likely will be—she instantly assumes he must know what he's doing. But remember your imaginary opponent? Without a doubt, he is a monster and a creep, but is he also an expert? Most criminals are pathetic losers. To think that all of them are crackerjack, know-it-all, hotshot fighters is ridiculous.

If you are ever thrown into the ring, go in with confidence. Remember ninety-three-year-old Soya and her iron grip. Go in fighting. And by all means, go ballistic.

Nobody does it better than you do.

Defense Dos and Don'ts

- Don't be intimidated by your attacker.
- Do realize inexperienced women often win physical battles.
- Don't think you need special training or a black belt to protect yourself.

Power Point!

If anybody can do it, you can.

McCall's Story

It wasn't the first time McCall was sexually assaulted.

Years before, when she was thirteen, her family had attended a company picnic at a Beverly Hills park, where a man who was naked from the waist down grabbed McCall in a public rest room. As she wrestled to get away, he rubbed himself against her arm. She broke free and ran to the safety of her three brothers and the rest of the group. She reported the assault to her parents, but the pervert managed to slip away.

Two decades passed. McCall was married with two sons. She worked as a flight attendant, traveling around the world and dealing with all kinds of people. The next time danger struck, it was in her very own home.

"It was a really hot day, so I had the top of our Dutch door open to let in the ocean breeze. We lived in a nice beach community in Southern California. Of course, I was fooled into believing that we were always safe in our neighborhood."

McCall was the only adult in the house for the first time in months. Her husband had returned to work after recovering from back surgery, and their housekeeper had the day off. Her toddler was asleep in his crib. Her four-month-old son had also fallen asleep, so she went to lay him down on her bed in the master bedroom.

"When I passed my older son's room, I paused, because I thought I'd closed his door earlier. Now it was open. That was my first clue. But I still didn't think anything was wrong."

When McCall went into the master suite to lay her son on the bed, a man came out from his hiding place behind the door. He threw her down on the bed beside her baby, then climbed on top of her.

"I've got a knife," he said threateningly.

McCall remembers thinking, "Hey, I don't care what you've got. There is no way you're raping me!"

Then he pulled out a large butcher knife.

"My baby started crying next to me. All I could think was that this guy would stab him because of the noise he was making. That's when the adrenaline took over. I went absolutely crazy."

McCall went on the attack. With every ounce of energy and might, she began to fight her assailant: hitting him, punching him, kicking, pushing, doing everything she could do to get him off of her. Instead of just fighting to escape a rape, she now wanted to kill him with her own bare hands. The guy soon jumped off of her and ran as fast as he could for the front door.

"I was out for blood at that point. Like a mother lion with her cubs. I ended up chasing him out of my house and halfway up the block. Then I suddenly stopped in the

middle of the street and thought, 'Wait a minute. What am I doing? He's gone, and I've got to get back to my babies!' "

So McCall ran back into her house, locked the Dutch door behind her, and quickly dialed 911.

"It was then that I realized just how hard I had fought. All of my fingernails were broken. I had peed in my pants. My contact had popped out of my eye. And I had a puncture wound in my left arm from the knife. There was a hand towel from my bathroom on the bed with my lipstick and makeup on it. I hadn't even realized he'd used it earlier to put over my mouth and stifle my screams."

The police were there within a few minutes. McCall immediately helped officers with a composite drawing and a neighborhood drive-through. The next day a detective spotted a construction worker doing a job on the house behind McCall's home, and he resembled the composite. McCall later provided the positive identification. The police believed he'd been stalking her for a while. Eventually McCall's attacker was convicted in court, but she believes he served only about six months in prison.

13

DECIDE YOU MAKE
THE RULES

Thorough preparation makes its own luck.

JOE POYER,
AUTHOR AND MILITARY AFFAIRS CONSULTANT

Y ou are in charge.
    There are codes to live by and boundaries to live within. These two elements lay the groundwork for your personal set of security rules. For every woman, rule number one is to make the rules and draw the lines. Rule number two is to abide by them. The guy who's attacking you or following you or stalking you or trying to close in on you or threatening you in some way is not the one who decides this. You are.

    Let's say some guy is crowding you and getting in your space in a public place. When that guy presses against you in a crowded room, you know exactly what to do. You've already made your rules regarding this. You have a rule for keeping a stranger a certain distance away from you. Now this guy doesn't even know about the rules. He has no clue that a woman like you even needs to make rules. He would never guess that you have a rule for situations just like this. There's no way he would know that, one day long ago, you made the decision to remain in control, even in crowded places where some men start pressing in closer to women. So when you suddenly start moving, gaining distance between the two of you and getting away from him, even if it means leaving the place altogether, this guy would never guess that you're doing more than getting yourself out of a suffocating situation. You're following one of your life's rules by protecting your personal boundary line.

Some Basic Security Rules That Women Often Decide to Create and Follow

- They always keep their doors locked at home.
- They activate the security alarm day and night, even when they're home.
- They get into their cars and immediately lock the doors.
- They don't drive or leave their homes alone after dark.
- They always keep pepper spray or another weapon handy.
- They check to make sure they're not being followed.
- They won't allow a workman in their home without a husband or friend present.
- They never open the front door no matter how innocent the visitor may seem.
- They show instant displeasure when men discuss certain topics.
- They insist on a neutral place when meeting a man for the first few dates.
- They don't drink from an open container without assurance of its safety.
- They inform someone of their continual whereabouts in case they end up missing.
- They never leave home without their cell phone.

Make a set of rules that you can follow at home, while driving in your car, and when you're working at the office. You should have rules in place when you're shopping, running errands, or visiting with friends. You definitely need rules for dating. Rules should be in effect when you travel, and even when you're relaxing or sleeping. Your rules can be made apparent to others by the way you dress, the way you speak, and the way you carry yourself.

I broke quite a few of my rules one night a few summers ago.

My teenage son and I were in the family truck, driving through a rough and often dangerous section of a town as we headed to a baseball game where we were to rendezvous with my husband and younger son. We were late, our directions to the park were sketchy, and I suddenly realized the gas gauge was on empty. It was hot so our windows were down. When we came to a four-way stop, I grew alarmed because right at the corner next to us stood a pack of shady-looking characters. They were ogling us, checking out the truck, and breaking glass bottles against the curb. I quickly advised my son to roll up his window. He was oblivious to the immediate danger, and he argued with me instead. He told me not to worry about it. But I was plenty worried. At any moment I was sure to run out of gas, and I still hadn't found our destination in this scary area of a strange town. I wasn't even sure we were driving in the right direction. There were no gas stations in sight. Even if there had been, I was not about to stop and fill up the tank in this neighborhood. And now one of the guys at the curb was walking toward our truck with a broken bottle gripped in his hand. I pushed on the gas, sped through the intersection, and drove off. Within minutes we reached the park where my husband and son were waiting for us.

By the time I got out of the car, I was spitting mad. I was furious with my son for not realizing the potential danger, for not following my instructions, and then for arguing with me. Though I've talked about issues of personal security with him his whole life, and often for his benefit, it was obvious that he hadn't understood the precarious nature of our situation. He definitely had no clue how it felt to be a woman when a bunch of men, armed with broken glass, were leering at her and her son from a few feet away. I verbally blasted my son for what could have happened to us back at that intersection, reminding him why it was imperative that he always listen and obey me, no matter his age or I.Q.

Truthfully, I was a hundred times more infuriated with myself. I'd managed to break so many of my personal security rules all in one evening; it boggled my mind and shook me to the core. For crying out loud, I knew better than to allow myself to get in a situation like that. Because of scheduling issues that night, it was impossible for our family to travel in one car, but that could have easily been rule number one. Knowing exactly where I was going and having a full tank of gas would've been smart moves on my part. Being on time so that I was not already distracted when I ran into those guys would've helped, too.

This whole experience was a great reminder that conscious effort is necessary when making and following your rules. Sometimes it takes a little extra energy on our parts to keep the rules intact. There are situations where we'll need to go the extra mile at a prior time in order to observe the rules later.

The bottom line: our safety rules are successful only when we regard them as serious guidelines and then choose to follow them regularly.

When you make your rules, be sure to include the creation of invisible lines around your physical body as well as your personal, emotional, social, and professional well-being. Once these lines are in place, you must always be aware of them. Imagine how they are positioned and utilize them as perimeters for what is safe, appropriate, and acceptable behavior from others.

After practicing this for a while, it will become quite obvious when someone trespasses across one of your boundaries. If this occurs, you'll immediately know that it's time to speak, act, bolt out the door, or run down the street. When one of your lines is violated, you'll find yourself doing exactly what is necessary to get him away from you. Or you'll do something to send *him* back across that line and out of the territory he violated with his presence.

Take, for example, a career or social boundary line you've created to keep a rule about a certain level of professionalism for yourself within the workplace. Then Joe, your coworker, says something inappropriate, something that could qualify as sexual harassment on the job. His comments make you very uncomfortable. But let's say you know Joe is sort of a jerk who has the reputation as the big joker around the office. You also know that he's married. Are you imagining that he's coming across your line? All too often this second-guessing prevents a woman from shoving a man back to his side of the line and out of her territory. Who cares if he's a jerk and everyone knows it? Who cares if he's the office joker? Who cares if he's happily married? If you're uncomfortable, that means he's out of line. It also means that he's crossed *your* line.

Too often women fail to believe that some guy really said what they think he said. We question if he really meant what we heard. Sometimes we're willing to give total slimeballs the benefit of the doubt just to keep *them* from embarrassment or to prevent a roomful of people from witnessing an uncomfortable situation. We don't like to rock the boat. We protect everyone but ourselves as we refrain from revealing our true strength. We know all too well how office politics work. We know that there are men who won't accept this type of brush-off, and they'll portray us as paranoid lunatics instead of women willing to stand up for ourselves. We assume that people will consider us too serious, too mean-spirited, and too aggressive for our own good. We believe we'll be accused of being unfeminine or overtly masculine. We fear that we will jeopardize our position, the money we earn, future career goals, and our entire life should we lose our jobs. We think we need to take time to digest the incident and analyze it from all angles.

While it's true that we need time, the time is now, not when the room is full of your coworkers eyeballing your showdown with the jerk. Draw your lines today, and it will be crystal clear when someone crosses over. Your response doesn't have to be bad-tempered or malicious. There are unlimited ways to get your point across to someone in order to force him back across the line you've established.

You can be calmly assertive. "Joe, I'm uncomfortable with the comment you just made."

Or your remarks can be blunt, almost humorous. "Hey, Joe, you may live happily in your own personal gutter, but I'm not going there, not even for a visit."

Speaking your mind clearly and honestly can be one of the best rules to have and an effective way to handle a bad situation, or you can just come on strong, perhaps something to the tune of, "Joe, you're nothing but slime. Your wife would kill you if she knew the stuff coming out of your mouth around this place. I'd like nothing better than to staple your lips together and throw you in the outgoing mail bin."

But seriously, if you're going to reprimand a fellow coworker, be sure to examine your own office demeanor. Your rules should definitely include one that prompts you to act properly on the job. That alone will aid you in deflecting many strange advances and inappropriate comments from others. If you happen to be the office floozy or the company party girl, most of the men around you are going to think anything goes in your presence anyway. Right or wrong, that's just the way it is.

Along with personal, emotional, social, and professional lines, there are the highly critical physical lines you must draw to create optimum personal security. As we continue with our choices, we'll discover the dimensions and the diversities of our personal space (coming up in chapter 24, "Decide to Protect Your Space"). For now, begin to create these lines around your physical well-being. Envision them surrounding you from two or three feet away. Strangers should, for the most part, stay on the other side of those lines. When they cross over, they are either going to make you break one of those rules you just made or they are going to get the boot.

It's been years, but I can still see one creepy man's hand coming across my physical boundary line.

Strangely enough, it happened at my wedding reception. Late in the evening a male guest grabbed my breast and shook it roughly. This shocking occurrence took place right in front of my new mother-in-law, father-in-law, and brother-in-law as we stood in a circle chatting. The whole thing came entirely out of left field. I'd never said more than ten words to the jerk. We were not standing there talking about how my wedding gown fit at the bodice. I did not complain that I had an itch and, boy, would I kill for someone to give it a good scratch. This creep simply helped himself to what police officers would describe as a sexual battery.

There were a few reasons that I didn't block him. For one thing, I wasn't trained in the martial arts yet. Second, I wasn't even looking at him. At that particular moment, I happened to be facing my mother-in-law and answering a question she'd just asked me. Also, as the bride, people had been reaching for me all evening to give me a hug, to pull me to the dance floor, to take a picture, or to stop and visit.

When this jerk's hand reached out and groped me in such a disgusting manner in front of my new family members, I actually saw in my peripheral vision the moment in which he crossed my line. Then I had a purely visceral reaction. In a flash, I moved close enough to punch him in the face. Reverting back to the tetherball punch (the hammer fist) that my dad encouraged me to use back on the sixth grade bully, I brought my fist across my chest and backhanded him with it in the nose three times. I remember thinking, "Wow, I'm punching somebody out at my wedding! Right smack in the face, too!"

After three punches, I paused, then thought, "Well, that wasn't enough. I'm the bride, darn it!" And so I went back for more. Same transition move closer to him. Same backhand hammer fist straight into his nose. Same punch three more times. Only this time my new father-in-law had come to life and was starting to make his move. After his initial shock and hesitation, he had stepped over to this creep with the intention of ushering him away from me and out the door. But my father-in-law's new position had placed him in the direct path of my fist. So I accidentally clipped *his* nose as I threw the first of my second set of punches.

By now things were starting to get downright comical! My brother-in-law had jumped in to shove the guy around. Then my husband glanced over from across the room and started complaining about his kid brother fighting with the wedding guests. The creep was quickly tossed out the back door of the country club, with his humiliated wife and son following behind. Our guests wondered what on earth had just happened.

"I heard it had something to do with Lori's boob."

"Lori's boob?"

"Surely if some guy was looking for boobs, he could have hit table number seven over there."

Okay, you get the picture.

But here's what I discovered. Frank was furious, for weeks actually, mostly because he hadn't been able to do anything to the guy. This creep had left the reception by the time Frank was told the details. For me, however, the incident ended as soon as my line was crossed, my rules were broken, and I went into action with the hammer fist.

———

Consider your rules and boundary lines as absolutely vital to your well-being.

This is exactly where you will win or lose. This is what will keep you safe and alive. It's where the power exists and where the power can shift. If a guy crosses your line and, for whatever reason, you break a rule and allow him to stay, you've just given him all the power. But if he comes across and you shove him back where he belongs, you've not only retained the power, you've probably heightened it.

When your lines are drawn and someone crosses over, you will need to act or speak up immediately. You might need to get physical in order to rescue yourself from the situation. Make it clear he is no longer allowed to stand this close to you or to speak in that tone or on a topic that's causing you concern. Let him know he has moved from neutral territory into personal territory. Tell him to get packing. Or just get the heck out of there on your own.

If someone is acting physically aggressive with you, he is crossing your line. If a man pushes you around, he is invading your territory. When some creep makes a sexual comment, your rules are being ignored and your line is being violated. If he touches you in an uncomfortable way, he's just trespassed illegally. Handle it. If he puts up a fight, take it for what it is, a battle over your personal rules and a contest for the power of that moment.

You're not demanding that everyone be perfect in your presence, you're simply asking that they not come into your territory and jeopardize your security. In most cases, messing with your rules and crossing your boundary lines means the guy is either clueless, seriously misunderstanding you, or up to something.

You're an artist and an architect. Start drawing some lines.

You rule.

Defense Dos and Don'ts

- Do create rules and boundary lines for optimum security.
- Do take precautions to keep your rules intact and working on your behalf.
- Don't fail to respond firmly when someone crosses your line.

→ *Power Point!* ←
Lay down your laws.

◄ 14 ►

DECIDE TO LIVE LIFE IN A STATE OF AWARENESS

Require not just a moment of perception,
but a continuous awareness, a continuous
state of inquiry in which there is
no conclusion.

BRUCE LEE,
*JEET KUNE DO: BRUCE LEE'S COMMENTARIES
ON THE MARTIAL WAY*

S ee it and believe it.

For years we've been told to be aware. Our mothers advised us to "Look around and see who's near you." The experts lectured, "Observe your surroundings at all times." But what exactly does this mean? Most women try to be aware. Many women think they are very aware. They may glance over their shoulders a few times as they head to the car with their keys between their fingers. They may check out the strange-looking guy who is roaming around the neighborhood. Too often, though, that is the extent of their awareness.

Remember the definition that awareness is 90 percent of self-defense? Awareness needs to be increased to the point that it *becomes* your lifestyle. It needs to be a tool you use every waking moment of the day.

Webster's dictionary describes the word *aware* as "on one's guard, vigilant, knowing or realizing, conscious and informed." But let's give it some muscle, shall we? Let's call it "a constant state of readiness." The woman who clenches her keys, beelining it to the car with a few sideways glances, doesn't exactly sum up "a constant state of readiness."

The woman practicing "a constant state of readiness" is a force. To watch her would look something like this:

There she goes, striding through the parking lot as she heads for her car. She sees everything: her vehicle, inside and underneath it, the entire 360-degree view, the guy over there in the phone booth, the elderly lady one parking row over. She sizes up the guy on the phone. She lets him see that she's looking at him. She lets the whole world know she's looking at him and at everyone else as a matter of fact. She notices he's a skinny guy with jeans and a black cap. He's about ten feet away from her car in that phone booth. She takes her eyes off him for a second, then looks back at him. She unlocks her door. The elderly lady is putting groceries in her trunk. A store clerk comes outside to round up shopping carts. She looks again at the phone booth guy. She sees a car pull past the store entrance. She opens the driver's door. The guy in the phone booth hangs up the phone. Now, if that guy suddenly decided to pounce on her, she knows he could reach her in less than three or four seconds. If so, she would see him coming in her peripheral vision, drop her shopping bag, grab something heavy she has stashed in her car, scream like a wild monkey, and face him straight on.

But the guy just stands there. He leans back against the phone booth. The elderly lady is still wrestling with her bags in the trunk. The clerk heads toward a shopping cart two aisles over. She climbs in the driver's seat, locks the door, and puts the key in the ignition. The guy at the phone booth thumbs through his wallet. She starts her car. That guy could still get to her quickly, but she mentally adds two seconds to the previous calculation because he's leaned back in a relaxed posture now. If he approached her, she wouldn't be at all surprised, because she knows anything can happen. If he surged in her direction, she'd never unlock her door or open her window. She'd put the car into gear and drive away. She's betting that her actions, attitude, and continual study of this guy will probably cause him to stay put. Sometimes, all bets are off, and she knows that, too. She pulls the car out of the parking space, still watching the guy in her rearview mirror as she drives away. A few blocks later, she checks her mirror again.

Now that's what I call "a constant state of readiness."

I have a confession for you. If all the men I've spoken to or stood behind in line or pumped gas next to had any idea what was on my mind, they'd think I was a complete loony tune. If they knew how often I calculated the number of steps or seconds it would take to get into position to punch my fist through their throats, they'd deem me certifiable. But these are the thoughts of a woman committed to a lifestyle of awareness. A "state of awareness" makes the day full of interesting mental exercises. It sharpens your senses. Timing and distance are factored. Choices are analyzed. When forced to, your awareness mechanisms will process this vital information quite easily all day long.

Perhaps the best advantage of awareness is that it packs a spiffy two-punch. It becomes both your edge and your double-edged sword. You use it to watch and realize, and simultaneously, it goes to work on your outward appearance. Awareness is certainly not some secret or covert tactic that you'll need to keep under wraps. Instead, it's something to deliberately flaunt. Let the entire world see just how aware you are. As you practice awareness with your mind, it is exhibited in your mannerisms and body language. When you're being aware, you'll look more confident, sure of yourself, and less like a target. The bad guys are out there studying women and choosing victims. Like predatory animals, they wait in the shadows before striking. They are not looking to pick the woman who spotted them first, the one who's already watching them, or the one who looks directly into their eyes several times. Women who look aware and constantly ready are the least likely to be chosen as victims.

Very early in my karate study, my instructor used an entire evening session to speak to our class about awareness. To me, this was a waste of my workout time. I thought I knew all about being aware. Hadn't most women been preached to enough on the topic? What a yawn, I thought, figuring there was nothing new for me to learn.

Two days later I was standing in a long line at the bank. My two very young sons were with me. One of them was inspecting a potted ficus next to the door. The other was helping himself to a few business cards from a tray on the loan officer's desk. I was keeping an eye on my kids. I was figuring out which bills I would pay when this deposit was recorded. I was planning what to cook for dinner that night. Finally it was my turn to step up to the teller window. I conducted my business, rounded up my sons, and headed for the door.

Outside I ran into a girlfriend, and we stopped to chat. Within moments the door of the bank opened behind me and out walked my karate instructor! I nearly fell over. He had been standing two or three people behind me in that bank line the whole time. As he passed by me, all he said was "It looks like you need to work on your awareness, Lori."

Of all places to be lazy about awareness! The bank! A place that actually gets robbed with some frequency! Years have since passed, but without fail, I think of that incident each time I step foot in a bank or wait in any line. The memory causes me to check out all the people around me, to inspect the entire place, to observe the mood of the employees, and to note the atmosphere in the room.

———

Granted, it's impossible to be aware twenty-four hours a day. After all, we do have to sleep sometime. But when you hear a noise or smell an odor that just doesn't compute, you need to be ready. When your neighbor is on your porch and there's something goofy about him, you need to be ready. When you're out on a date and the conversation gets uncomfortable, you need to be ready. And when that guy back in the parking lot phone booth starts after you, you'd better be aware.

Awareness is a lifestyle. Get ready. Start keeping an eye on things.

Defense Dos and Don'ts

- Don't hide your awareness from others.
- Do observe and be mindful of your surroundings.
- Do notice what the people around you are doing.
- Don't ignore unusual behavior.

 *Power Point!* ◄

Wake up your senses and wise-up your consciousness.

◄ 15 ►

DECIDE TO MASTER
VERBAL SELF-DEFENSE

Speech is a mirror of the soul;
as a man speaks, so is he.

PUBLILIUS SYRUS,
FIRST-CENTURY LATIN WRITER
OF MORAL MAXIMS

Words are powerful weapons.

This is another one of those self-defense decisions that can simultaneously work for us in two different ways. To put it simply: we hear the things we need to hear, and we say the things we need to say. As a result, this verbal self-defense will keep our personal security intact.

These are strange times. Women are being attacked by their friends and acquaintances. They are brutally raped by the men they are dating. Aside from the fact that there are bad guys out there with serious issues concerning violence, there also appears to be a breakdown in communications. While it's impossible that each bad guy might be controlled by words, or that every violent situation could be resolved with a little chat or even some bold dialogue, it's worth noting that many men out there need to know what women are truly made of. Words are a great vehicle for exactly that. It's also important to understand that, if you listen carefully to his words, a man will often provide tangible clues about himself and his intentions.

Verbal Self-defense Is a Dual Process

1. Listen in order to understand exactly what is being said in your presence.
2. Say precisely the things that will allow others to understand you.

First of all, you owe it to yourself to fully absorb the dialogue of the men who populate your world. I'm not talking about hanging on to their every word with bated breath. Instead, pay attention to any verbal signals that will alert you to impending danger. In other words, allow his words to showcase his true persona. Don't ever ignore verbal clues that reveal characteristics that might be problematic later.

Some of the ways in which a man will verbally cue you of suspicious or dangerous tendencies:

- He will exhibit vulgar, profane, defaming, disgusting, or violent talk about women in general.
- He will show a lack of respect when speaking about any woman.
- He will speak of violent or destructive acts he's committed in the past.
- He will come across as pushy and controlling by trying to make decisions for you, or by attempting to run your life or schedule.

- He will use a dismissive tone when speaking to you or about you, as if unable and unwilling to seriously consider your feelings or requests.

Likewise, you also owe it to yourself to be heard. Whenever you speak, you want to convey to the world that you are made of some really powerful stuff, including strength of character and a sturdy backbone. Take full command of the language, especially when you need to get a point across. Often you can keep a situation under control simply by saying what is necessary right from the start. Say what you mean, and if need be, back it up with action. Always use your vocabulary to convey strength, confidence, and decisiveness.

Your voice can save you in the following ways:

- *Set the tone.* Whether it's a friendship, relationship, or a chance meeting on the street, always let a man know what kind of woman he is dealing with.

- *Speak up.* When something is going wrong, express yourself. Say it quickly and loudly if you feel the need. You don't have to behave like a challenging, insulting witch. Just use your words to display firmness and strength.

- *Involve others.* Let those around you know what's going on. Include the people nearby: the couple sitting at the next table, the guy on the bus next to you, or the people walking past you on the sidewalk. Allow them to hear that you are being harassed. Tell everyone within earshot if you think it will help. Start shouting the whole story out loud if you want to. Who cares if you feel like a fool? If something does happen, these people may be your only witnesses to the event.

- **Put a stop to it.** Get up and get out. Tell him to leave. If he puts up a fight or gets pushy, his true colors will be exposed, and you'll know it's time to get rid of him fast.

- **Pick up the phone.** Call 911 and inform the emergency operator that you are being harassed or threatened. Or report it to your parents or a friend. Do this right in front of the bad guy if you like. Let him hear you speaking about his rotten behavior as you're attempting to distance yourself from him.

No matter how much you grow to appreciate the results of verbal self-defense in your life, do keep in mind that there are some things to vocalize and others to keep under wraps.

In the martial arts, there are secrets. The standard secret question in many dojos is "What did you do in your black belt test?" The standard secret answer is "If I tell you, then I'll have to kill you." This little joke forced us to remember that some things were better left unsaid. In this case, silence was an absolute necessity for maintaining the integrity of that highly important examination.

Likewise, our instructors urged us to keep quiet about our karate skills when out in the world, especially in the company of people we didn't know or trust. Sometimes the identity of the enemy is unclear. By not discussing our training, we keep the proverbial "card up our sleeve" just in case we ever need to use it.

You don't want to accidentally tell the bad guy all about your best self-defense moves, the cool getaway technique you just learned, the sledgehammer you sleep with every night, or the one crime that scares the daylights out of you. You don't want to tell that new guy you're dating that you're reading a book about decisive self-defense. You don't want to share your decisions with that guy on campus who seems to watch you a lot. Let him think you know zip about all this fighting stuff in case your forearm needs to blast through the air and crack his jaw apart someday. Then, as that shock is registering, if he doesn't back off, bust up a couple of his ribs. When he's wondering where you learned that, give him a kick between the legs. And so on.

I have two friends who used verbal self-defense with courage and utter brilliance. One used many words for a long period of time. The other used very few words within seconds. Both methods worked beautifully.

Here are their stories.

A total stranger approached Alice in an underground parking garage. He forced himself into her car and made it very clear that she was going to be raped. So Alice started talking. And talking. And talking. Exhibiting calmness and patience, Alice desperately tried to connect with her attacker, both verbally and emotionally, on a level of communication he perhaps never expected from a victim. She used that connection for all it was worth. She shared thoughts about herself and encouraged him to open up and do the same. Suddenly Alice was no longer his victim. She was his confidante. After a couple of hours, he released her unharmed.

Melissa remembers her use of defensive words from a frightening incident as a young girl. She was walking home from school at the age of twelve with two schoolmates. A man pulled up in a car beside them. When the girls glanced his way, they saw he was naked from the waist down, masturbating as he urged them to come closer to the car. Melissa walked immediately to the back of his vehicle and began shouting the letters and numbers of his license plate, over and over again. She screamed so loudly, people in homes up and down the whole block heard her. One of them called the police and reported the license plate number. The man took off, but officers located his vehicle and apprehended him. The girls gave a positive identification. At just twelve years of age, this adolescent girl showed she had "the stuff" and "the smarts" to effectively use the power of her words against an adult.

It's been more than thirty years, but Melissa can still accurately recite that license plate number.

Some college girls recently gave my verbal self-defense some extra muscle. They informed me about "code words" that their families had come up with for emergencies. One girl told us certain code words used by her parents meant that something was wrong and the kids should go immediately to the designated safe room of their home. One girl was encouraged to use a particular code word on the phone to her mother when an evening babysitting job was over, but the girl didn't feel comfortable accepting a ride home with the man of the house. Another explained that if anyone out of the ordinary ever tried to pick her up from school, they had to recite the family's code word before she'd get into the car.

Now here's the last word about verbal self-defense.

The dumbest thing a bad guy can ever say to you is "Lady, I'm gonna kill you." Or, "Take off your pants. I'm going to rape you now." Or, "I'm going to stab you, torture you, then cut you up into little pieces, cook you in a big pot, and eat you for dinner."

When the bad guy is stupid enough to tell you his violent, lethal intentions, he's just called you up for active duty. He's given you your only option in this world. In doing so, he's sure to unleash a wild animal. You will be fighting for your life like a crazed maniac.

His words will take you exactly where you needed to go anyway—absolutely nuts! If a bad guy should ever tell you in advance the horrific scheme he has designed for you, don't hesitate to believe him. Let his words ignite your inner fire until you explode. Defend your life as if there's no tomorrow. Why? Because he's not lying. And even if he's the equivalent of pond scum, this is the one time when you should believe what he's saying and take his word for it.

Keep your ears open and your mouth moving.

Defense Dos and Don'ts

- Do listen to what a man is really saying.
- Don't make excuses if it's not what you were expecting or hoping to hear.
- Do speak your mind with confidence and certainty.

→ *Power Point!* ←

Hear it. Tell it like it is.

16

DECIDE TO DEVISE
A STRATEGY

A sly rabbit will have three
openings to its den.

CHINESE PROVERB

You need a game plan.

You need a one-way ticket out of every sticky situation you can imagine. This calls for escape routes. In your home, these are like fire drills. If a fire's burning the back door down, you don't just stand there looking at it and wondering what it will do next. Instead you hustle out the front door as fast as you can.

Let's say a man breaks his way into your home through the front door. While another woman might think, "Oh, no, I can't believe this is happening to me," or, "What am I going to do now?" you should already be mobile, moving through an outlined plan you schemed up long ago. Perhaps his presence at your front door frees up your back door and your side door. Now, you have a choice. Since your back door is closer, your cell phone is recharging right next to it, and your pepper spray is hidden there, too, that's the route you want to take. Perhaps there are weapons near both of those exits that you could grab on your way out to safety. Maybe you've thought about this enough to know the bad guy could be working with another bad guy, so you need to be on guard as you exit your home. If your children or roommates are home, round them up as you move steadily in the direction of the exit you've selected. Suppose you've already identified a shortcut through your backyard to the neighbor's house or to the street. These are the types of plans you need to have in mind at all times. Think of them often as you walk through your home.

When you arrive at a public place, a crowded club, for example, notice the location of the exits. If you make this a routine plan in all unfamiliar locations and there happens to be an emergency, you're going to be one of the first ones out. In a restaurant, always keep an eye on the door. In fact, sit facing it if you can. Always know where the back door is in case you need it for a quick escape. The same thing goes for shops or stores. In large department stores, keep track of what floor or level you're on and how you would get out quickly if you need to.

These aren't difficult concepts to apply to your life. You certainly won't have to draw up an artist's rendition of how to get the heck out of your house, around and away from someone on the street, or out of the driver's seat of your car. You do need to consider your options in the quiet times as you're walking through your home, workplace, or parking lot. Soon it will become natural. You'll simply enter a room and see the escape route stretched out before you, and you'll make a mental note of your best plan of action.

The key word here is *escape,* so try not to trap yourself in a dead-end room such as a bathroom. (There are a few exceptions to this rule, like the one coming up in "Kate's Story," when a bathroom happened to provide the necessary resources for escape.) Usually the bathroom is not the best room to head for. In movies, they always show women running from the bad guy and hiding in the bathroom, only to be left looking in the mirror at their own scared little faces. Bathrooms are prisons. There's no door to the outside street. There's nothing to hide behind. The windows are usually too small to climb out of. There aren't any decent weapons in there unless you've got a knack for disabling someone with a roll of toilet paper or a bar of soap. (Or unless you stash a few tools or weapons, which I'll discuss in chapter 29, "Decide to Use Props.")

If you must board yourself up in a room, choose one with weapons, a phone, and a window large enough to allow your escape. Plant these items in some of your rooms ahead of time. Create a panic room, or a safe room if you like. It doesn't have to be some elaborate construction project. You can turn a walk-in closet into a panic room with a dead-bolt lock, security hinges, a jam lock, a battery-operated light that you touch to turn on, and a cell phone. The main thing is that you have a plan in place.

All this strategy is bound to give you an edge. In your home, however, you already have huge advantages from the get-go. After all, the bad guy doesn't live in your house. You do. He doesn't know this hallway leads to nowhere or which drawer contains the ice pick. He has no idea where you keep one of your seven canisters of pepper spray. He would never guess you planned ahead and have an extra key for the car stashed near one of your exits. There's no way he would know the baseball bat's behind the door, or that you even have a fifth door that leads outside from the upstairs study.

Vivian's strategy worked quickly to her benefit one scary morning.

When she heard the knock at her door and looked out the peephole, Vivian immediately knew this guy didn't belong at her house. She would later discover that her gut was right, because this man was completely deranged and attempting to get inside. He was covered with sweat, and he kept looking around and over his shoulders as if he was fearful of being discovered.

Vivian didn't open the door. Instead, she turned around, picked up her phone off the hall table, dialed 911, and quietly explained to the dispatcher what was happening as she proceeded down the hall. She then scooped up her infant, who was sleeping in a bedroom.

Heading for the back door, Vivian kept glancing out the windows. She suddenly spotted the man again, but now he was in her backyard. She switched directions, telling the dispatcher that she and her baby were now going out the front door. The dispatcher assured Vivian that a squad car would arrive at any minute and that he would stay on the line until Vivian and her child had gotten safely away.

Vivian ran up the street with her baby in her arms, knowing which of her neighbors would be home at that hour. They watched from a safe distance as several police units arrived. Soon after, the escaped criminal was spread-eagled on Vivian's front lawn and surrounded by law enforcement officers.

Vivian's decisive strategy worked. She made her way through her house with the only two things that mattered—a phone to the outside world and her child.

Make the best plans for the worst predicaments you can imagine:

- *Car jackings.* Decide ahead of time what you would do whether he had a weapon or not. No second locations— ever! This means aim for getting out of that car however you can. Toss the keys several feet away, forcing him to go get them. Jump out of the car with zealous cooperation. Grab your child out of the backseat. Start running. Or, if he's heading in the driver's door, climb over into the passenger seat and out that door.

- **Abductions.** Again, no second locations. If someone tries to grab you and take you somewhere, start moving with all of your strength. This is a Force Level Four lethal attack, so your immediate defense measures should include targets such as the eyes, groin, and throat and any item nearby that could qualify as a weapon. Make plans that no matter where you are when an attempted kidnapping occurs, you'll fight to get away and head for the nearest populated area.

- **Home invasions.** Your goal is survival, and the best way to accomplish that is through your exits, which include all the doors and windows in your home. Be sure to plant props and weapons ahead of time. Focus on their efficiency and location long before the bad guy ever comes through the door.

- **Rape attempts.** You should know by now whether you'd fight a rapist. If so, what moves would you use against a rapist in your home or elsewhere? Again, this calls for a Force Level Four response, so aim for those serious targets (the eyes, groin, and throat). Plan for emergency procedures that include items stashed around your home and others you carry when you're out. Never lose sight of your path to escape. Getting away is always your best strategy for any attack.

Make your own similar blueprints for altercations with street thugs and for workplace or school violence. Plan for as many scenarios as possible. Share your plans with family members so they will be in sync if they happen to be participants in a crisis with

you. Talk about your plans with your friends so they will understand your motivation. These plans are not only good when used
for escaping bad guys, but they work well for fires and other emergencies, too.

One effective tool for planning strategies is to play a game called
what-if. It's a game where anything can happen. Decks are loaded.
Wild cards are scattered across the board. Big-time gambling is going on. Life and death are the stakes.

What-if is a game that you should be practicing regularly. You
should play it in your home and out on the town. While you're
with other people and when you're alone. You should think what-
if as you sit in your car at the stoplight and as you walk along the
avenue to window-shop. Pretty soon, you'll be so used to playing
what-if, you'll be able to do it anywhere, anytime, and with very
little effort.

I play what-if almost all the time, not in some freaky, paranoid way, but with observance and awareness. I'm playing it right
now, as a matter of fact. As I'm typing on the keyboard of my
computer in my home library, I'm asking myself a question I've
asked and answered a thousand times. What if a bad guy is in my
house right now? What if he came bursting into this room and attacked me?

Without wasting one second of precious time to see what he's
up to or to think about how creepy it is that this bad guy invaded
my home in the first place, I'm planning to be up and moving. After all, this is familiar territory for me. This bad guy has been part
of my game for years. I've seen his hand before. There shouldn't
be too many surprises, because I've known all along that bad
things happen to good people and that I'm my own bodyguard.
I'm well aware that this horrible sort of thing could happen. So,
instead of waiting to see what he wants or wondering what on
earth to do, I'm already throwing something at him, then moving

in with a weapon I keep by my side. No questions. No excuses. No apologies.

What if your situation is similar? Let's say you also work at home at your computer. What if you had to fight off an attacker in that room? What if you had some interesting things right at your fingertips? Things for throwing, beating, or stabbing. An iron lamp. A telephone. A heavy stapler. A pair of scissors. What if the bad guy managed to get all the way into the room, sneak up on you, and choke you from behind? What if you could get your hands on a sharp item? The scissors, for example. What if you could stab him and free yourself enough to turn around? What if you picked up a chair and threw it at him or threw it out the window to attract attention, surprise him, or change the dynamics of the situation? What if you punched him in the solar plexus, smashed his nose in, and lunged at him with those scissors? What if you kept all your defenses on overdrive for quite some time? What if you lined up fifteen different fight techniques, one after the other? What if a few of them actually worked? What if you bought yourself enough time to escape?

What if you actually won this game?

What if this isn't a game?

Believe it or not, this is how the most important game you might ever play must be visualized in your life.

At a store, it's what if that guy pulled out a gun and held up the cashier? What would I do? Comply? Wait for an opportunity to escape? Stand there with my hands up? Yes, most likely. But how about if he put the gun to my head and started dragging me out of the store with loot from the cash register? Well, I've played this game enough to know I'm fighting when it comes to that second location. Once I put up my fight, I'm running. And I'll do so in a zigzag pattern to make myself a more difficult target, diminishing his chances of shooting me as I race to get away.

At home, it's what if I was awakened from a dead sleep by a guy trying to climb on top of me? What if I was attacked while on the toilet or in the shower? Are you prepared to fight naked? It may seem crazy, but all women must think about this, and here's why: for females, the threat of rape makes fighting naked or partially dressed a tremendous possibility. One of the first things a rapist tries to do is remove some or all of his victim's clothing. As the woman is cringing with humiliation, the rapist is instantly achieving the power he so desperately needs. By the way, fighting naked is no different from fighting when dressed. It's just cooler and breezier.

Playing what-if will make you aware of your limitless options. You will begin to recognize effective strategies, new avenues of escape, and interesting weapons within reach that will aid in your fight. The process of playing what-if will force your mind to prepare itself.

Get in the game. Create the strategies you'd use against invading enemies. Come up with all the battle plans you can and go out fighting.

Defense Dos and Don'ts

- Do imagine the worst scenarios in order to rehearse for the best outcome.
- Don't ignore the possibilities of an attack anywhere, anytime.
- Do plan the routes for escape in your own house.
- Do play what-if often to consider alternative strategies.

➤ *Power Point!* ◄

Find a way out every time. Make it happen.

Kate's Story

The last person Kate expected to meet that afternoon was a maniacal stalker. She was standing in line at the military credit union where she conducted business regularly. Surrounded by men in uniform, she felt anything but vulnerable.

He said he was a former Marine. And a former cop. He even showed Kate his badge. As a former member of the law enforcement community herself, she was no pushover. His badge was the real deal, so she deduced that he probably was, too. Besides, he seemed like a nice guy. Attractive. A tall man with a muscular build. They exchanged phone numbers and met for coffee a week later. They had dinner a week after that. He kissed her good night in the parking lot before Kate drove herself home. She wasn't one to offer her home address right away.

Late one night the following week, Kate was cooking in her third-floor condo in a resort community that overlooked a golf course. She was preparing pasta sauce to serve to friends who would be arriving in town the following day. It was nearly midnight, but her kitchen trash was overflowing, so she decided to dump it in the communal bin outside.

"I opened the door and, to my horror, he was standing there! I'd never given him my address, yet he was on the landing right outside my front door. And he was armed. He made sure that I saw the 9 mm in his waistband. With his enormous strength, he immediately shoved me back into my condo. His push knocked me to the floor and my head bounced backward on the tile. Trash flew everywhere. Meanwhile, he'd slammed the door and locked all four of my dead bolts."

Kate realized she was trapped, but spoke boldly to him, "I don't think I invited you here."

"I'm here because I'm supposed to be here," he answered.

In the kitchen the man began a series of sexual assaults on Kate that lasted for more than a couple of hours. Each time he touched her, he grabbed, pinched, bruised, and groped her intimate body parts.

Kate responded by instinct. In a drastic attempt to level the playing field, she met him move for move, aggression for aggression. If he grabbed her roughly, she grabbed him back with equal roughness. This went on for what seemed like an eternity. At one point he forced Kate to perform oral sex on him.

"He was not in his right mind, and I intuitively knew that if I showed any weakness, he would take me down. To him, his physical aggression against me was some sick form of foreplay. To me, it was a matter of life and death."

Kate thought about the knives on the countertop, but felt certain he'd shoot her if she went for one.

So she tried another approach. "You've got to be hungry!" She posed the words as a statement rather than a question.

He was hungry. Kate poured him a glass of wine and proceeded to boil pasta.

"This act of cooking a meal for him seemed to derail him. It slowed him down. He began behaving in a more controlled manner."

After eating the entire meal, Kate managed to get him out of the kitchen and into the living room where she offered to give him a back rub.

"I have some massage oils in the bathroom. I'll get

them." Again, she made a statement, and she didn't ask for permission.

Kate walked past the front door, wishing she could escape. But if she attempted to unlock all four of those dead bolts, she knew that he'd certainly have time to shoot her.

Once in the bathroom, luck was suddenly with her. Kate had left her purse there earlier, and it contained her cell phone. She quietly locked the door behind her and dialed 911 while also removing the curtain rod's dowel to use as a wedge of security between the doorknob and the cupboard. She went through the bathroom's drawers and cupboards, collecting sharp fingernail files and aerosol sprays, anything she felt she might be able to use for defense. She placed the laundry hamper under the doorknob, then sat back against it with her feet braced against the wall.

"I whispered to the dispatcher, but I was very specific with instructions. I told him to send officers armed with a battering ram in order to bust down that front door of mine. I also encouraged him to send officers as fast as possible. After about five minutes, my attacker started banging on the bathroom door. I didn't say a word, but I did keep the dispatcher on the line. The situation was deteriorating, and I wanted everyone to understand the threat I was facing."

Ten minutes after locking herself in the bathroom, the condo's front door was leveled, and Kate's home was quickly infiltrated by dozens of police officers. The man with the gun was taken into custody. Police later discovered his real identity, that of a deranged mental patient with a completely different name and life story. His personal history included numerous institutions and psychotic breaks with additional violence against women, but no Marine Corps or police work.

"They jailed him, and during one of his first nights in custody, he stabbed himself through the wrist with the prongs of a dinner fork and bled to death." Kate continued, her voice rich with irony, "His family actually tried to sue me. They insisted that because I'd met him for coffee and dinner, I must have encouraged him and brought the whole thing upon myself."

Kate sought medical and psychological recovery after her ordeal. As a result, she was able to resume her normal life, to reclaim her career and creative passions, and to embrace her strength and survival.

17

DECIDE WHAT YOUR STRENGTHS AND WEAKNESSES ARE

Sometimes it is more important to discover what one cannot do, than what one can do.

LIN YUTANG,
CHINESE WRITER AND INVENTOR

You need a reality check.

Chances are slim that you'll come off looking like Wonder Woman. You're probably not built like the Rock. I doubt you can twirl ladders above your head like Jackie Chan, execute Bruce Lee's one-inch punch, or wipe out an entire village of bad guys faster than Chuck Norris. No way. You're just out there in the world winging it like the rest of us. You'd be happy to run away or scream for help or hit one target out of ten with great force. Heck, you'd be happy not to pass out on the floor.

Join the club.

It's time to analyze our strengths and weaknesses.

When it comes to weaknesses, I've had the humbling experience of discovering and digesting my shortcomings quite a few times in my life. I often think I've got plenty more than my share, too. Many of these deficiencies were revealed to me early in my life. As a kid, I certainly wasn't the smartest student or the best athlete. Then, as a journalist, it was apparent that I wasn't the most aggressive interviewer, the most talented writer, or the most gifted producer.

But when it came to karate training, my weaknesses seemed more obvious than ever. There I was, five feet four inches tall, a woman surrounded mostly by men who were stronger and, in most cases, more skilled and experienced fighters. I tackled that great divide the only way I knew how to—by working my butt off. Each day I practiced karate for up to three hours in my garage dojo. As the years passed, the moves were burned into my psyche. When someone else forgot his kata or technique, I remembered. When a kick needed that extra snap, mine somehow managed to have it. When we closed our eyes to practice lengthy forms in complete darkness, facing an opposite direction, I continued, unshaken. When a partner blanked on a self-defense move, there I was, plowing ahead, perhaps weaker, perhaps feminine, but getting the job done anyway.

In karate class we all learned a great deal about personal weaknesses from a big guy named Mike. Six feet seven inches. Three hundred pounds. Pure muscle, but with the personality of a teddy bear. Doing self-defense with him seemed more like a comedy skit. When aiming punches to his face, we'd lose all of our power just trying to aim so high.

So what did our instructor say? "Figure it out." He'd call to us, "Aim lower."

Somehow we learned to adapt our techniques to Mike's enormous size and brute strength. We'd strike low—groin, knee, abs, kidneys, ribs, knees, and shins. We'd move quickly. We'd do the best we could. Then we'd get the heck out of there.

Mike's tremendous size was his strength. It probably had been one of his greatest advantages all of his life. But with fortitude, the rest of us somehow managed to use our smaller-sized energies against him. We applied speed, finesse, knowledge, memory, determination, and agility in our attempts to equalize the situation with him. Time marched on. We managed to elude his punch, to "slip" his kick, to squat low in a horse stance, and counter to his solar plexus.

As hard as things were with Mike, I'm forever thankful for the experience of facing a "brick house" of an opponent. After all, you never know how big the bad guy might turn out to be.

Early on in this book, you were encouraged to get to know yourself in order to win fights. One of the best ways to do so is to figure out your strengths and weaknesses. Be honest with yourself. If you don't think you have any qualities you'd define as strengths, think again. You definitely possess advantages that other people do not, so begin to consider what those might be and then get serious and organized about them.

Decide what strengths you'd utilize if the need arises.

Ask Yourself

- Are you strong? Are you fast? Are you feisty? Are you determined to save your life at any cost?
- Can you fight? Can you shoot a firearm? Can you think clearly in the midst of a crisis?
- Do you know how to punch someone? Do you know how to kick someone?
- Could you scream bloody murder until help arrived?
- What is your greatest physical strength? Is it size? Are you muscular or strong?

- What is your best mental advantage? Are you one smart cookie? Do you remember details?
- What psychological gifts do you have? Can you size up people?
- Are you an intuitive individual? Can you sense when trouble is brewing?
- Are you able to talk yourself out of danger?
- Are you an escape artist?
- Are you ready?

Perhaps you are unskilled as a fighter, but you can handle a gun like an expert. Okay then, that's what you build on. When you make your security strategy for your home, it should definitely include your legally registered gun. Maybe you have weak wrists or hands, but after months of Tae Bo, you can execute some awesome kicks now. So kick the snot out of some bad guy. Aim for his knees and do as much damage as you can. If your weakness is a total fear of fighting, could your gift of gab help you talk your way out of a tight spot? You might have physical limitations, but perhaps your awareness skills and safety measures are over and above anyone else's. If so, those are the strengths to build on. Maybe you're not too quick on your feet, but you've been helping your husband build a gazebo for the backyard and you've learned how to swing a mean hammer. Hey, that could turn out to be a great weapon in a crisis, so make sure you stash a few around the house. Perhaps you've never punched a man, but you were a track star in high school and you're still a fast runner today. So run like the wind.

Running, by the way, is a wonderful self-defense technique. The experts say that statistically it's the best chance you have of saving your own life.

In my late teens and throughout my twenties, I ran thirty to sixty miles a week, so I've always considered running to be one of my strengths. One night, in a scary moment, I used this strength to my advantage.

I was attending a show at a comedy club. The parking lot was not well lighted, so I practiced awareness as I got out of my car and locked it. Two huge men suddenly turned the corner and started walking straight toward me in the dark. It was obvious they were going to approach me. I immediately sprinted in the opposite direction. I'm sure I did so based on a decision I'd previously made, that running was acceptable in any ordeal and something I happened to know how to do. What made this unusual was that, at the time, I had no idea I was even running! Then I heard one of the guys call out to me, "Hey, you don't have to run. We're not going to hurt you." But there I was, already hauling butt through the parking lot before I even computed the fact that I was doing so! With quick reflexes, I used my strength (running) to overcome my weaknesses (being female, alone, and small, with two large men approaching at night) and ended up safely at the entrance to the club.

Now, not a lot of women would have run right then, thinking it would incite a chase, insult the men, or make her look crazy, stupid, or fearful. Who cares? Is there anyone really keeping track of all the ridiculous things you do? Let's hope not, because my list would be endless!

Okay, after some close and not particularly pleasant scrutiny, I see my strengths and weaknesses: I'm only five-four, 112 pounds, but I do have a fighting spirit. I'm not the greatest fighter on the block, but I am trained. I'm not made of muscle, but I can execute moves. I'm not the fastest physical specimen, but I love going nuts in a fraction of a second. I'm not the smartest cookie in the jar, but I have thought through the bad stuff. I'm not sure of everything in this crazy world, but I have made my personal security decisions. I don't come out of the gate first, but I don't give up, either. I have no clue what the future holds, but I know the location of my favorite weapons.

How would you describe yourself? List your strengths and weaknesses. What talents and attributes do you have that you might use against an assailant? If you know you're not good at something, consider it a weakness. What *are* you good at? Do what our sensei instructed when facing big Mike: "Figure it out" and "Aim lower."

You can't be a whiz at everything. Build on your strengths.

Defense Dos and Don'ts

- Don't dwell on the weaknesses in your life.
- Do figure out what your greatest abilities are and how they would aid your fight.
- Do remind yourself often of your mighty strengths.

→ *Power Point!* ←
**You know what you do best. Use that
knowledge and those skills.**

◄ 18 ►

DECIDE TO ACT
ON YOUR INSTINCTS

The art of life lies in a constant
readjustment to our surroundings.

OKAKURA KAKUZO,
JAPANESE SCHOLAR, ART CRITIC,
PRESERVATIONIST, AND CURATOR

Start believing with your body.

When God was busy giving man all those rock-hard muscles, He endowed woman with something even better—intuition. This female characteristic is truly a gift. To ignore it would be a shame. To take it for granted would be sad. But never to act upon it would be absolutely crazy.

When your inner security system sounds the alarm or flashes the warning lights, don't dismiss it. These are cues from your intuitive self. Our instincts are some of our most valuable attributes, but if we suppress them or distrust them, they're useless. Heck, if we behave in that manner we might as well be men without as many big muscles, right? If you know you're instinctually wired or if you've learned to tap into your intuition already, then consider yourself lucky. If this is not the case, start paying more attention to what your sensory prompts might be trying to tell you.

It's time to take our intuition to the next step; we're going to start acting on it.

You've probably tried this before. Perhaps you obeyed your instincts, but hardly even realized it. A situation may have felt a bit odd one day. Something seemed out of place, perhaps even dead wrong. You couldn't put your finger on what was so unusual, but you trusted your instincts anyway. You took a different path or street. You asked a friend to come along when you went to meet a stranger. When the guy seemed "off" to you, you decided not to deal with him or hire him or stay in the same room with him. You chose not to go into a building or room, because it just didn't feel right.

To act on a gut feeling is simple. You're going about your day in a state of awareness. Then everything changes. Something starts bugging you. You may not see it, smell it, hear it, or completely understand it, but you feel it. There doesn't seem to be a logical reason that you feel a certain way.

Two perceptions are now fighting within you.

One is rooted in your *logical* self. She's busy telling you that to take that different path or street, to change course midstream, would be weird, noticeable, embarrassing, time-consuming, insulting to someone, not part of the schedule, or whatever. But your *instinctual* self is also communicating. She's begging your body to do something unplanned. You feel her warnings: "Pay attention to this. Leave this place. Get away from him. Move. Go fast!" Or, "Wait, don't go yet!" Or perhaps, "Something is wrong. Beware."

In many cases, you might be seeing what's wrong in a very clear, visual manner, but your brain may not be computing it in a rational way. Often, we perceive the things around us, but we don't always process the information correctly, especially if we're tired or distracted. But perhaps you're instinctive enough to realize that the same guy you saw an hour ago has suddenly reappeared. Or you know someone is watching you, and even though you're not one to jump to conclusions, there's something bothering you about this. Or someone seems to be lurking about, and there's this little feeling deep inside you that he could be waiting for you.

These intuitive clues could be as simple as a flash of something in your peripheral vision. A sudden movement. A look on someone's face. The smell of a foreign substance nearby, such as strange cologne or cigarettes. Whatever the case, your intuition picks up on it, starts banging the gong and waving the red flag. Now it's your body's turn to respond.

So what are you waiting for?

Get going. Act on it. Always believe your gut feeling. If this means putting some distance between you and what you believe to be the threat, do it. You'll have a whole lifetime to fix whatever it was you disrupted in that particular moment in order to act on your gut feeling. Maybe it will cost you some time or energy, or you'll be late for a meeting or embarrassed that you fled with no explanation. None of that matters.

Pam was a high school teenager going out on a date with a guy she'd known back in junior high. They'd just run into each other at the shopping center a few days earlier. After catching up for a few minutes, he asked her out.

He was nicely dressed when he showed up. He spoke politely to her mother at the door. His car looked buffed and polished for the big night out.

But as soon as he began driving, he lit up a cigarette and turned toward Pam. Then he sneered at her. There was something about that look on his face that sent a shiver up her spine. Pam knew she needed to get out of this guy's car immediately. She feigned sickness and asked him to take her home before she threw up all over his passenger seat. He did so right away.

Pam relied on her instincts to make excuses and bring about a safe return home.

. . .

Eva got a gut feeling as she stepped into an elevator that was occupied by a lone man. Suddenly, she felt as if something or someone was telling her not to ride with him. She knew she had to get out of the elevator fast.

Impulsively, Eva glanced at her watch. On the pretense that she'd suddenly remembered a forgotten item or appointment, she jumped back out of the elevator just as the doors were shutting. Instantly, the man started cursing at her. Eva quickly dashed away from the vicinity and chose an alternate route to her destination.

It took her a few minutes longer, but she never doubted her intuition was right that day.

Now, here's what's so frustrating about acting on our instincts. There's no payoff. We hardly ever receive satisfaction that our quick change in plans was the correct thing to do. We don't get to find out when we've done it well. Most of the time we have no clue if our intuition even comes close to being right.

Pam never found out for sure if her sneery-looking date would have done something bad to her. All Eva was ever certain of was that the guy in the elevator used raunchy language. There's no way either woman will ever know if these guys might have been brutal attackers intent on causing physical harm.

When we act on our intuition, we often keep ourselves secure. That's a really great thing. But the not so great thing is that we rarely receive verification that our hunch was right. By shifting our plan and changing our intended action, we avoid danger and stay safe, but without confirmation of that smart move we just made, we begin to lose faith in the very powers that could continue to keep us out of harm's way. After a while, we might become lazy or wonder if we weren't a little crazy to run away from a man or a particular situation. We ask ourselves if we shouldn't lighten up and start trusting people again.

But sometimes we are validated. Pam felt good just to be back home again. Eva felt justified as she stepped out of the elevator and heard that man's verbal abuse.

I once received overwhelming proof that my instincts rang true. The story below is not about bad guys or self-defense, but has everything to do with how acting on a gut feeling possibly saved my life and the lives of those I love.

I'd won a travel writing contest and a cruise to the Caribbean for two. My husband and I planned to take the cruise, which would sail to Belize and the Bay Islands of Honduras during the last week of October 1998. We tentatively booked the trip, adding a cabin for our sons. The cruise agent asked me to call back the following week and confirm with a credit card.

For the next week, I continually woke up during the night with my heart pounding. All I could think about was the boat we were supposed to cruise on, the *Fantome,* a beautiful sailing vessel once owned by Aristotle Onassis. After several sleepless nights, I finally told my husband that I had a weird feeling about the trip. We decided to pass on the prize trip and take a more secure land vacation to Cancún, Mexico, during that same time frame—the last week of October 1998. Two days before we departed, Hurricane Mitch started churning up the waters of the Caribbean. Rather than forfeit the cost of the prepaid trip, we flew to Cancún and hoped for the best. The minute we arrived and saw how bad things were, we spent two difficult days trying desperately to get back home. This normally beautiful tourist destination was battening down the hatches and preparing for the worst storm ever. It was a nightmare. By the time we returned to L.A., we were exhausted.

During the entire ordeal we were glued to the Weather Channel. The most horrific activity was off Belize and Honduras, exactly where we'd originally planned to cruise. I couldn't help but wonder how the *Fantome* had fared. Certainly the ship wouldn't have sailed under such harrowing conditions.

Our third day back, my travel agent friend called. "You'd better sit down for this one," she said. "The *Fantome* sank on the very trip you were originally supposed to be on. Although the passengers got off alive, the crew of thirty-one died." The *Fantome* had gone down in fifty-foot waves. Chills ran up and down my spine for days as I recalled the sleepless nights I'd spent contemplating that very excursion. Call it what you wish: a gut feeling, women's intuition, or a message from above. In this case, I surrendered to my instincts, shifted gears, changed my plans, even gave up a free vacation worth thousands of dollars. As a result, my family avoided great, if not fatal, danger.

You don't need evidence that your gut is right. Your instincts *are* your verification. Trust them. Become a believer. Be willing to prove it with your actions.

Defense Dos and Don'ts

- Do live attuned to your inner voice.
- Don't be afraid or embarrassed to follow your gut reaction.
- Don't think you need proof of danger before acting on your instincts.

→ *Power Point!* ←

Feel it in your bones.

DECIDE TO RECOGNIZE THE THREAT OF THE INITIAL ATTACK

**When you see a rattlesnake poised to strike,
you do not wait until he has struck
before you crush him.**

FRANKLIN D. ROOSEVELT

You've got to see it coming.

The only time a bad guy can attack you is when he's near you. In most cases, he's got to be really close, skin to skin, breathing down your neck, and sometimes right on top of you. An attacker with a gun needs to be within shooting range. After all, a murderer isn't much of a threat three blocks away, and a rapist doesn't pose a danger if he stays across the street. When you think about it, the bad guy's got his work cut out for him. He understands the importance of proximity, so he's busy trying to figure out how he's going to get right next to you or in your face or in your house or in your car. If he's a stranger, he's got to be creative and convincing, because he has no business being this close to you. He knows it. And deep down, you know it, too.

It all comes down to his steps. There's a series of maneuvers the bad guy must undertake in order to get close enough to you to commit a crime and transform you into a victim. As he's progressing through these steps, he's attempting to close the distance. If you're paying attention, his advance becomes obvious.

Sometimes it's only a *physical distance* that will begin to diminish with his steps. You might feel as if your personal boundary line has been crossed or that your space has been invaded. Other times, his steps will reduce a *relational distance.* He may try too hard to strike up a friendship, or he might attempt to move it along too quickly. He might be too helpful or attempt to isolate you too soon. His steps can involve trickery, a cry for help, or an acting performance that would rival one given by a Hollywood star. Remember handsome serial killer Ted Bundy? He was a pro with disguises, luring his targets with casts on his limbs, car trouble, and other seemingly innocent inducements employed to disarm his victims.

The bad guy is the one with the tough job here. He has to fool you. You, on the other hand, can just up and decide you don't happen to like him. Or you might feel uncomfortable about his behavior, his physical closeness, or how fast he's moving. Or you may feel you're being snow jobbed or duped into something. Never fail to recognize these signals for what they might be: an initial move by someone who might attack or harm you later. Individually, his steps may not physically injure you. They may not seem all that threatening at the time, but they very well could be a part of his pre-attack positioning. And while you shouldn't and legally can't respond to his initial steps at a Force Level Four, Lethal Attack elevation, regard them seriously, because they could be a prelude to danger ahead. Perceive his steps for what they are—warning signals. Then get ready, because now it's your turn.

Your response to these initial threats must be immediate and fiercely determined. Your goal is to get away from him or to get him away from you. So tell him off. State your intention to leave— without him. Turn around and walk in another direction. Run away from him at full speed. Shout for help. Shove him back. Do something. Do anything!

Be prepared for a potentially bizarre response to your rejection. He's just been busted. Let's face it, it's quite possible it's for one of three things: he's pursuing you sexually and romantically in a way that makes you uncomfortable, he's preying on you with the intent of seriously harming you, or he's just a total wacko. Plenty of them are running around the planet. Whatever the case, you have just called him on it and rejected him for it. If his intentions were innocent, this is the moment during which he'll show his true character. If he's an okay guy or a gentleman, he'll bow out and back off. A bad guy is not always so polite.

Take this guy's reaction very seriously. It might include anger, frustration, persistence, not taking no for an answer, over-the-top friendliness, or desperation. You'll know this perfect stranger is a jerk when he tries to make you feel bad or guilty for not instantly trusting him. Why on earth would you? You don't even know him! Another variation is that he might be trying so hard, you'll actually feel embarrassed or sorry for him. His reaction is important to watch, but it's ultimately completely irrelevant to your next move. As we already know, there are no apologies in self-defense. His feelings are neither your concern nor your responsibility. Your only job is to secure your own safety.

Consider your advantage here. You can sit back and watch carefully for those steps. If a man keeps himself on the other side of that boundary line you've drawn for yourself, you'll probably be fine. But when he takes a step, closing the distance, you must respond. This doesn't mean you snap the guy's neck and leave him for dead because he's a little too friendly. Simply tell him to back off or start moving yourself. Get some distance between the two of you, just as I did several years ago.

I was alone in an airport, preparing to board a plane for home. I'd been a martial artist for several years, so I was actively working on my awareness and personal security. As I stood in line at a desk near the departure gate, a man positioned himself right behind me. He stood too close, in my space. I moved forward and away from

him. He immediately began to talk to me, asking me some ridiculous question that only an airline employee could answer. I told
him to ask the person at the desk and turned away from him. When
the line moved up a space, he suddenly grabbed my carry-on bag
off the floor and, despite my immediate protest, he carried it and
placed it beside me in the line after we'd all moved forward.

This was pre-9/11, so there wasn't the heightened awareness
about luggage back then, but I was concerned enough to tell him,
"You don't need to do that. I've got it."

When the line shifted again, he jumped to move my bag to the
next spot. This time I said firmly, "Really, don't. I'll handle my own
luggage."

But the man persisted. Every time the line moved forward, that
guy was on my bag. Then he always placed it beside me as we
waited to move again. He tried starting conversations, but I remained aloof and kept a close eye on my bag—and my back.

Finally, I was at the front of the line. I conducted my business
with the agent at the desk, grabbed my bag, and hurried off
to stand among a group of people positioned next to the departure gate.

There were no assigned seats on the flight, and the plane was
about 25 percent full. I boarded the aircraft prior to Mr. Bag Grabber and sat in an aisle seat near the rear of the aircraft. If anybody
wanted to sit next to me, he would have had to climb over me.
When Mr. Bag Grabber came aboard, I was well aware of his presence but tried to look consumed in a magazine. There were numerous rows of empty seats for him to choose from. But guess what?
He came directly to me and asked if he could sit in the seat next
to mine.

That was it. Even though he'd crossed my line long ago, he'd
escalated his pursuit once again. Now I had to do something
about it.

I answered his question at full volume so that everyone could
hear me. "No, you can't sit here! What for? To harass me and bother

me the way you just did in the airport by talking to me and pick-
ing up my bag? I told you to leave my carry-on luggage alone, but
you kept grabbing it anyway. You're a complete stranger, and I don't
want you near me. As far as I'm concerned, you're threatening me,
and I don't like it. I want you to get as far away from me as possible. Get out of my face! Go!"

Talk about busted! He reacted by calling me a nasty name
while acting confused and ticked off. As he walked away, I heard
him mutter, "What's her problem?"

There wasn't another peep out of that guy the whole flight. Half
the passengers overheard me as I berated him. What I found most
interesting was the instantaneous, overwhelming support I received from them. I learned a great lesson—giving my fellow passengers the whole story in detail and in the loudest voice I could
muster, I had successfully managed to involve them in my ordeal.
They weren't simply witnesses. They'd become my allies in what I
felt could've been the threat of some initial attack. Everyone sitting
nearby turned and nodded their approval. A woman gave me the
thumbs-up. "You tell him, honey," somebody said. Never mind his
response. Their response was amazing!

Someone went so far as to report the entire incident to the flight
crew. Once the plane was in the air, a flight attendant knelt beside
me. "Is it true that a man was harassing you?"

"Yes." I identified the man and provided her with the parti-
culars.

She assured me she would include the information in her flight
report. "I only wish you had told us before we departed," she said,
"If it ever happens again, tell the crew before takeoff. He'll be
kicked right off the flight."

I couldn't believe it. "You would kick some guy off a plane because he handled my carry-on bag several times and acted in a
way that left me feeling harassed?"

"Absolutely. Like that!" She snapped her fingers. "Any airline would. Nobody wants to be flying around in the sky with a person who poses a threat to another passenger or the crew. We have too many other safety concerns."

And now, thanks to the tragic events of 9/11, passengers are very aware of this particular reality.

The truth is, I almost blew it. As this guy attempted to close the distance with numerous steps, I responded as a woman so often does: I did not do enough.

Here are ways in which I could have stopped him much sooner:

- When he invaded my space the first time, I should have left the line with my bag and waited elsewhere.
- When he grabbed my carry-on bag, I should have grabbed it back from him and called security.
- When he grabbed my bag again, I should have alerted the ticket agent at the gate or picked up my bag and moved away from him.
- I should have boarded the airplane and immediately reported his actions to the flight crew.
- I should have waited for him to select his seat first, then chosen mine as far away from his as possible.
- I should have insisted that he be kicked off the plane.
- I should have twisted off his testicles and shoved them down his throat. (Oops, there I go, getting carried away again. Fortunately, that was hardly necessary, as I wasn't seriously threatened.)

What I did do correctly was recognize the appearance of an initial attack. I watched and felt each step this guy took in his attempt to cozy up to me. Something was wrong, and I knew it. Just how wrong, I never learned. I did learn, however, that it's perfectly fine to be rude and impolite to someone who's threatening me. Ditching my manners is always acceptable when my safety is on the line.

The second correct thing I did was to apply some of that verbal self-defense we learned about. I let everyone on the aircraft within shouting distance know that this guy was up to no good. I gave them all the details they'd ever need to instantly take my side in the matter. Dozens of people turned around in their seats just to take a look at him. Whatever he had planned for me or any other woman, for that matter, stopped the moment I verbally assaulted him. He became part of the official flight report, for crying out loud. If a woman had been bothered, stalked, followed, raped, assaulted, or killed that night anywhere near the airport, guess who the police would've picked up for questioning?

Wait a minute, you might be thinking. Isn't this is a little unfair? Somewhat paranoid, perhaps? Shouldn't we give this guy the benefit of the doubt? Well, since my gut feeling at the time told me I shouldn't, it doesn't make sense to do so now, but for the sake of argument, let's say he was just some lonely guy. Maybe he was a little weird. Perhaps he wanted to date me. Maybe he was just pathologically friendly. We all know that there are cemeteries and rape treatment centers filled with women who didn't want to be rude to the weird guy, the friendly guy, or the too-helpful, couldn't-get-the-message guy. What if this man *was* evil? What if he was banking on the idea that he would gain my trust and friendship by the end of the flight? Would he have said, "Oh, I'm parked right over there, too. I'll walk you out"? Would I have reassured myself, "Oh, it's okay. He's just a lonely, helpful guy. And we did sit together on the flight. I practically know him now"? There was no way Mr. Bag Grabber could've known that three people waited for me at the airport—my husband and my two sons. But what if my family had been late or stuck in traffic? Would I have been in danger, unable to shake this guy?

When that jerk walked away to find another seat on the plane, wondering aloud what my problem was, I never did answer. So here goes: my problem is that too many women are constantly hit on, scoped out, eyeballed, and ultimately preyed upon, victimized, and often killed by creeps who move in on them in exactly the same manner as my airplane guy. Some of these fellows are innocent. Many are pathetic losers. There are plenty of men who can't take no for an answer. And then there are those who pop up and seem like Mr. Nice Guy right before they turn around and kill an innocent woman who was too kind to insult them. Some men are just clueless. Others want one of two things: sex or a crime fix. There's not a guy on the planet who's dying to lift anybody's travel bag six times for exercise or have a nice little chat on an airplane with a married woman who's made it more than clear that she's not interested. The threat and the steps are obvious, but it's the hidden motive that's truly sickening. But perhaps the sickest part of all is that women are constantly bombarded by these assaults from creeps who just don't "get it." So that's my problem, Mr. Bag Grabber. In truth, it is the problem that all women face and a reality that has been stated by countless personal security experts.

If a man's intentions are decent, your requests should be honored and your feelings valued. If you maintain your distance, he should respect your desire to be left alone. Some men will back off even more in order to reassure you. The good guys are in no rush. They have time to pursue you for bona fide romantic reasons. The bad guys have an agenda. They push for instant closeness and familiarity. Every step is a push that gets him closer to his goal. Take this behavior clue for exactly what it is: the threat of the initial attack.

When it comes to recognizing the threat of the initial attack, there are exceptions. You will never be able to see it coming if it's a complete surprise attack or if you're sleeping. But everyone must sleep, and we don't have ten eyeballs wrapped around our heads to prevent every attack that comes out of nowhere. If a bad guy wakes you up in your bed, it's impossible that you could have anticipated the threat of the initial attack. But, in other cases, he will be taking those numerous, obvious steps, and you're going to be able to detect them.

Spot him from a mile away. Then stop him in his tracks.

Defense Dos and Don'ts

- Don't just stand there and allow initial threats by suspicious people.
- Do react when anyone tries to close in on you in a *physical* or *relational* manner.
- Do consider his attitude and actions as clues to what may happen next.
- Don't wait. Get moving and gain back your distance.

 *Power Point!*

You can't foresee the future, but you can see him coming.

◄ **20** ►

DECIDE TO FACE
THE FALLOUT

**They only can force me who obey
a higher law than I.**

HENRY DAVID THOREAU

S ay it like you saw it.

Imagine this . . . a rapist has just picked the wrong victim—you. He pops out of the bushes next to your front door as you're letting yourself into your home. Grabbing you from behind, he throws you to the floor of your entry hall, then bends over you. You manage to keep your wits about you. With a sharp jab of your finger, you poke deeply into his eye. Then, rising quickly to your feet, you elbow him in the ribs. You kick him in the kneecap, grab the back of his head, pull it forward and down, slamming him face-first into your rising knee. He's now stunned, but he's still coming at you, so you grab a heavy vase next to the front door, crack it over his head, and even slash him in the abdomen with one of the broken pieces. He takes a look at the blood appearing on the front of his shirt and passes out. You call 911 on your cell phone while running out the front door and over to the neighbors' house. The police arrive within six minutes.

An hour later, he's in the hospital because your knee happened to dislocate his jaw. His eye needs medical attention. Your elbow cracked his rib. He's got a bump on his head and a slice to his abdomen from the broken vase.

You, on the other hand, are going downtown for some serious police questioning.

That's okay, because you are going to tell the whole truth and nothing but the truth. Then you're going to repeat your story a dozen times more. Different police officers are going to question you at different times, but nothing is going to shake you from your truth. As you're answering the officers' questions, you're going to explain very carefully the threat you faced. You're going to articulate how serious that threat appeared to be. You're going to share the fact with them that this man was the perpetrator of a home invasion in your house. You'll explain why you thought he would rape you and possibly kill you. You'll tell them how you knew you had to be brutal in order to save your life. You will tell them how frightened you were. You will let them know that you thought you might even die if he had his way with you.

You will tell them everything.

As a new martial artist, I was shocked to learn that when the cops are called to a fight, everybody's going downtown. Bad guys, good guys, all the participants.

A fellow karate student learned this the hard way.

He and I were both orange belts. Neither one of us really knew that much about this new hobby of ours—martial arts. One night at class he told us of a frightening incident that had occurred just days prior. He was walking through a grocery store parking lot, minding his own business, when he saw an elderly lady open her car door and a young thug attack her from behind. As she leaned over to get into her car, the thug pushed her headfirst into the vehicle, and she went fanny-up, sprawling inside.

The thug immediately went for the lady's purse. My friend

ran to her rescue, and he and the thug started fighting. Meanwhile, someone called the police. The fight continued, and my friend managed to connect with several good kicks and punches.

In the end, my friend was unharmed, and he felt that he'd won the fight and, better yet, that he'd saved the day. But the elderly woman was so confused, she was unable to tell the police what had happened. She wasn't even sure who had attacked her. She had absolutely no idea if the bad guy who assaulted her from behind was my fellow karate student friend or the thug. That left the police to interview both men for several hours at the police station. The truth finally came out, and my friend was finally released with no charges filed.

He left the station house feeling as if he'd just finished fighting his second battle of the day.

Most law enforcement officials will tell you that the evidence speaks for itself. After an assault, a victim will end up wearing the proof of his crime against her. Likewise, she'll wear the signs of her defensive efforts. Often, so will the attacker. This evidence is displayed all over her body and on that of her attacker's. Telltale signs are gouges, red welts, scratches, black-and-blue marks, and, in worse cases, more serious damage such as broken limbs and vaginal injuries. A victim might have her attacker's hair and skin beneath her fingernails, his sperm inside her, and his DNA evident on her body and clothing.

But in self-defense, there is always the chance you will end up causing some pretty serious pain and trauma to the bad guy. There's also the possibility you'll be suspected of inciting the whole event yourself. The cops might even think *you're* the bad guy. You might be accused of inflicting unnecessary injuries on some criminal, regardless of what he tried to do to you or planned to do to you. The bad guy might even try to sue you.

Unfortunately, that's the chance you must take in order to save your own life.

My karate instructors spoke to the heart of self-defense: "If the courts and the justice system don't see it my way, if they can't fathom my need to use self-defense in the manner I felt necessary, with the degree of intensity I chose, I would always know in my heart that I had responded in truth to the rules of a higher law."

Amen.

Learning to defend ourselves and survive a fight is one thing. Avoiding legal trouble afterward is yet another.

In chapter 7 we learned how to recognize the Four Levels of Force as vital elements of our personal security. We discovered that an effective counterattack meant matching the strength and force of our opponent, sometimes even going higher and harder in order to survive and escape. But each level has a lawful elevation for response, and it is up to each of us to understand and abide by this. Counterattacks come with a weighty responsibility—a proper response.

Now consider the great advantages for female defenders.

First of all, our instincts are rarely wrong. If we need to defend ourselves in a certain manner with a particular amount of intensity, our guts will instantly deliver the message. I always tell women, "If a guy grabs your arm, you can't turn around and kill him. But if he's grabbing your arm and dragging you off somewhere to get you alone and possibly rape or kill you, you should be fighting lethally with every bit of fierceness, determination, and skill you possess."

Now here's another female advantage. The plight of a lone woman defending herself against a bad guy takes but a few seconds to capture the attention of law enforcement officials. While countless men out there don't "get it," the police officer usually does. He's been called to enough rape scenes to get it. He's seen enough women who've just been beaten to a bloody pulp to get it. He's scraped enough female corpses off the floor to thoroughly get it.

The police understand the vulnerability that women face daily. They know from experience that, for the most part, women are the recipients of brutality from bad guys and not the other way around. That doesn't mean you won't need to prove your point, explain your case, and describe the intensity of the threat against you.

It just means you have to do the right thing.

Here are three points to remember in order to act correctly and legally with any assailant:

1. Avoid physical fighting. Don't engage unless you have to.
2. If you must fight, do so with enough force to gain your escape.
3. As soon as you are out of danger, stop fighting. Get out of there.

What you don't want to do is poke out the rapist's eyes, kick him in the knee, knock him unconscious with the vase, then walk into the next room, locate your gun and shoot him dead, reload, and then shoot him dead some more. That little scenario is called premeditated murder.

However, if the bad guy is still coming after you or your family members in your home and you use the gun as your only means to get away from him, then you are acting in a legal and just manner. This is simply exercising your right to take up arms and protect yourself and your loved ones. After all, the bad guy is in your house. You didn't invite him there, so he's guilty of a "home invasion," which happens to be one of the most frightening and deadly crimes against residents these days.

But if he's lying there unconscious in your home, you cannot get up, find your gun, and then go back and shoot him. Detectives will later determine that, if you had the opportunity to get the gun, you could've headed straight for the door and gotten out of there.

Always utilize any opportunity for escape with wisdom. Put up your fight. Do what you need to do. Get him down. Render him defenseless if you can. Then make your escape. Always run away, even if it's out of your own home. Then tell the police everything.

It is not difficult to convince police officers of some threat or danger you just experienced from a criminal. They recognize scum when they see it. They spend their entire careers trudging through scum up to their eyeballs just to be able to assist, rescue, and save the lives of people like you and me when danger comes our way. Describe to law enforcement officers the peril of your situation. Explain your injuries and how you expected to end up dead. Let them know the threat that was obvious to you and hazardous to your well-being. Women are at tremendous risk out there, and the police realize this better than anyone. They know the truth when they see it and hear it.

When facing the consequences, tell it like it was.

Defense Dos and Don'ts

- Do realize the threat against your life or physical health at all times.
- Do react defensively according to the danger at hand.
- Don't forget to make clear the intensity of that threat later to officers of the law.

▶ Power Point! ◀

In the aftermath, let the truth be known.

PART III
Physical Decisions

Strength is a matter of the made-up mind.

JOHN BEECHER,
AMERICAN ACTIVIST AND POET

21

DECIDE TO GET IN SHAPE

To strengthen the mind, you must harden the muscles.

MONTAIGNE

Your body is your weapon.

You've just made the mental decisions necessary to out-smart and out-think your opponent. Your mind is pumping with new insights and information. Your head is telling you that you are prepared for anything. But if your body is in such poor shape that it takes you five minutes to get out of bed in the morning, you've already got a huge breach of security.

It's time to get real about your body. That means getting in shape.

Now, don't get me wrong, we're not talking about somebody's ideal of a great figure. No one cares how you look in a bathing suit or if you'll ever fit into your "skinny" jeans again. We're talking about high-energy, kick-somebody's-butt-if-you-had-to shape. If that means losing forty pounds, do it. If it means gaining ten, happy eating. If you need medication or vitamins or more sleep, what are you waiting for? If you need protein throughout the day, start snacking. If it's been ten years since you set foot in a doctor's office for a checkup, make an appointment. If you haven't exercised in three years, it's time to put on the sneakers and head out the door for a nice run or a brisk walk. If you are in the habit of medicating yourself with drugs or alcohol, get some help. If you need to quit smoking in order to take a deep breath, do so.

No excuses, right? Because, as we now know, there are no excuses in self-defense.

You don't have to kickbox all day, enter the Ironman Triathlon, or turn into some out-of-control health freak. But do take an honest look at your physical condition and your body's ability to perform. Being in a healthy, more agile, and flexible body will be a benefit in matters of self-defense, as well as every other area of your life. If you never exercise, your reflexes may be slow and unsure. If you're critically overweight or ignoring warning signs about the state of your health, you're setting yourself up for trouble, possibly even danger.

Here are some great ways to start shaping up your body for security.

- **Get physical.** Pick up the phone and schedule an appointment for a physical and any other examinations you may be overdue for with specialty physicians (gynecologists, dermatologists, and so on). Think of this as your fresh start, the one from which you will springboard into a new healthy regimen.

- **Clean your palate (but not necessarily your plate).** Dump anything in your refrigerator the diet police would define as unhealthy. Go to the market and buy "fresh" food, including fish, chicken, vegetables, fruits, cheeses, whole grain breads, and yogurt. If you still want the desserts, heavy sauces, starches, and red meats, feel free to indulge, but do so in moderation. Drink eight glasses of water each and every day.

* **Pop pills.** Take your prescribed medication as directed. Load up on enough of your daily vitamins.

* **Get up and go.** Make plans, either by yourself or with a friend, to walk, run, hit the gym, or attend a yoga class starting tomorrow. You can get on the treadmill or exercise while watching TV. Schedule the rest of your exercise periods on the calendar for the week. Figure out what type of exercise you like and when you enjoy doing it. Try sticking to it at that time every day. When you miss a day, think of it as a little break. The next day, get right back to it.

* **Put food in the fridge, not on the throne.** The bottom line—it's just food. It fuels your body with energy and satisfies nutritional needs. That's it. It will never make you happy, loved, or complete. It certainly won't save your life when you defend yourself from a bad guy. It's just going to feed your body and, after a while, make you feel full. You definitely need it, but not to excess.

* **Discipline is not a dirty word.** When it comes to health, food, exercise, and caring for your body, always embrace and enhance your willpower and self-control. Don't be afraid to be crazy about yourself and your health. The payback for such an attitude is tremendous.

* **Dump the garbage.** Eliminate all the bad things such as cigarettes and illegal drugs. Cut way back on alcoholic beverages, fats, and sugar.

- *Fall in love with your earth suit.* You don't really have much of a choice but to love and accept the only body you'll ever possess. Make peace with it. Accept your flaws. Everybody's got them. Most people are so concerned about their own flaws, they don't even notice yours.

- *Decide to stay in shape.* Being in good physical shape has lifelong advantages. Your metabolism and energy will increase. Your muscles and bones will strengthen. Your heart will be healthier. Your blood pressure and cholesterol will decrease. You'll sleep better. Your skin will improve. And that's just the beginning!

I was eighteen years old when I noticed I was getting a little flabby. I started running every day and swimming during the summers. A lifetime of daily exercise began. I ran up to sixty miles a week for ten years. I cohosted *Jack La Lanne and You* in Los Angeles, and did aerobics, weight lifting, regular swimming, and more than a decade of extensive karate training with practices often totaling fifteen hours per week. I've walked between two and five miles a day for years. I've also studied yoga, Pilates, and tai chi.

I know from personal experience and decades of commitment that exercise is more than skin-deep. You need to make it a non-negotiable part of your life. Besides feeling healthier and looking better, it truly is one of the fastest, easiest ways to positively change your life both physically and mentally.

With all this exercise, it's quite sad that I've never had an hourglass figure or some fabulous body from a magazine. I certainly hate shopping for bathing suits as much as the next gal. But I can honestly say that this is a body I love. I loved it enough to meet my walking group at five o'clock in the morning when the wind was whipping through the dark sky. I loved it when I got the snot beat out of me in a sparring match on the mat and again when my hand sliced through bricks as if they were melted butter. I loved it when I climbed out of the pool after two hundred laps.

I love it enough to fight for it.

If it's been a long time since you were in shape, it's going to take that kind of love affair with your body to get yourself going. Start with a simple stretch. Everything we're talking about is a stretch, so go ahead and reach. Extend yourself.

Just do it.

Defense Dos and Don'ts

- Do adopt a healthier lifestyle in order to increase your personal security.
- Don't aim for perfection, but strive for high energy.
- Do rid yourself of all that's holding you back from optimum physical well-being.

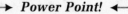 **_Power Point!_** ◄
Exercise your amazing capabilities.

Holly's Story

Holly saw him coming from a mile away. Literally.

"This was a few years ago, when I was in my early twenties. I was just starting off with my first job. I didn't have a car, so I walked the main road of a rural area every morning to get to work as a day care employee. On that particular day, a man was walking toward me, coming from the opposite direction on the same road. As we passed each

other, I called out, "Good morning!" like I did with every-body all the time." She paused and then admitted, "I was so naïve."

Holly still cringes as she remembers what happened next.

"He took a gun out of his pants and pointed it at me, de-manding that I come closer and get down into the bushes right next to him. I was so shocked. But gun or no gun, I knew I was not going down into those bushes."

Holly shudders as she recalls her choice.

"I decided to run. I'd always been a fast runner, so that's exactly what I did, almost immediately. I felt like it was the smartest thing I could do in the circumstances, maybe the only thing."

Holly took off running full blast down the road. The man with the gun started to chase her. She opened her mouth in an attempt to scream, but no sound emerged from her. Since the area was so desolate, she figured screaming might waste some of the energy she could put to use running instead.

"The whole time I was running, I expected to hear the gun go off. I thought for sure he'd take a couple of shots at me. That was the worst part, I think, running like that, but believing that, at any second, I was going to be shot from behind. The realization that he was still coming after me was overwhelming. I could hear him behind me. I kept wondering if he would ever stop chasing me."

Holly reached a driveway on the road and saw that it extended for a long way up to a home at the top of a hill. She started up that driveway praying that someone would be in that house to help her. She banged on the door a few *times and then turned the knob and ran inside, locking it behind her. A grandmotherly woman was coming toward her, looking both confused and concerned. Holly fell into the woman's arms, sobbing.*

"That poor lady," Holly said. "Talk about brave. She had no idea who I was or what I was doing in her house, but she hugged me anyway. I guess she could tell that I was scared to death and in some big trouble. Then we both looked out the window to see if we could see the guy with the gun, but he was gone."

The two women called the police, who responded within minutes of the ordeal and then conducted a helicopter search for the gunman.

"They looked for quite a while, but never found him."

After the incident, Holly's parents purchased a car for her so that walking alone along that rural roadway wouldn't be necessary. It took years for Holly to feel comfortable about being alone. Today, she has numerous personal security rules in place.

22

DECIDE TO MOVE

Chance favors those in motion.

JAMES H. AUSTIN, M.D.,
NEUROSCIENTIST, AUTHOR,
AND ZEN PRACTITIONER

G et the lead out.

When danger rears its ugly head, many women go into instant lockdown. They become frozen to the point of paralysis and are unable to think, let alone able to respond in a deliberate, action-packed way. It's interesting to note that the amount of energy used to stand there rooted to the floorboards, scared to death, with adrenaline pumping, is about the same needed to deliver a ferocious counterattack and take off running.

So what exactly is holding us back?

Fear.

By the truckloads. Tremendous fear. Numerous fears. A fear of the bad guy. The fear that we don't know exactly what's happening or what will happen next. Fear of doing the wrong thing. Fear that we don't know what we're doing to begin with. The fear that we can't breathe, that we'll throw up or pass out. The fear that our bodies have forgotten how to move.

Fear is a natural human emotion, and it's certainly not

something we would routinely boast about. But the cool thing about fear is that it triggers these physical responses that send glandular secretions into our nervous systems. This results in something very advantageous called the fight-or-flight reflex.

The fight adrenaline (epinephrine) aids the person who cannot run or avoid danger. This is the one that people are speaking of when they describe suddenly attaining superhuman strength and an overwhelming resistance to pain. The fight adrenaline can make a person stronger, quicker, and able to continue fighting, despite injuries and serious discomfort.

The flight adrenaline (norepinephrine) makes a person more alert to her surroundings and more tuned in to danger. A person experiencing flight reflex can run sooner and much faster than normal.

In an attack, the best thing to do is to run to safety. But if you can't get away, your next best option is to break through the fear with immediate movement. Think of propelling yourself into full-force advancement right from the get-go. Even if there's just a hint of fear inside you, you're going to have some of that potent fight-or-flight adrenaline to back you up. This is how fighting like a girl gets its legs. As a result, you'll be faster, quicker, and stronger.

When the bad guy attacks, start moving. Run. If you can't run, get your feet loose. Keep your body fluid and alive. Breathe. Get your hands above your belt (in case you need to block his grab or punch). Put your hands in his face. Get your mouth moving—talk, scream, call out for help. Do anything. Do crazy things. Throw something at him. Pull his T-shirt up and over his face. Kick him in the groin. Kick his knee out. Start poking at his eyeballs. Go for different strike zones, one after the other.

In a word, *move.*

In karate class, our instructor would introduce a new technique and then call us one by one to demonstrate what we had just learned. Now this could be rather disastrous because half the time we'd be up there trying to demonstrate something we could barely remember, let alone perform with any sort of finesse. It never failed that some student's nerves would get the best of him. He'd stand before us, his mind completely blanking on the technique he'd just learned. Usually he'd get so flustered, he'd forget everything he was supposed to be doing.

That's when our instructor would call out the one thing that matters most when it comes to self-defense. "Move! Do something! Quick! This guy's going to kill you! Why are you just standing there?"

That's when it all would kick in, and with a vengeance. The student would either remember what he was doing or, better yet, he'd improvise and create a whole new defense technique far deadlier than the one he was supposed to do, because now he was furious with himself for forgetting.

Improvisation was highly encouraged in the dojo. The point is that it's "better to move like a wild lunatic with bad form and lousy techniques than to stand still and take a beating." Improvising is a big lifesaver for fighting in the real world, too. It happens to be exactly what everyone's doing all the time anyway.

It does require one very important thing from you, however—the immediate commitment to move.

One of my worst character flaws is an extreme lack of patience. If I cannot fix everything wrong in my life in two seconds flat, I come unglued. However, when it comes to self-defense, and while some martial artists would disagree, I believe a lack of patience is like a drawn sword or a cocked gun. I have very little patience with threatening people. I have no patience for anyone in my space. I don't have one extra second of time for the guy who's crossing my line.

I realized long ago that in self-defense the only thing patience would give me is more time. The only thing more time is going to buy me is additional fear and hesitation.

When I was seventeen years old, I worked at a clothing shop in a strip mall in a small Northern California town. One night, my boyfriend picked me up after my shift, and we went to the record store next door to my workplace. My boyfriend was browsing on one side of the store, and I was on the other side when the telephone rang. The manager yelled from the counter, "Hey, Lori, there's a phone call for you."

Right away, I thought that was a little weird, because nobody would have had any idea I was even there. Our decision to check out the record shop was a last-minute, spontaneous thing. I wondered if something had happened at home and perhaps my parents were calling some of the nearby shops, hoping to locate me.

I picked up the phone. "Hello?"

The unfamiliar voice of a man began to speak. "I'm in the phone booth in the parking lot. I'm watching you right now. I have a gun. This is what I want you to do—"

Before he could continue, I was already moving. With great exaggeration, I pulled the phone from my ear, backed up several steps, and, in complete view of the full-length windows lining the front of the store where he claimed to be watching me, I threw that telephone against the wall as hard as I could. I quickly grabbed the store manager and my boyfriend, and we headed for the office in the back of the store. I told them what had happened, and we called the police. The story ended there. The phone stalker was never caught, and I never heard from him again.

After the call, I questioned the store manager. "What exactly did that man say to you anyway? Did he ask for 'Lori'? Did he sound like he knew me?" The voice of the caller was totally unknown to me, but the manager had called me over to the phone by my name.

"No," the manager said, "he just asked for the blonde in the blue outfit. Of course, I called you to the phone by your name, because I know you."

Though I barely knew what I was doing at the time, this phone-hurling reaction to a stalker's frightening request was my way of breaking through fear in an active and immediate manner. Even at seventeen, I seemed to know that listening to that jerk for one more second would have locked me into fear.

I vividly remember one thought going through my head: "I can still get out of this if I don't hear what he has planned for me. If I don't listen to him, he can't put me under his spell of fear." What if I had listened to his comments or demands, and I'd heard something that shook me to the core? Would I have been so frightened that I would've felt I had to comply with his orders? He'd told me he had a gun. That was scary enough. I knew I didn't have the nerve to find out what on earth he wanted from me. Since he was watching through the window, I thought, "Okay, then, pervert, watch this!" as I hurled the phone at the wall.

Two other women I know were teenagers when they faced traumatic ordeals, but in both cases, fear left them paralyzed. Here are their stories:

Norah was sleeping over at her girlfriend's house when she woke up in the middle of the night to find her friend's older brother sprawled atop her. He was rubbing his body on hers, fondling her breasts, and kissing her. Norah was instantly wide-awake and petrified.

"What . . . ?"

"Shhh," the boy said, sounding angry. Norah immediately felt intimidated. She barely knew this guy, and here he was on top of her. He'd never paid much attention to her before, not even when she was at his kitchen table having dinner right across from him.

Norah smelled liquor on his breath.

She wanted to cry out, but then wondered what good that

would do. After all, she was in *his* house. She remained beneath him, frozen, scared, and praying he'd leave her alone.

He escalated the intensity of the kissing and fondling. Still Norah didn't move a muscle. The boy eventually got off her and made his way back to his own bedroom.

Thirty years later, Norah still wonders why she did nothing.

Debra found herself in a similar predicament when she was about seventeen.

She was walking to her car after school when a boy from her English class caught up to her and asked her for a ride home. After he described where he lived, she agreed. It was right on the way to her house.

Debra didn't really know this guy, but he was in her English class. She concluded it was okay to drive him in her car.

Up and over the hill, Debra shifted gears. She suddenly felt her classmate's hand on her breast, fondling her. Then he shifted his hand to her other breast. Soon he was groping her crotch.

"Please don't do that."

But he kept fondling her. And, for some unknown reason, she just kept driving.

"Hey, please, I asked you to stop. Stop it."

Debra was cringing inside and pleading, "Please, you gotta stop this." She knew she had to get this guy out of her car, but the only way she could think to do that was to drop him off at his house.

He continued groping her until they reached his house.

"Okay, this is the place. Thanks."

She watched him exit the car. He acted as if he didn't have a care in the world. Until later that night when the police showed up.

Debra may have been too scared to do anything while the assault was under way, but she had the nerve to go home and tell her parents. They hit the roof and raised holy heck. The boy was questioned by officers. He admitted the whole thing and even spent time in juvenile hall.

Debra still wonders about her reaction that day. She'd been so scared and intimidated, she could only think to politely ask him to "please" stop what he was doing. But that didn't do any good. Why on earth didn't she do anything more drastic?

Two assaults. Two frozen women. Two main reasons for their paralysis. They were full of fear and had no clue on how to handle their situations. Unfortunately, this inability to respond is all too common for many women. During an attack, if a victim becomes shocked, scared, anxious, panic-stricken, angry, or confused, she often stays still, wondering what she could or should be doing. All that was necessary in Norah's bed and in Debra's car was movement, the very thing these young ladies did all day long without thinking about it. For Norah, a move like rolling the guy off and onto the floor, then stepping on his face on the way to his parents' room to tell them their creepy son was desperate for supervision, would have worked nicely. For Debra, a quick backfist to the nose before pulling over and kicking her passenger to the curb would have been effective. Fortunately in each case, the aggressor stopped on his own before they were seriously injured.

One great way to get moving no matter how shocked and scared you are is by realizing ahead of time where your energy comes from. This source of great power and strength is what the martial artists refer to as ki (Japanese) or chi (Chinese). Imagine this ki located right in the center of your body, deep within your mid-section. Think two inches below your belly button, but straight back into the middle of your torso. This is the nucleus of your power. It works like the ignition of a car—from nothing to full throttle—instantly! In an attack, you will be the more effective fighter if you can draw from this power source, then explode from the inside out.

This is not difficult to do. You just dig in deep and release that ki energy. Cause it to blast you into movement at the very start of your actions.

You must consider your option to move always, anytime, anywhere, and with any degree of strength you wish. Criminals will come at you in a variety of forms and intensities. They try the strangest stuff. There's no method to their madness. You can listen and comply, go along with them, try to give them what they want, and they'll still leave you dead as a doornail. Or you can take your chances right at the get-go with the sheer power of fierce and immediate movement from the core of your fighting spirit.

In the Los Angeles television newsroom where I worked for many years, our group of employees had a term for going out in the field to cover a breaking story when things had gone berserk and we were short on manpower and completely out of time.

"Do it quick and dirty!" the assignment editor would order the crew over the phone. That meant the crew was to get there, tape what they could as fast as possible, and then get out of there even faster.

Quick and dirty. This same phrase could apply to the business of defending your life. Be quick and dirty about it. The bad guy is never going to wait around for you to find your nerve and figure out what to do. You're going to have to break through fear with courage. You're going to have to muster up the energy of the fighter within. Move. Do anything. Improvise. Let your ki get you started.

Or keep in mind what my sensei taught: "Better to move with bad form and lousy techniques than to stand there and do nothing."

So bust a move. Explode into it. Come out swinging and keep moving until you are safe. Fight or flight—it's your choice.

Defense Dos and Don'ts

- Don't lock down or freeze up when you are alarmed or confused.
- Do use instant mobility when facing an opponent.
- Don't be overly concerned about how you move, just move.
- Do call upon the strong power source deep inside you.

→ *Power Point!* ←

Fight fear with immediate movement.

23

DECIDE TO LOOK LIKE THE ANIMALS DO

Man, I can assure you, is a nasty animal.

MOLIÈRE

Welcome to the jungle.

In case you didn't already know, the fight is in your eyes. You just have to start looking like it is.

We can learn a lot from Mother Nature about protecting ourselves. In the animal kingdom, members of the cat species consistently prove they are some of the best fighters in the world. Perhaps you've observed them while watching television documentaries. They're the ones with the full stomachs at the top of the food chain, licking their paws. They're not exactly losing any fights.

Because of their finesse with fighting, there are many references to cats in various styles of the martial arts. There are cat stances and panther strikes and many katas (or forms) with tiger poses and names. If you've spent any time paying attention to cats, you know they're carnivores and sometimes man-eaters.

Once I learned about the connection between cats and the art I was so diligently practicing, I started studying our family's cat, Tigger. Like many other cats, Tigger is not winning any popularity contests. She trusts no one and refuses to befriend any of us. But what has me particularly interested is her body language. Her lithe form moves effortlessly and silently through our home as if she's some undercover agent. The retractable claws she uses to threaten our golden retriever (just for being alive and having the audacity to breathe the same air as she does) are out on a second's notice. She exhibits perfect balance. Every single move she makes is preceded by a glassy-eyed stare. Each of her actions is cool and covert.

Tigger always turns her head to look before she takes a step in any direction. She whips her eyes to focus on exactly what she's going for, and then she pounces into action. She creeps around in the dark. She hears things from the other side of the house. She sits still, waiting. Even though she's fourteen, she continues to prove that she's quite a huntress.

In self-defense, each of the five senses is important, but what we do with our eyes is absolutely crucial. Like cats, we snap our heads to see our opponents. We move. We size him up. We go forward. We watch him. We read him. We react to him. We eject the claws. We never take our eyes off him.

Cats have always known that the fight is in their eyes.

Then there's my golden retriever, Sparky. While this dog is as smart as heck, there's not a whole lot about him to make me think he might open a can of whoop-ass on any given day. But the Rottweiler across the street—Bossanova—is another story. Just looking into his eyes gives me the willies. I instinctively turn my head for the irrational (he never hurt anyone) fear that he'll bite my eyeballs right out of my face. He nails me to the wall with those things. I've come to learn that Bossanova is a master of something my karate instructor called "mad-dogging."

One night after class, this instructor told me I should be making eye contact with every man I come across.

"In fact," he said, "you should be mad-dogging each and every man you see." He went on to define mad-dogging as staring right into someone's eyes in a deliberate way and then holding on for a bit.

Now this idea struck me as very odd, and the women I've since discussed it with always initially feel the same. To look boldly eye to eye at every man seems rather unnatural. Most women wouldn't dare, considering that throughout history females have been taught to be subservient, to look downward in the presence of men. These days we might glance in their direction before turning our gaze elsewhere, but that's about it. Women know that a long look at a man can easily be misconstrued. He might think she's loose, aggressive, improper, or unladylike. We know how a man can be. You give him too lengthy a stare, and he thinks you're hot to trot. The next thing you know, he's following you around, begging you to go home with him.

But my instructor went on to assure me, "When you mad-dog someone, you're giving him this look." He walked toward me, staring intensely with a slight frown and a *Dirty Harry* squint. He continued to stare even when it felt prolonged and impolite. While his stare was bold and assertive, it was not at all threatening or suggestive. I wasn't very comfortable with it, though, and that was exactly his intention.

Here's the message mad-dogging sends. It says, "I see you. I see you good and clear. I will remember you. I would identify you and pick you out of a lineup if I had to. You stay over there and don't you move, because I'm watching you. I don't particularly like what I see, but make no mistake, I see you."

I decided to put mad-dogging to the test. It only took a few times to realize that this concept not only works, it changes everything. Combined with great posture, a sure-footed, striding walk, and an overall awareness of your surroundings, mad-dogging is one zinger of a physical defense tactic. For one thing, it takes very little effort. We're talking about a look, an expression. You can perform this one with four bags of groceries and two kids in tow. Another plus is that mad-dogging has the ability to transform your

appearance into that of a totally assertive woman. This air of intensity will make you look on top and in charge. Mad-dogging also
changes the actions of some of the men you encounter. I've
watched countless times as men have grown uncomfortable under
my gaze due to mad-dogging. They seemed almost nervous, as
though I was actually intimidating them with very little effort.
"What's she looking at?" they seemed to be thinking, glancing over
their shoulders to see if I was directing my look to someone else
right behind them. Even my seventy-plus-year-old mother started
"mad-dogging," and she was amazed at the results.

Don't plan on having a lifelong stare out with everyone you
meet, but mad-dogging is one terrific tactic to use if you are alone
and you suddenly find yourself in a vulnerable situation. It's perfect for "keeping somebody over there" on the other side of that
wall you built and across that line you've drawn. It works while
heading past a group of men in the parking lot. Heck, it'd probably
be an excellent entrance to a staff meeting at work when you've got
a tough proposal to pitch. I used it recently when a girlfriend and I
exited a theater and found a man loitering near my car. I let him
have it mad-dog style. Instead of intimidating us, he backed off and
headed in another direction.

Perhaps cat-watching and mad-dogging will inspire you to take
on a little animal behavior.

A couple of years ago, I was up early to walk in a beautiful residential area of Montecito, California. As I came to a curved intersection, I found myself face-to-face with a cougar. This cat was
slender, but at least tall enough to reach my thigh. It stood about
twenty feet away from where I'd stopped dead in my tracks.
Though the cougar was absolutely beautiful, I knew from recent
television news accounts that this cat could be quite deadly.

At the risk of sounding like a woman who hadn't made the decision that something bad could happen to me, I'll admit saying
one thing to myself: "All this time I've been preparing to battle a
man, and now it comes down to a fight with a humongous cat!"

I couldn't remember what any of the television documentaries had suggested for a jam like this. Was I supposed to stretch my hands over my head and look huge? No, that was for bears or something. Was I supposed to run for dear life? No, that felt like the worst thing to do. Sudden movement would've surely provoked the animal to chase me.

One thing I knew for sure, that cat was moving very slowly and smoothly.

And then it hit me. That was it. I would emulate a cat. I would behave like this cougar. I would try to make him think he was looking at something not far from his own kind. I would act like Tigger, for crying out loud. Why not, right? What did I have to lose?

I looked the cougar straight in the eyes. With a sleek motion, I reached to the front pocket of my sweatshirt. Ever so slowly, I pulled out my brand-new, very large canister of pepper spray, cocked the trigger into the ready position, and pointed it at the cougar. Then I began moving backward, smoothly stepping one foot behind the other.

For an entire block, I continued this backward cat walk, every second of it slow and deliberately unruffled. My eyes were glued to his. The cougar looked at me. He watched me for a few seconds. I kept stepping back with the pepper spray ready. He looked at me again as I kept up the cat act. Our gazes were locked as we watched each other. My gut feeling was that he didn't seem interested in me. Perhaps he wasn't hungry. The cougar finally slipped into the bushes. I continued moving in reverse until I was safely back, all the while watching the bushes that lined the street.

Incidentally, at the time I was unsure how effective pepper spray would've been on the cougar. A police officer later informed me that defense sprays work quite well on animals, including large, threatening dogs such as pit bulls. He insisted that the spray would have been a sufficient force against the cougar. That morning, I knew it was all I had. That and a little cat-titude. (Sorry.) But essentially that is what this whole animal thing is about. Attitude. In the wildest sense.

If you want to avoid a few fights, take a look at our friends in the animal kingdom and then start emulating them if need be.

Go ahead, let the cat out of the bag. Put the dog out while you're at it.

Fight with your eyes.

Defense Dos and Don'ts

- Do get physical with your eyes.
- Do use your facial expressions to show your assertiveness.
- Don't take your eyes off your opponent or someone who seems suspicious.
- Do mad-dog in situations where you feel vulnerable.

→ *Power Point!* ←
Take a walk on the wild side.

◄ **24** ►

DECIDE TO PROTECT YOUR SPACE

**Therefore good warriors cause others to
come to them, and do not go to others.**

SUN TZU,
THE ART OF WAR

L ocation is everything.

Personal space is an ever-changing element. You create it,
claim it, protect it, and use it as a measuring device. Violators are
kept out, avoided, or escaped.

When dealing with strangers, the best rule of thumb is to keep
them at least two to three feet away from you. But the instant some
guy comes up and gets in your space, the solution is really quite
simple. You just dump that old space and claim new space. All it
takes is a step in the right direction. Or the left. Or backward and
out the door.

One of my favorite discoveries of all the martial arts concepts
was that a true warrior never fights over the same thing as his opponent. Though usually aware of what his opponent has committed to, the warrior always looks for opportunity elsewhere. By
steering clear of the exact same goal that his enemy is pursuing,
the warrior can choose what's open and available.

This idea easily applies to our space, the air we breathe, and the ground we happen to be standing on. While it's highly important to protect your actual physical body, the space it inhabits is a different thing all together. If you think about it, it's actually a piece of the earth or the atmosphere. As soon as it's invaded, just go get new space. Relocate. Give that guy your old space. Give him all the space he wants. Take yourself three steps back, across the room, out of the building, and into the next zip code if you have to. That space might have been nice, but so is the next patch of grass, carpet, or cement. You didn't own that piece of the floor at the grocery store. You were just passing through. Let him have it.

Again, the key idea here is to move. Someone's presence in your space means it's time to get going.

Distance is also a factor. When the fighting hasn't started but the threat exists, greater distance is always your objective. If he can't reach you, he can't exactly fight you, so try to put as much distance as you can between you and the bad guy. Remember the number one goal for any personal security incident is to escape. That's why distance is a good thing. That is why it's okay to let him have your old space as long as you've moved on to new. It's why running away is always a valid escape technique as long as the guy is not right on your heels.

There's no need to defend your personal space with your body or your life. After all, it's just a piece of asphalt or a section of air that you stopped to breathe for a while. When you decided in chapter 9 what was worth fighting for, I'm guessing that dirt and air were probably not topping your list of valuable possessions. So never choose to stand still like a stubborn fool, thinking, "He cannot make me move. I refuse to move for him." If he keeps invading your space, you'll need more drastic measures. By the second or third time, he's making it clear it's *you* he's after and that he's willing to keep coming at you even though you've moved backward to claim new personal space. Now you'll need to articulate a verbal warning with your hands up to his chest to give him a light or hard push back (depending on the situation).

Again the idea is to *move* and/or to gain some *distance*. Once you do, your options are numerous.

Let's say you're at a cocktail party. Some creepy guy manages to get you alone over by the hors d'oeuvre table. This guy's already had too much to drink. He's getting closer and closer to you, and moving in on you with every sentence. All you have to do is take a step back, allowing him the space he wants so badly. If it happens again, move again. If it happens a third time, let him have it. Say, "Okay now, bub. Back up. You're in my space." Or, "Okay, I'm going over there now. Bye."

He may get offended, but oh, well. If apologies existed in self-defense, you might have cared.

A new guy you're dating comes to your apartment to pick you up. You sit down on the couch to chat before heading out the door to a movie. He inches nearer to you again and again. You do a good job relocating, scooting farther away from him each time. Finally, you're at the end of the couch, and he's practically sitting in your lap. Now you must move with more drastic intentions. So stand up. Let him have the whole couch. Pace across the floor. Walk to the other side of the room. Adjust the CD player. Let your pit bull into the room. Free your boa constrictor from its cage. Summon your roommate. Make a phone call. Open the front door for him and tell him, "Good night."

Nothing like a space invader to suddenly make you crave an evening alone, watching a video.

Let's say your boss is a real jerk who has the tendency to come up behind you and lean over you as you're sitting at your desk. It's beginning to feel like sexual harassment because your legs are trapped under the desk and he's breathing down your neck. Leave that space and seek a new locale. You might want to roll your chair right over his foot and bump into him as you stand. (It's easier to protect your space on your feet, and it gives you a more powerful demeanor.) You could toss a file folder on the floor and then ask him to pick it up for you. You could tell him to move. You could mention a close friend who has an interesting sexual harassment lawsuit currently being tried in the courts.

You might want to consider getting up, walking out the door, and looking for a new job.

You're in the parking lot at the mall and some knucklehead thinks he was first in line for the parking space you just pulled your car into. He unravels. As you lock your car, he gets out of his and walks over to you, yelling and cursing the day you were born. Keep moving away from him. You'll need more than a three-foot safety zone with this stranger. Get your hands up above your belt, because you may need them. Keep your keys in your hand, because they're good for smashing into his face and poking in his eyes if this ordeal escalates dangerously. Order him to back off while you call 911 on your cell phone. Keep walking. But better yet, ask yourself, "Do I really need to be here? Do I need this ground, this territory, or that parking space?" You can easily say to him, "Okay, I'll give you the spot." Jump back into the driver's seat, lock your car doors, put the vehicle in reverse, and give him the geographical location you once inhabited.

Gain distance. Get away from him.

Your personal space will always be in transition.

It will change depending on where you are, who's near you, and what's going down at any particular moment. When you're with someone you know, you'll allow him to come closer. When you see a guy panhandling in the alley, you'll keep him several yards away. When six gang-bangers are heading up the sidewalk toward you, your instant goal is more space and greater distance. Drastically shift your geographical location by crossing the street and heading far away. Give the bangers your old territory. Give them the entire sidewalk.

Moving somewhere else in order to keep you in your safety zone shouldn't feel like surrendering to the opposition in some war. As long as there is plenty of space between you and the person you're concerned about, you're winning the battle. The place you never want to be is where he is. Go after what's available and leave the old space behind.

Get a move on.

Defense Dos and Don'ts

- Don't ever think that your space and your body are one and the same.
- Don't fight over your personal space. Simply move instead.
- Do protect your space with distance.

➤ *Power Point!* ◄

Space—the first frontier for fighting like a girl.

25

DECIDE TO REMAIN ACTIVE VERSUS REACTIVE

Have the courage to act instead of react.

EARLENE LARSON JENKS

L ive in the moment.

The worst day of your life has arrived. You have no idea that a rapist is hiding in your home. You settle down in front of the fireplace with a cup of hot tea. The bad guy emerges from the hallway, rushes over to you, hits you in the face, and demands that you take off your clothes. No matter how much you think you will lose your mind, you need to keep your focus right here, right now, right smack in the middle of your biggest nightmare.

If you ever find yourself fighting for your life, it is absolutely vital that you remain *active* instead of *reactive*.

We learned in chapter 22 that when a woman is attacked, she'll often go into an instant deep freeze or straight into lockdown mode. This is when she could be described as being *reactive*. Translation: she'll start going either *inside* or *outside* of herself. This shut-down mechanism is a survival tactic that her brain attempts in order to escape the horror of the moment. She's mentally trying to "check out" of the whole ordeal. Rape victims will often later attest that their minds left their bodies during penetration as a means of survival. If a woman checks out completely, she's left numb, immobile, and unable to do anything to save herself. These are the women who are found a few hours later in a fetal position, completely traumatized.

As we compare reactive versus active, let me clearly state that it is essential that you *react* in any fight scenario and that you do so both mentally and physically. But don't ever allow yourself to go into a reactive shutdown mode. Instead, stay completely active. To stay active means to stay in the present. To stay in the game. To stay in "the here and now."

The bad guy might be as dumb as dirt, but he does have a few things figured out. One of these is that if he can get you into a reactive state, you are no good to yourself or anybody else. If he can get you reactive and no longer active, he possesses absolute power over you. Thus, he's in complete control of your entire life for the time being.

Some bad guys know how to use this concept to their greatest advantage.

They'll come at you in full-tilt active mode in order to put you into your most intensely reactive state. They realize that getting you reactive will put you out of commission for the time being, so they make a point to jack you up good and hard right at the start, hoping to thrust you straight into reactive mode. Once they accomplish this, they are pretty much in control of the situation.

How does the bad guy get his victim into a reactive state?

He uses pain, humiliation, fear, confusion, shock, surprise, and extreme violence.

An example would be the bad guy who walks into the room, quickly makes his way toward you, and immediately slaps you across the face. Now, it's very natural for you to become reactive.

You'd be wondering, Who is this joker and what is happening? You'd be thinking about the residual sting in your cheek. You'd probably put your hands to your face to wipe the blood from your lip. You'd definitely be trying to figure out what this guy wants from you and why he is inflicting pain on you.

Pain is one of the most expedient ways for the bad guy to push his victim into an immediate reactive state. A man's fist flying toward your face can feel like a medicine ball, and his arm like the trunk of a tree. There are women who break their forearms just trying to block a man's punch. Take a moment to contemplate the hurt you'd possibly experience if that strength was directed against you. In any physical fight, there is going to be pain as a result of his powerful force, but you must not allow this suffering to send you into reactive mode. Decide that pain won't have the power to shock you or lock you into fear, paralysis, or submission. Refuse to surrender. After all, pain is no picnic, but it isn't going to kill you, either. The worst thing about pain is that it's as uncomfortable as heck. *Injuries* are what you want to avoid with a ten-foot pole. Always remember—your goal in any fight is to escape. If you must engage and defend yourself, try to do so while experiencing the least amount of injury, or no injury at all. Then make your escape.

The reality is that all fights hurt. The pain is something you can count on. You're going to be sore, scraped, and bruised. You might break all your fingernails, get some of your hair pulled out, rip your pants, pee your pants, chip a tooth, twist an ankle, break your nose, or receive a black eye. He could break your arm or jaw. You might bleed all over the place, or he could start bleeding and his blood might get on you and that may very well freak you out. All of this is creepy, horrific stuff. Tomorrow you can visit the doctor, the dentist, the plastic surgeon, the nail salon, the beauty shop, and the dry cleaners. You can go to the police station and report the crime. You can obtain psychological counseling and attend group therapy. But today, in the middle of all that pain during this worst-case scenario circumstance, you have to take that guy down.

No matter what, you must survive.

Another example of being sent straight to reactive mode is when a rapist attacks by immediately stripping you naked from the waist up. There you are, standing bare-chested in a state of complete humiliation. Any woman in her right mind would go reactive in such a situation. She'd be using her body in reactive stances and postures, while trying to cover herself. In doing so, she'd be unable to use her hands or arms for any physical self-defense techniques. She'd be tempted to think dozens of reactive thoughts beginning with "I don't have my shirt on," continuing with "Oh, no, I'm going to be raped," and ending with "Is he going to kill me after he's raped me?"

A deputy sheriff informed me that rapists often try to strip off a victim's clothes immediately. This is done not only to begin satisfying their violent control issues, but also to keep their victims in the disabling condition of total humiliation and embarrassment. They do it to keep victims under their management. Rapists know, either consciously or intuitively, that a naked victim will most likely be locked into reactive mode for the next few hours.

Fortunately, we've already played a game called what-if. In that game, one of our rounds included the question, "What if I had to fight a bad guy naked or partially clothed?" If a man ever manages to overpower you and strip you down, you know you need to be mentally ready to stay active and fight for your escape.

In any fight, you can be sure you've slipped into reactive mode if you become physically frozen or find yourself locked into one of the following two mind-sets:

1. *You are thinking about the past.* "Why did I open the door to this guy? I knew I shouldn't have told this man where I live. How did he follow me home? I never should

have come home early. Did he just break my tooth? My ribs are killing me. He really messed me up with that punch."

2. *You are thinking about the future.* "What am I going to do if my children walk in and see this attack? When is my husband coming home? What will this guy do to me next, kill me? I'll never see my family again. How will I ever identify this guy when he's wearing a mask? I'll never live to see my thirty-fifth birthday."

Most times, all it takes is fear to render people totally reactive. Make the decision to break through the fear and get active and stay active. Again, this can be translated to one word—move! If you feel yourself slipping into reactive mode, think of getting back into the present immediately. Start moving again. Get back into the fight for your life. Look for an opportunity to escape. Ask yourself, "What is happening right now?" or even better, "What am I doing right this second to get myself out of this mess? What lethal counterattacks am I using on him to save my life? What am I doing to this slimeball to get him into a reactive mode that he can't recover from?"

This is a perfect example in self-defense when everything is up for grabs. This means anything being used against you can also be used against him. Turn the tables. Force him into a reactive mode. He's expecting you to be horrified, victimized, and too scared to fight back. Go ahead, rock his world.

For added power, try using the element of surprise to get him into a reactive mode.

Surprise is one of the greatest advantages and most frequently used tactics in any battle situation. Military strategists all over the world continually implement surprise in their battle plans. They'd be crazy not to. Without the element of surprise, the invading troops might as well be calling out, "Yoo-hoo, we're coming to get you!"

In the dojo, we practiced hundreds of self-defense techniques. Many incorporated what we called a distraction or surprise move at the beginning of the counterattack. If our uke grabbed one of our wrists, first we'd shock him by poking his eye with our available hand, then we'd quickly transition in with the stronger, more deliberate defenses. If the uke grabbed both wrists, we'd shock him with a kick to the shin or a stomp on his foot before proceeding with additional techniques. These distraction moves weren't powerful enough to take anybody out in and of themselves. They were designed purely for shock value, to surprise him and render *him* reactive.

The bad guys have the surprise thing pretty well figured out, too. They know that if they can surprise their victim, they'll immediately have the upper hand and the control by sending their victims into a reactive state. But you're always entitled to surprise him right back! Remember the bad guy has a plan, and there's a good chance he planned on your acting like a victim. He is not prepared for your deliberate active mode. He wasn't banking on your ability to respond assertively or to fight effectively. The last thing his plan called for was a bigger surprise coming back at him.

How Can You Surprise the Bad Guy?

- Be the woman who's prepared for him.
- Break through your fear with instant movement.
- Poke him in the eye, the face, or the nose.
- Kick him in the knee or the shin.
- Pick up something and throw it at him.
- Scream at full volume in his face.
- Have strong counterattack measures ready to put in action.
- Stay active, mobile, in the present, and in the game.

- Keep moving like a woman who's gone mad.
- Shock him with some bizarre actions or behavior.
- Deliver a surprise that sends him straight into reactive mode.

While speaking about the surprise factor to a group of females, a woman named Abby waved her hand and called out, "I've done that!"

Then she smiled, adding, "And boy did it work!"

She explained to our group that she had been dating a guy for several months when things started going downhill. On this particular night, however, they took a drastic turn for the worst. "We hadn't really been getting along for a few weeks. I'd been seriously thinking about breaking things off with him. That night when we were talking at his apartment, he became extremely volatile. He began ranting and raving about inconsequential things and his mannerisms grew very threatening. I thought I was about to be hit, smacked around, or even raped.

"I started fearing tremendously for my safety. All I wanted to do was get out of there. But I didn't see how I could, because he was standing between me and the door. I felt completely trapped. Meanwhile, his bizarre anger and behavior seemed to be getting worse. I knew I definitely had to do something."

Abby recalled glancing around his apartment, thinking she had better come up with a way of defending herself in case his anger escalated to violence. A couple of feet away there was a hammer on a console. She figured he must have been using it to fix something earlier.

"Just when I couldn't stand it anymore, I moved quickly over to that hammer, picked it up, and then deliberately walked over to his aquarium. I took the biggest swing I could and slammed that hammer into the glass, shattering it completely."

By now she had us pretty surprised as well.

Abby shook her head with a smile. "Everything changed that very moment. Glass was flying. Water was splashing all over the place and spilling onto the carpet. Fish were dying on the floor. And all he did was stand there in total amazement, almost in a daze, as if my behavior was now so much worse than his. It actually shocked him enough to diffuse the whole situation."

Abby saw her opportunity to head for the door and, without delay, she dashed out to safety.

With one swing of a hammer, Abby managed to change the dynamics of that evening's end and deliver her boyfriend straight into a reactive state. She turned the tables on him, using brute force and the element of surprise in a most brilliant manner, aided only by a simple tool from the hardware store that each of us probably has in the garage. No telling how many fish were surprised to be dumped onto the carpet that night. By the time her boyfriend realized the damage, Abby was already heading down the road. She never saw that guy again.

Self-defense is one big balancing act. In the martial arts, the Japanese judo term *kuzushi* (kah-zoo-she) is used to describe getting your opponent off balance. The bad guy knows that if you're off balance, both physically and mentally, you will be the easiest victim he could have picked. He's aware that when you're off balance, you're shocked, surprised, scared, and rattled. You're wondering what went wrong and what might happen next.

A woman experiencing kuzushi is in a reactive state. She's too off balance to protect herself effectively. She won't be throwing that boiling cup of hot tea in the face of the bad guy threatening her life in her own house. She won't be using her thigh to rupture his testicles. She won't be slamming his nose deeper into his head with her forearm. She won't be grabbing him by the hair and shoving his entire skull right through the brick fireplace. She won't be taking necessary steps to protect herself.

Remember that when any fight is going down and you are involved, you need to be an active participant. You need to surprise him with some strong counterattacks and self-defense measures. Going reactive will lead to your injury or death.

Stay in the present and never settle for anything but total victory.

Defense Dos and Don'ts

- Do stay active in any threatening situation or fight.
- Don't let pain, fear, shock, or confusion give you a bad case of kuzushi.
- Do surprise your attacker and get him reactive with your powerful self-defense.

➤ **Power Point!** ◄

Active defense is the only defense.

Ivy's Story

The cashiers at the grocery store were worried.

Ivy overheard a few of them talking to one another about some creep in an overcoat who'd been loitering in the parking lot that evening. But Ivy was too busy to be concerned. She was a single mom with teenagers waiting at home for her return. It was her daughter's boyfriend's birthday, and she'd promised to bake him a cake.

"I worked during the day, so I always had to do my grocery shopping at night. It was dark in the parking lot as I put my things in the car. Suddenly, as I sat down behind the wheel, a man in an overcoat flung open the passenger

door. With his hand in his pocket, he said, "I've got a gun and I'll kill you if you don't take me to the bus station."

Ivy tried starting the car and putting it in reverse before he could get in, but the man jumped in the passenger's seat and shut the door.

"Take me to the bus station, or I swear I'll kill you."

Ivy had no idea where the bus station was located, but she started driving as if she knew exactly where she was going. She headed onto the freeway. Her carjacker reminded her over and over that he had a gun and he wasn't afraid to use it. Ivy still had yet to see the actual weapon.

"I didn't have a clue how to get out of this situation," Ivy later said. "He was a big man, and I was quite sure I couldn't overpower him. All I could think to do was to talk to him. So that's exactly what I did."

Ivy started telling the man about her strong religious faith and about her two terrific kids. She told him how much she loved those kids and that everybody was back home, waiting for her to return from the store and make a birthday cake.

"I need to get back home because they're waiting for this birthday cake," I informed him. "He was just sitting there extremely agitated. In fact, the whole time I was with him, he was highly agitated, but I just kept right on talking. I figured my only shot at getting out of the situation was to make this as personal as I could. I told him all about myself, my life, and my childhood. I tried to be as human to him as I could."

Ivy remembers being very calm and clearheaded. She determined that her passenger was mentally "off." "He was definitely not dealing with a full deck. But there was something about him that told me I needed to be very afraid of him."

After driving for a while, the man motioned Ivy to exit the

freeway. "Get off here," he snapped, and then, "Turn here."
Now they were heading up a hill to a restaurant that Ivy knew
was closed for renovations. The road dead-ended up at the
top of the hill. At that point, she made the decision to flee.

"It was a now-or-never moment. I had to take the
chance."

Ivy suddenly announced that she was going to throw
up. Then she flung open her car door and jumped out. She
landed in a ditch, scrambled to her feet, and started running as fast as she could away from the headlights. It was
now raining.

The man climbed into the driver's seat. After grinding the
gears of her stick shift vehicle for a while, he finally took off.

Down the hill Ivy tried flagging cars down to help her,
but no one stopped. She couldn't exactly blame them. With
her long hair crazy and standing on end and her clothes
muddy and wet from landing in a ditch, she didn't exactly
look like anyone you'd want to pull over to help.

One young college man finally did. He drove Ivy to a
coffee shop, where she called the police. Officers arrived
quickly and issued an all-points bulletin. That moment, a
few miles away, the carjacker ran a stop sign in full view of
two officers in a squad car.

"He was immediately taken into custody," Ivy said and
then shook her head. "It turned out he was an escapee
from a mental institution in another state. He had already
raped and killed two women. The police kept telling me
how lucky I was, because he hadn't left anyone else alive."

Months later, Ivy testified in court. Several criminal
counts were added to his record, including those of kidnapping and carjacking. He was sent out of state and, once
again, institutionalized.

26

DECIDE TO GET UP CLOSE AND PERSONAL

**Unless you enter the tiger's den,
you cannot take the cubs.**

JAPANESE PROVERB

Y ou've got to make a commitment.

Like it or not, self-defense is an act of intimacy. Masters of the martial arts often go so far as to define the dynamics of a fight as a "relationship." Not exactly the most pleasant thought that takes you straight to your happy place, right? Yuck!

Let's say you've been successfully drawing your boundary lines and protecting your space, but one day, you don't see him coming and you suddenly find yourself in the midst of a serious attack on your life. This is now a fight scenario with him holding you tightly, dragging you somewhere, and to your horror, you find yourself unable to pull free because of his brute strength. Guess what? The moment of extreme dedication has arrived for you. Just when you'd rather be anywhere else in the universe, preferably on another planet, or at least as far away as you could possibly get from this guy, it is now time for you to *move in closer* to him.

In order to fight any opponent, you've got to be in his face and right under his nose. You must be within close proximity to the body parts that you'll be targeting for counterattacks. You're going to be close enough to smell what he ate for lunch that day. Think about it now. Be prepared for the most terrifying of intimate relationships, one that you'll need to commit to totally in order to end.

Fights take place at close range. The reasons for this are pretty obvious. The most important one being that you can reach each other. Another significant reason is that the techniques will have more power. You don't want to barely tap the bad guy with your fully extended punch. You want to be one foot away as you plant your punch deeply into him and complete your delivery full force. That way, there's still plenty of power to the punch. If he's a full arm's length away from you, blasting a punch at him is worthless. You'll just have executed your punch into thin air. You'll be lucky to tap your fingernails on the buttons of his shirt.

However, if your punch is coming from twelve or fourteen inches away from him, this could very well give a solid pounding to his solar plexus. It might knock some of the air out of him. Or you could aim for the Adam's apple and do some serious damage. Your goal is to punch right *through* the target you're aiming for, instead of just attempting to reach it. Try punching and kicking a heavy bag for twenty minutes at the gym and you'll see what I mean. The same idea applies with kicks, karate chop–style strikes, and grabs of any kind. Get close.

So what do you do if you're too close to him to escape, but too far away to fight him effectively? Once again, the magic word is *move!* This particular move in the karate world is called a *transition*. Transitions take you from here to there smoothly, quickly, and effectively. Take a long reaching step with your right foot and slide your left to follow. In one second you can be two feet closer to your opponent with a transition step.

There are many other ways to transition, and anything you can think to do at the time is okay. You can *rush-run* right into him, grab his lapels, and bring your thigh right up into his scrotum. You can leap to his side, put up a guard hand, and strike his ribs or kidneys with a vertical punch. You can throw something above his head like your cell phone, transition in with a slide step, and punch your knuckles straight into his trachea while he's looking up at the phone. You can hopscotch, tap-dance, leap from foot to foot, dive through the air, or swing over on a vine. Anything goes when it's time to get close to him.

Just get there.

As with any committed relationship, the up close and personal fight contains vows. Here are some of the promises you need to make to yourself before engaging in battle with a bad guy.

The Up Close and Personal Vows

- When he intends or begins to harm you and you are unable to escape, commit to fight and save your life.
- Make your commitment both mental and physical.
- Once committed, move in or transition right next to him.
- Plant your feet close to his in a wide stance for balance.
- Immediately strike him as hard as you can.
- Strike as many times and in as many target areas as you possibly can in order to win the fight.
- Don't stop, give up, or back off until you've earned an opportunity to escape.

With a commitment of this magnitude, there is no turning back. Once you're in close and nose to nose with the bad guy, you need to be battling. If you're not, he's going to have all the control in the situation. If you've been threatened, moved in on, and forced to transition up close and personal to your opponent, you'll need to fight with everything you've got before you start moving back out of that shared space.

Incidentally, up close and personal is exactly the style of fighting needed to perform a knife, gun, or club take-away. Not that any of us want to attempt that unless absolutely necessary. It's best to break out running as fast as you can. Weapons are the worst-case scenario, and fleeing rather than fighting a person with them remains your number one goal. Staying clear of people who shove a weapon in your face should be a way of life. Decisions regarding weapons will take our full concentration, and we'll delve into that subject in chapter 33.

As we discovered in chapter 24, distance always works to your advantage. As a result, your goal should always be to put major distance between yourself and the bad guy. But if it's too late to get distant, or he's already on you and you can't break free, then get closer. If there's no way out, commit and get intimate. Then, break it off fast and furious. It's the only way to fight.

Your best defense can only be executed close-up.

Defense Dos and Don'ts

- Do run away if you can. If you can't, get closer to him.
- Do think of fighting as a serious commitment.
- Don't hang back so that your punches, kicks, and strikes can't reach him
- Do realize that once you've committed, there's no stopping until you are free.

→ *Power Point!* ←

Get right up in his face and fight.

27

DECIDE TO GO "NUTS"

I never saw a wild thing sorry for itself.

D. H. LAWRENCE

You are the bomb.

One minute you're Miss Congeniality and the next, you're exploding all over some poor slob who's mistaken you for his next victim. Going "nuts" is like setting off a grenade. When you've decided to detonate this bomb inside you, everything you are, were, or ever will be must join forces to fight on your behalf. Every ounce of energy, strength, passion, and adrenaline is necessary for the battle at hand.

Absolute madness is your only key to survival.

You will never win this fight if you attempt it as the person you are right now: the brilliant college student, the friendly waitress, the sharp businesswoman, the talented artist, the computer specialist, or the loving wife. Your attacker is an animal. In order to match his force, power against power, you will need to go to a place within yourself that you've perhaps never visited. It is a place where fierce animals tread. This man—a criminal, a murderer, or a rapist—is coming after you on a different physical plane. It's there that your battle must be fought because the truth is you'll never be able to stop him with anything less.

Deciding to go nuts is your license to explode. If you make this decision today, you'll be able to go nuts if you ever need to. But you must choose to muster up strength you never knew you had. You must release the fighter within, a woman so wild, so horrific, you'll probably be as shocked as the bad guy. When the explosion occurs, guttural sounds may come spewing from your mouth. You may find yourself screaming and ripping at somebody's eyeballs, then quickly moving on to bury your fist all the way to the back of his throat. You may strike his temple with a blunt object you never before dreamed you'd swing at anyone. You'll find other targets to strike, to kick, and to hit that you've never before realized. You must put every muscle into play. Each bone in your body must cooperate with your defense. You might find yourself biting into flesh, punching, ripping, snarling, and scratching all at once.

Perhaps some slimeball's top layer of skin isn't exactly something you're dying to sink your teeth into. Let's say you're a mildmannered woman. You might take pride in your self-controlled, gentle nature, and going nuts might sound like quite a big stretch for you. This is one of those times you'll have to give yourself permission. How many seconds or split seconds would it take for you to get nuts? How nuts would you become? How would you move, defend, and fight? You may need to practice exploding in private once in a while, but when the time comes, your body will know what to do—how far to go and what actions are necessary. Take care of this now, in an ordinary moment, and you will gain peace of mind.

Without question, there are the obvious situations when you will need to set the bomb off and go nuts instantaneously. These include Force Level Four attacks, worst-case scenarios, and circumstances where someone is attempting to transport you to that dreaded "second location."

An assailant who's attempting to drag you elsewhere or push you into an automobile is leaving you with one single option—to fight for your life with everything you've got as fast as you can. You must get away immediately. Decide that the only place you're going is nuts, and that you will break the speed limit to get there.

If the bad guy has a weapon and he's trying to take you somewhere, you need to think seriously about taking some tremendous chances. Try to escape at the very start of the attack while you're still in that first location. Your odds of dodging a bullet by running in a zigzag pattern or escaping from this criminal at the get-go are often far greater than surviving some sick horror he has planned for you at the second location.

If it's a gun he's got, keep in mind that a bad guy often uses a firearm as a "power tool" rather than as a killing instrument. He'll be happy to wave the gun to achieve his goal, but he doesn't necessarily want to pull the trigger and leave any dead people around. Or, consider the statistic taught at the self-defense school Impact Bay Area—that 90 percent of the people who are shot survive, and that most shooters in an adrenaline-pumped condition cannot hit a moving target.

Is it worth taking your chances right at the beginning? Many people believe so.

If you stop on the street or at a red light, and from out of nowhere some guy suddenly opens your car door and climbs into the passenger seat with a gun, you have three choices:

1. Follow his demands and end up at the destination this slimeball has chosen for you, praying all the while that you'll live through the ordeal.

2. Pretend to cooperate with him. While driving, look for a window of opportunity for escape, perhaps by getting in a fender bender, jumping out of your car, or whatever it takes.
3. As soon as the guy gets into the car, burst through your fear with ki energy and fierce movement, and immediately attempt to get away from him by jumping out your side door and running off in a zigzag pattern.

All three choices are risky on your part. The differing factor is in the timing, or specifically when you decide to take the risk. To make an immediate escape would put you in tremendous danger right at the start. But to stay with him, biding your time for a chance later, could possibly place you in worse danger down the road. To end up at a final destination with this guy could certainly mean your death. When and where would you rather take your chances? How much time do you really want to spend with this monster?

Always keep in mind that the first location is the one that you selected. You might have friends nearby or on the way. There might be more people around, hence a greater opportunity to attract attention and unnerve this guy enough to prompt him to back off. If you allow yourself to go with him, your chances for survival rapidly diminish.

The first location is a fight scene. The second location is possible death. Do anything and everything to keep from going there with this man.

Get mad, get nuts, but most of all, get yourself out of this.

Male martial arts experts often advise their students to stay away from anger. Many of them say anger is self-defeating, that it can cause the loss of one's focus, and in some cases, the entire fight. But women are vastly different from men, and these differences also enter the fighting arena. Women are often described as emotional creatures, and anger is one emotion that will often get a woman riled up enough to protect herself. Rage can be pure fuel for any fight. It can get her from nowhere to nuts in record time.

If some bad guy takes it upon himself to threaten your safety and screw up your life for a while, you've got some good reasons to be angry. If he terrorizes you, you can certainly allow yourself to be mad. If he attacks you or hurts you, let fury charge through your entire body. Use that emotion and the adrenaline it produces for all it's worth.

Think of that scene in the movie *The Patriot*—the one in which one of Mel Gibson's sons has just been killed by the redcoats and another son, played by Heath Ledger, has been taken captive. The redcoats take off with their young prisoner, but Mel and his remaining two sons make a plan. They run like lightning down to the creek to head off the redcoats. Mel has brought his weapon of choice, a crude-looking tomahawk from previous legendary battles. His young sons aim their rifles and prove to be excellent shots. Finally, Mel runs right into the throng of redcoats.

And then he goes absolutely nuts.

By the end of the battle, everyone is dead except Mel and his boys. Mel turns to the camera. He is covered with the blood of at least twenty redcoats. And there's the unmistakable look in his eye of a man who's just crossed over into madness.

You might think it's impossible that you would ever fight as well as Mel. You might think you'd never be able to go nuts. But now we know about this thing called fight adrenaline—it's real and raw and enough to start you down the path to nuts. We've all heard about the meek and mild mother who lifted a car off her kid or some other gal who wrestled herself free from a wild animal. It *is* possible to go nuts and call upon strength you've never experienced. Decide today how big of an explosion you'd cause if you ever had to.

It's not about how big and strong you are. What matters is that the bomb goes off. So get mad. Get nuts.

You are full of explosive material. Set yourself off.

Defense Dos and Don'ts

- Don't stifle your anger when you're dealing with danger-ous individuals.
- Do imagine going nuts in order to get there swiftly if the situation ever arises.
- Do fight like a woman gone mad, not like the woman you are.

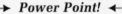

➤ *Power Point!* ◄

When it's time to go nuts, detonate the bomb inside you.

28

DECIDE TO GET HORIZONTAL

**It isn't important to come out on top.
What matters is to be the one
who comes out alive.**

BERTOLT BRECHT,
GERMAN WRITER

Chances are you're going down.

We usually imagine fighters in the upright position with their dukes up and doing all that fancy footwork. But the reality is that, in a fight, you are more than likely going to be grounded. Laid out. Floored. Parallel with the earth. You can almost bank on it. This could easily happen right away, seconds after the fight's begun. One minute you and the bad guy are on your feet, and the next thing you know, you're on the dirt, the cement, or the floor.

We need to be fully prepared to end up in a horizontal position, and we need to figure out how to fight once we're down there.

There are many reasons that a woman may have to fight on her back.

In chapter 4, you learned that one of the four most common attacks against women is the ambush. This is when a woman is jumped. A man may use every bit of his weight to pounce out at her or on top of her. Often the woman will end up horizontal, either on her stomach or on her back. These attacks may cause her to think that she's in a pretty tough position for counterattacking and getting away. But each of us needs to be ready for exactly this type of fight.

The following women were both prepared to fight horizontally, each in her own unique way.

Grace was walking from her college campus to her apartment one night when a man started trailing behind her. He was several feet back, but calling out and trying to get her attention. Grace gave him the brush-off and pretended to ignore him by refusing to answer. But she knew she was in danger because he didn't stop following her and trying to talk to her as she continued on the path ahead. She tried walking faster, but he sped up, too.

Finally, the man made his move. He rushed up behind her and pushed Grace to the ground, then knelt over her. Grace fell to one side and then rolled onto her back. She started moving wildly, squirming and punching him with both of her fists. Then she used her legs to kick him as hard as she could. When her attacker was struck by her foot in the stomach, he paused, and she was able to scoot away from him. Jumping back onto her feet, Grace ran away.

Later, Grace admitted that she thought she was done for when she found herself on the ground with her attacker, especially so soon after he initiated the assault. Then, realizing she hadn't even tried to fight back yet, she decided to give it all she could.

Heather woke up to find the figure of a man towering over her bed in the dark. Then suddenly his entire body weight was straddling her on the mattress.

"Why haven't you returned any of my phone calls?" he demanded, his angry voice right next to her ear. To Heather's horror, she recognized him. It was her ex-boyfriend, Travis, a guy she'd broken up with several months before due to a string of disturbing social and emotional behavioral traits. He had scared her back then, but now she was petrified. Heather realized the only way he could have entered her room was to have climbed the outside wall onto her second-story balcony and then through the sliding door.

Intuition told her that if she fought back, Travis was likely to rape her. So instead, she began speaking gently and softly. She pretended she was genuinely pleased to see him again. Several moments later, he'd calmed down enough to slide off her body and lie beside her. After a while, Heather was able to get up. A few more minutes passed and she turned on a light. Finally, he left by way of the front door. But the ordeal took an hour to play out, and the entire time Heather feared for her safety.

Two women flat on their backs. One went nuts and fought for her life. The other acted on her intuition, using verbal self-defense to perfection. Each escaped a rape or possibly worse. Both fought horizontally and lived to tell about it.

Don't ever give up just because you've bottomed out and landed on the floor. It doesn't mean you've lost the fight. You're just grounded for a while with new techniques to try on him. In order to save yourself, you've got to think fast or immediately move and keep doing so until you are clear of your attacker and on your way to freedom.

Techniques for Solid Ground Fighting

Take the fall. If a bad guy pushes or pulls you to the ground, "take the fall" or "go with it" or "roll into it" using a somersault or a side roll. This way, you'll suffer less injury from the fall itself. Don't forget to tuck your head chin-to-chest as you roll forward.

Roll out. If he's throwing you on your back, use the momentum of his toss to redirect your body, rolling sideways or even backward. If he's throwing you on a bed or couch, try to bounce right off it or over to one side or right back into his face with a good counterattack such as a jab to the eye or nose. Move with utmost speed and use your elbow and arm to push up. Take a fighting stance as soon as you're back on your feet. A fighting stance is feet apart with one foot slightly in front of the other (left in front of right if you're right-handed). Your left fist is out front, guarding your face and left temple. Your right fist is guarding your chest and ready to power punch.

Crab-crawl. To defend yourself on your back when he is still standing or coming toward you, crab-crawl or spider-crawl (belly-side up) away from him until you can get back on your feet. The crab-crawl can go in any direction. If he gains on you or gets too close to you, kick out at him hard and fast to keep him back. Aim for his groin or knees or try to sweep one of his feet out from under him. But be sure to pull your leg back in quickly so he doesn't grab it and hold on. If he does, twist your body until you break the attacker's hold. Buy yourself some distance by crab-crawling, then jump up when you get the chance. Now you're on your feet again and back in your fighting stance.

Smash out. Your attacker has just climbed on top of you in your bed. As far as you can tell, he doesn't have a weapon, but his body weight has you pinned to the mattress. Start jerking your entire body to get space between the two of you, especially twisting your hips around to knock him off you. Spit in his face. Bite him. Do anything you possibly can to get him reactive and to cause him to loosen his hold on you.

Then work an arm or hand free and use it immediately. This person wants to rape or even kill you, so feel free to rip that eyeball right out of its socket. If you get two hands free, use one to pull his hair and yank his head back, and the other to punch him through the throat all the way into next year. Or start jamming your thigh into his testicles. Or head-butt him. Bite into his nose or his lips.

Pelvis up. If you're pinned on your back by a man who's in more of a sitting up position with his legs bent on each side of you, pull your knees up, keeping your feet on the bed or the ground. Then lift your pelvis and twist fast and hard to one side. Try to thrust your arms in the direction of the twist. This will cause your attacker to be thrown off balance and, consequently, off you. Be sure to counterattack with a strike to the eyes.

If you end up in a self-defense ordeal someday and find yourself dumped on the ground, don't let the reality knock you for a loop.

When you hit the floor, your fight goes with you.

Defense Dos and Don'ts

- Do be absolutely prepared for ground fighting.
- Don't give up when your fight bottoms out.
- Do practice constant movement in this new position.

➤ *Power Point!* ◄

Be prepared to think on your feet, but fight on your back.

29

DECIDE TO USE PROPS

There is a homely adage which runs:
Speak softly and carry a big stick;
you will go far.

THEODORE ROOSEVELT

B lunt objects are a girl's best friend.

On movie shoots, props are what the showbiz folks call everything that ends up in the footage of a production, all the way from a matchbook to an airplane. Directors enhance the scenery with these objects in order to add visual creativity and realism.

Now it's our turn to get real about setting the stage for our personal security. With this decision, we'll enhance our scenery with some creative ideas about fighting with props.

Props are backup. They are added insurance for the female fighter. Fighting naked, fighting with one's fists, fighting "the way of the empty hand"—that's all fine and dandy, but you're going to feel a lot better if you're swinging a baseball bat when that intruder comes around the corner in your hallway.

This concept of backup has its roots deep in the martial arts of ancient times. In Okinawa centuries ago, rulers and invaders banned the people from arming themselves with weapons. This left the Okinawans to rely on their karate skills alone, but they knew they needed more. So they began using farm tools as fighting instruments, because they could carry these around all the time. Just as the sai could poke a hole in the earth for planting a seed, it could also stab through an opponent's midsection. The bo may have done a nice job of balancing across the shoulders with a bucket on each end, but as a weapon, this long staff could also poke, strike, or trip an opponent.

These days, our props work for us in the same way those ancient farm tools did for the Okinawans. If you were to look for household objects and tools, what would you find? What kinds of things do you have right at your fingertips that could save your life in a brutal fight? Is there a heavy iron lamp beside your reading chair? A fireplace poker on the hearth? A walking stick in the hall tree? A vase on the table? A wine bottle on the kitchen counter? Chopping knives in the drawer?

Props are good news for women who need to defend themselves. They are some of the most effective weapons you could ever hope to get your hands on, and they are absolutely everywhere. Without ever visiting your home, I can already tell you that you have props all over the place. I'm sure many of them exist in almost every room. In the rooms where there are none, you can easily throw in a few.

Starting today, begin noticing the props you have in place already. Make a mental note of where they are and pick your favorites in terms of force. Decide which ones might be easiest for you to handle. Decide what you would use when dealing with the various levels of force coming against you.

Take a fresh look at the props in your home and how you might use them:

- *Hitting props.* The baseball bat and hockey stick in your son's room.

- **Spraying props (to be used in the bad guy's eyes, nose, and mouth).** Hair spray, deodorant, cleanser in the bathroom, and ant killer in the kitchen.

- **Stabbing props.** The knives in the kitchen (though you might not want to display them for the bad guy's benefit in one of those nifty knife holders), the knives in your son's pocketknife collection, your rat-tail comb, the metal fingernail file on the bathroom counter, your husband's fishing knife in the tackle box in the garage, your sewing scissors in the den, and your knitting needles.

- **Throwing props.** A phone, keys, clothing, anything. Throwing an item is a great distraction technique. Usually, if something is flying through the air at a person, he will try to catch the item or to block it from hitting him in the face. It's a natural reaction. While his hand is reaching, that side of his body is open for your counterattack—a punch to the ribs or kidneys perhaps. You can think of these throwing distractions as ways in which to buy yourself a few seconds of time. With that time you can move out, gain some distance, and start running for the hills. Or you can transition and move in "up close and personal" to properly fight him.

- **Blocking props.** Throw a chair at him to slow him down. Push down a garbage can or a table to trip him or force him to slow his pursuit of you. Get something sizable such as a table between you, to keep him from being able to reach you. Pick up a vase or whatever happens to be on the table and throw it at him. Take that opportunity to run to safety.

Walk through your home and observe the props in their various locations. Take them one by one in your hand to feel their weight and texture. Make a few practice swings or jabs or sprays with the props. Try this in each room. See how many seconds it takes for you to leave your favorite position on the couch, run to a prop, and ready yourself to use it. Glance around the room. Do you have enough effective props stashed all around you?

Once you begin to recognize household objects as props, you'll begin to realize that almost anything can be used to help you in a fight. The laundry room has brooms and mops for swinging upside his head, even cleansers and chemicals to spray in his face should you get the chance. The dining room has cast-iron candlesticks and your grandma's old plate collection for smacking him around. The living room has a row of family pictures in heavy frames that you could start throwing at the guy. You could pick up the side table if you had to and use it to block his path. The game room has the pool cues and the dart set. The entry hall has the walking sticks and umbrellas. Props can be stashed in all the bedrooms, beside the bed, and under the bed. You'll need a prop at your side in the bathroom as you're showering (think *Psycho*) and while your ability to hear is diminished if you're using the blow-dryer. The garage has everything under the sun. Besides the garden tools and nasty bug sprays, there are enough items in the toolbox to take out a small army—screwdrivers, hammers, wrenches, and so on.

Once you recognize the props that fill your home, take this same idea into the workplace. Are you an artist or a draftsman? Perhaps you always have an X-Acto knife by your side. Are you a hairstylist? You must have plenty of scissors at hand. Are you a chef who could quickly arm herself with a chopping knife? Even a writing pen is a usable prop for stabbing through a guy's throat, and we could carry one of those around all day long.

Now take the idea of props into your cars. And your purse and briefcase and backpack and gym bag.

But don't stop there. Start noticing the props at your friends' homes, in your favorite restaurant, the café, and the mall. Pretty soon you'll be amazed by the objects that are available everywhere for your self-defense. Remember, though, if you choose to use a deadly prop such as a butcher knife or an ax, you're jumping to a Force Level Four counterattack, so the threat against you had better be life-threatening. If a guy is harassing you and following you down the street, spraying perfume in his eyes would be the better choice rather than stabbing him with your scrapbook scissors. If a bad guy has broken into your home and is attempting to murder you, the scissors are the smarter choice.

These days we have a wonderful prop at our fingertips almost all the time. It is the cell phone. Young women and teens are continually armed with this prop; in fact, they can't seem to survive a second without it! Like the Japanese yawara (an extremely short, wooden fighting stick), the cell phone is easily carried in the palm. It can strengthen the hand with interior armor. Poke a half-inch to an inch of your cell out the outside edge of your hand and you'll have added reinforcement as you pound a hammer fist into your attacker's temple, ribs, nose, or jaw.

Always keep in mind that the bad guy can turn the tables (and every other prop out there) on you, too. He's able to use them just as easily as you are, so if you're going to take care of business with a prop, be "quick and dirty" about it. Once you've shoved the broom handle up his nose and smacked him upside the head with it, get away fast and call for help. If you don't, he might come after you again, and this time with the props of his choosing. If you start thinking about all this today, you'll have the advantage of knowing the location of your props and against what threat and force level they should be used.

Many years ago, when my father was working as an officer for the Burbank Police Department, a call came in one night reporting a domestic disturbance. He and his partner raced to the location and noticed that the altercation had moved outside and onto the street. They were surprised to find the feuding couple running up the middle of the avenue completely naked! The woman was chasing her husband and quickly gaining on him. My dad and his partner stepped on the gas to catch up just as the woman raised her hand. With what my father later described as "a flick of the wrist" against the back of his head, the woman managed to lay that guy out, straight down, face flat in the pavement! All my dad could think was that this was one tough, mad, naked lady! It wasn't until they got out of the squad car to investigate that they found the black cast-iron frying pan she'd used to strike her husband's head. The solid black color had made it impossible to see in the dark night.

Begin to think creatively about the objects around you. Remember where they are every day.

In a pinch, use whatever is available.

Defense Dos and Don'ts

- Do take note of all the props that surround you.
- Do decide which ones would be your weapons of choice in a fight someday.
- Don't forget or lose sight of where these household props are located.

➤ *Power Point!* ◄

If you can't get away, prop him up and stick it to him.

Dina's Story

Dina's only mistake was to walk alone across campus late at night.

At the time, the decision didn't seem like a big deal. Besides, she had to stay late after her night class in order to talk to her college professor. Usually, she and several others walked in a big group back to the dorms. But that night, she encouraged her friends to go ahead and promised that she'd catch up within a few minutes.

But the discussion with her instructor took longer than she had anticipated, so she set out by herself down a path sandwiched between tall trees, the campus on one side and a row of fraternity houses on the other.

"It just so happens that it was a Friday night after ten o'clock, so you can imagine the frat parties. They were in full swing, with the loud music and lots of rowdy guys. And, of course, the alcohol was flowing. Suddenly, I was sorry I hadn't asked my friends to wait and walk with me."

When Dina realized that the wild party scene was just on the other side of the trees, she figured she'd better be on guard. She gripped her keys but, more important, the church key that they were hanging from.

"My dad had given it to me," Dina explained. "He called it a church key, but really it was a skinny piece of metal with a can opener on one side and a bottle opener on the other. Remember when everybody used the bottle opener with the triangle-tipped edge that could also puncture a can of juice or pop open a soda bottle? That was it. I carried it with me everywhere I went."

It was then that two guys from a frat party beyond the trees started to follow Dina.

"They were heckling me in a threatening manner, talking dirty, and following me. They were out-of-their-minds drunk."

Then a third guy suddenly jumped out in front of Dina to block her path. She now realized she was surrounded by these punks and in serious danger. She sensed that something violent and ugly was about to happen. From their verbal cues and their physical aggressiveness, it quickly became apparent that they intended to rape her. Within seconds, she was ambushed by all three young men.

"The one who grabbed me from behind reached around the front of my body and across my chest. With the church key gripped firmly in my hand, I slashed his arm from wrist to elbow. Despite the poor lighting, I watched his flesh open right up. Suddenly his blood was everywhere. He screamed really loud, releasing me at just the same moment that I kneed the guy in front of me. It was a perfect shot to the groin, and he went down like a ton of bricks. By now, the third guy had backed off completely. Realizing I'd broken loose of all three of them, I took off running as fast as I could."

Dina ran almost a mile to her dorm. When she got there, she discovered her assailant's blood was all over her clothes. She immediately told the other girls on her dorm floor and the campus security guards what had happened.

"After that, all of us were on the lookout for a guy with a messed-up arm. The weather was warm. Everybody was in short sleeves, so we thought for sure we'd spot him on campus with a big bandage or covering it up with long sleeves. We never did, though. Security looked for this guy for weeks, but they never found him. We finally concluded

that he'd probably been visiting the frat party from somewhere else, another campus maybe."

After her horrifying incident with these multiple attackers, Dina was always careful to walk with others, especially
at night. She still has her church key today.

30

DECIDE TO USE YOUR NATURAL WEAPONS

Boldness sharpens the sword.

ANONYMOUS

Y ou are armed and dangerous.

In the last chapter we defined backup, and we began choosing tools and props that we would utilize if we ever needed some extra help in a counterattack with a bad guy. But if you can't get your hands on anything, no worries. You're already equipped. In fact, your body is a well-stocked arsenal. There are weapons all over you from head to toe. As long as you figure out what to do with them, these tools of combat will aid you in your battle against the bad guy.

Lock and load, ladies.

The first thing to remember about your God-given weapons is that anything goes. You may use any of them you wish against an attacker as long as your opponent is not already controlling it. This causes us to revisit something we discovered in chapter 24, one of my favorite concepts from the martial arts, the idea of what's available.

Remember when we learned that a true warrior never fights

over the same thing as his opponent? This can be visualized by the following.

If the bad guy grabs you by the wrist, forget that wrist. It's now *unavailable*. The last thing you want to do is waste time fighting him to regain control of that wrist. You don't want to yank your wrist trying to get it away from him. You don't want to pull on it as he tightens his hold. That would be silly. It would also be difficult to succeed because these bad guys can be very muscular and strong. Instead, let him have the wrist he seems to be so committed to, and with your other *available* hand, make a fist and release some of that potent ki you've got flowing up and out of your midsection. Throw your hips into it, give a spirit cry, and drive that available fist right through his nose.

Your goal is to plant that punch so deeply into his face that he'll feel some immediate discomfort and then release the wrist that had his attention in the first place.

For many years I've watched the what's available concept repeatedly misused on television dramas. It never fails—when the bad guy finally gets around to choking the woman he's been stalking, chasing, and pursuing throughout the whole movie, she always does the same thing. She tries with all her might to peel his fingers, often one by one, off her throat. Now, granted, when a guy has his fingers around your throat, you're on a strict time schedule. If he knows what he's doing in the choking department, you might be down to about seven seconds of air, but it's probably going to take much longer than seven seconds to remove those ten big fingers from your throat.

So what's a girl to do?

Well, you know right away that both of his hands are committed to your neck in the choke. Meanwhile, you've got lots of available weapons on your body. Two hands, two legs, two knees, two elbows, two forearms, ten fingers, and two feet. The only thing not available is your throat, and it's not one of your weapons anyway. Knowing that a choke is a lethal attack, a Force Level Four, you can go straight for the eyes on this slimeball. Poke them as hard as you can. Permanently scratch them. Blind him. Pull his eyeball out if you have to. But move fast and furious. You might have only seven seconds. Or box his ears nice and hard, poke his eyes with your index finger, and punch his solar plexus, pull him forward, and pump your thigh into his groin. Pivot your hips as you kick that thigh up. That way, your weight will be behind the move.

To punch properly, start palm up with a bent elbow, making a tight, solid fist. Pivot your hips slightly and begin straightening your elbow. Release your punch forward as far as it will go, with as much speed and force as you can muster. At the last second, twist your fist palm down to give it that added snap. Keep your wrist straight as you land the punch into your opponent. Your goal is to hit him with your first and second knuckles because these two are reinforced by the bones of your wrist.

You can also throw a vertical punch. This one pushes straight out and strikes vertically with palms and knuckles facing sideways.

And then, of course, there's my favorite, the hammer fist. This is the punch I used successfully on both the school yard bully and the jerk at my wedding. It's a punch that can be delivered by driving it across your body from the inside or the outside. Either way, your elbows stay down. Think of striking a tetherball.

A palm heel is an excellent weapon. Picture someone holding up his hand and saying, "Stop." This is the palm heel. With fingers pulled back (so you don't break them), punch out your palm heel by straightening your elbow quickly. Strike hard with the palm or fleshy, padlike area on the inside lower part of your hand.

The elbow is believed to be the strongest point on your body. It can be used in many ways and almost anywhere on your opponent. Just remember to shoot it out hard and fast. You can transition in with a sidestep up close and personal while elbowing the bad guy in the ribs. You can take the guy down on his back and drop down on his body, using your elbow as the striking object. You can elbow his spine in the same way if he's facedown. You can elbow his face if he's bent over, gasping for breath after the punch you just delivered to his solar plexus. You could stuff your elbow in his ear, his temple, or even his eye.

Also on the upper body are forearms for slamming into an opponent's face, fingers for poking eyes or pulling hair and ears, fingernails for scratching the eyes and face, and teeth for biting his nose or chomping into a finger if necessary.

Your lower body has weapons, too.

Our legs and feet can deliver mighty kicks. There are snap kicks, which are commonly used in counterattacks. This is when the leg is bent about knee-high and the foot shoots out fast, delivering the kick with the ball of the foot. (Don't ever kick with your toes or they might break.) The power here comes from the use of your midsection, the force of the hips, and the snap of the kick as it flies back into that bent position.

There are also side thrust kicks, which can be more powerful than the snap kick. This kick begins with the leg bent at the knee as if you're about to take a step up one stair. Then, with hips pivoting and the heel of your support leg pointing toward your target, thrust your kicking leg quickly sideways, pushing the knee straight with impact. Keep your eyes to the side on your opponent. The side thrust kick is an excellent one to use on your opponent's knees.

There are many additional kicks in the martial arts, but those listed here are the easiest for a beginner.

By the way, your shoes can either help or hinder your kicks. If you happen to be wearing tennis shoes, you'll have great mobility and flexibility. If you're wearing stiletto heels, you can utilize your heel and poke him with it as you kick, then remove it and beat his head in with it if you like (but please, only at a Force Level Four). Boots deliver some good power kicks as well. But many shoes, like clogs, mules, or fancy slip-ons, will present a problem for your kicks, so be sure to do the best you can and get rid of them as soon as possible. Kick them off if you must. Don't worry if you're forced to fight barefoot. This is exactly how martial artists fight all the time. Just remember not to kick with your toes.

The legs and feet can also be used for tripping and sweeping techniques. If you and your opponent are fighting and you can tell he's off balance, put your leg behind his and sweep it forward under his foot while pushing his shoulders back and sending him onto the floor.

Knees are great weapons. If you need to defend yourself by using a groin strike, try it with your knee. But as you do, grab his shirt or lapel and pull him toward you while simultaneous jerking your knee or thigh straight up into his testicles. By using your body's natural weapons to move concurrently in opposite directions, more power can be produced. It is produced when directional forces work against each other for the purpose of more power. Another example would be grabbing a bad guy by the back of the neck and pulling his head forward while at the same time slamming your other forearm into his nose. Or let's say you're standing side to side with the bad guy. You'd yank him toward you by his wrist, while simultaneously striking him in the ribs. This kind of motion delivers weighty impact every time.

Think about the natural weapons that you carry around at all times. Imagine what you could do with them if you ever needed to. Practice punching or kicking on the heavy bag at the gym or on nothing but air. Try to improve your techniques in terms of speed and force.

Think of yourself as heavily armed with weaponry.

Defense Dos and Don'ts

- Do always focus your fight on what's *available*.
- Don't hesitate to practice your punches, kicks, chops, and strikes.
- Do use elbow pokes, teeth bites, and finger jabs and pulls.
- Do think of yourself as continually armed.

 ***Power Point!*** ◄

Use your strongest weapons of mass destruction.

31

DECIDE TO STRIKE TARGETS

There is no need to fear the strong. All one needs to know is the method of overcoming them. There is special jujitsu for every strong man.

YEVGENY YEVTUSHENKO,
RUSSIAN WRITER AND ACTIVIST

Hit him where it hurts.

There are bull's-eyes all over the bad guy's body. Just as you discovered that you are endowed with weapons galore in chapter 30, this one reveals the flesh and bones targets arrayed all over your opponent's physique. If you see them, focus on them, and imagine what a power-packed strike might do to them, you can successfully hit them.

Think of it as going out for a little target practice.

First things first, let's lower our scopes to focus and point at the one target that most men would freely admit they're focused on twenty-four hours a day. The groin area. If women have heard one thing about self-defense, it's that they must kick the bad guy in the groin and run like the wind.

It's important, though, not to rely too much on groin strikes.

Since most men realize that the groin is highly sensitive and the first spot their opponent is likely to strike, they naturally treat it as their number one area to defend. And the groin is relatively easy to defend. For one thing, a man is quick to think about it, as we've already established.

Second, all a guy has to do in order to "protect the jewels" is turn his knee in. Most members of the male gender have mastered this protection technique. As soon as anything gets even close to the groin, the guy's knee is already turning in, with a rather spectacular efficiency, I might add. After all, they've been protecting this area of their anatomies all their lives.

If the woman decides to pack her knee into the bad guy's groin and he happens to turn his knee and leg inward to block her, she will then land her knee against the quadriceps running along the front of his thigh. The quads are some of his most powerful muscles. Consequently, this won't be a very effective move for her.

Don't let me dissuade you completely. The groin *is*, by far, one of the best targets to shoot for on your opponent's body, especially if you can get a clean shot. But it is important to always have other targets planned as well. A good idea is to get his focus off his groin. (Yeah, right, like that's possible.) Try planting a palm heel in his temple a few seconds before you execute the groin strike. Or stomp your stiletto heel into his foot just prior to kneeing his testicles. These surprise distraction techniques will allow you to sneak your groin strike in as his mind is registering the pain in other areas of his body.

When contemplating counterattacks, we should have many different targets in mind. Aim for ten, repeating some if necessary. Ten might sound like a lot, but if five connect where they're supposed to with power and effectiveness, and if three of those actually cause discomfort, and if one is really smacking the daylights out of him, you'll be in luck. Mix them up high to low to midsection if you can, hitting both primary and secondary targets. This will really have the guy distracted, reactive, and thinking about all the different areas of his body instead of what he had planned for you.

The primary target areas are located on the center line of your opponent:

- **The eyes.** If you hit the bad guy in the eye, it might impair his vision and cause both eyes to tear. Poking a finger in his eye can cause blindness. This target is to be used only in life-and-death circumstances.

- **The throat.** The trachea or windpipe is located inside the front of the throat. When that is hit, it can cause choking, unconsciousness, or even death. Once again, the throat is a target for serious battles only. If your life is not threatened, don't go there.

- **The groin.** When successfully executed, a kick to the groin can bring on extremely serious results, including pain, vomiting, loss of consciousness, and in very rare circumstances, death. This is a great way to drop your opponent and take off running, but again, this is a critical counterattack, and one used only for dangerous attack situations.

Now, here are some of the secondary targets you can shoot for:

- **The knees.** If you can kick someone's knee out, the fight's probably over. Any kick coming from the front or either side can cause serious damage to the bad guy's knee. Years ago, my father was talking to a neighbor on the driveway, and his two-year-old son wasn't getting the attention he wanted right then. So this little guy picked up a hammer, walked up to my dad, who was engrossed in the conversation, and he slammed that thing right into his kneecap. He didn't break my dad's knee, but he sure took him down for a minute. He finally got everybody's attention, too.

- *The kidneys.* The kidneys are in the lower back on each side. If hit significantly, they not only cause pain, they also release toxins into the bloodstream. This, too, can be considered a serious bull's-eye. A punch, palm heel, or elbow is effective here.

- *The ribs.* It takes only a few pounds of pressure to break ribs. When broken, they can be very painful, and it's often difficult to breathe. There are front and back ribs. Elbows are great weapons of choice for the ribs.

- *The temple.* A person's temples are on each side of his forehead. If they are hit with great impact, the individual will often pass out. A punch works here, but so does a shuto (karate-chop-style strike), or a palm heel.

- *The carotid arteries.* These are located on the sides of the neck. When hit very hard, a strike to this area can cause a person to pass out. The hammer fist or the shuto chop is effective on this target.

- *The bones.* Any bone on the bad guy's body that can be broken will lead to his impairment. Even if it's only a finger, it's going to help you immensely. With a broken finger, he won't be using that hand to grab you, and he won't be using that fist to punch you. If you have any type of prop nearby (that hammer, perhaps, or a two-by-four), smacking it into his hand or fingers is really going to hamper his ability to grab and hold you.

- **The solar plexus.** This is the "soft spot" high in the center of the abdomen, below the chest. It is very sensitive. When struck, it can knock the wind out of the person.

- **The nose.** When a bad guy's nose is hit with a closed fist punch or an open hand palm heel, he will usually experience watery eyes, a runny nose, or both. This can put the person out of commission for a while.

Don't forget to fight dirty. This means you're completely allowed to revert back to those free-for-all scuffles from childhood where scratching, biting, pinching were not only a matter of choice, but very effective weapons to use against your opponent. Pinch the loose skin of his inner arms or thighs. Pinch his ears. Pull his hair or his ears. Cram two of your fingers up his nose and yank it straight up.

And here's one not to forget. If he's reaching for you or grabbing for you with an open hand (not a closed fist or a punch), get ahold of that hand with both of your hands and spread two of his fingers apart hard and fast. If you direct him and put your body's strength behind it, surprisingly enough, that little move will take someone all the way to the ground. And as long as he's down there, keep him there and stuff the bottom of your shoe in his face. Another similar version is to grab his hand and pull his first two fingers all the way back—again very effective.

Whatever you do, make that total commitment that we discussed in chapter 26. It's full-force dedication at this point. Don't ever go at half speed or with hesitation or reduced energy. That will never save you against a violent attacker. Put your ki and its awesome power behind you. Go nuts as you explode with all your might.

How exhilarating it was to break bricks for the first time.

I remember the dojo falling silent as my instructor carefully placed a brick foundation on the floor. Then, he stacked support bricks in a perpendicular fashion, before finally placing the ones on top that we were supposed to break.

With our hands, mind you!

I was going along with the whole thing, but inside I was thinking, "Whoa! Are you kidding me? I'm so sure. There's no way I can drive my hand through a brick! I'll make a big fool out of myself when I get up there. Not to mention mess up my manicure."

Things seemed particularly quiet and serious right then in the dojo. One by one, we were called to the front of the class. After each brick was broken, the instructor took several minutes in between students to place the bricks in position for the next person. The men who went before me proved to be some superlative brickbreakers. They had those things crumbling all over the place. This only intensified my uneasiness.

Then it was my turn.

I took my stance. I began to breathe and slowly move through the breaking motion as part of my preparation. At that point I was just hoping that I wouldn't fracture my hand. Or that I would get lucky and put a little crack in a brick. But then my instructor said something ever so softly, but quite profound: "Your mind goes through it first. Let your mind take you all the way through."

So I took an extra moment. I tightened my mind on the task before me. I concentrated on moving *through* the brick, visualizing my hand going all the way to the bottom side of it, completely out, onto the floor beneath, and even beyond and into the earth. Several breaths later, I exploded and watched the brick fall apart before my eyes. I had gone through it. Twice. First with my mind, and then with my hand. It was amazing, on the borderline of miraculous. It was about as difficult as cutting through melted butter with a hot knife.

What a beautiful gift his words were and still are. *Your mind goes first.* Through any challenge, obstacle, danger, enemy, all aspects of self-defense, and much of life.

Send your mind through it first. All the way through.

This concept of striking through something is a good one to remember as you aim for one of the bad guy's bull's-eyes. If it's his nose, think of punching through it all the way to the back side of his head and into the wall behind him. Elbow strike through the ribs as if pushing them into the center of his body. Focus on kneeing or kicking his testicles all the way up and through his midsection and into his intestines.

Use your inner source of energy, your ki, for your explosion. Scream out as you plow through one target to the next. Breathe. See the bull's-eyes. Take aim. Fire. Throw your deliberate force into every move.

Let your mind go through first. Let it take you all the way through.

Defense Dos and Don'ts

- Don't rely completely on groin strikes.
- Do plan and contemplate the targets you'd try to hit and go through in a fight.
- Do vary your target areas from high to low and in-between.

→ *Power Point!* ←

Follow through to the bull's-eyes. Let your mind lead the way.

32

DECIDE TO FINISH THE FIGHT

Victory—a matter of staying power.

ELBERT HUBBARD,
AMERICAN PHILOSOPHER AND WRITER

It ain't over 'til it's over.

In the boxing ring, there's the count. In the race, there's the finish line. In the game, there's the clock, the bell, the buzzer, or the final out. In real life, there's you and some crazy maniac that you're still wondering about after you just managed to deliver a nifty counterattack kick, elbow, and head slam technique. Before you pat yourself on the back, however, there's something you need to consider. Is he down for the count? Or is he still coming after you?

In other words, is it really over?

In order to claim victory in a fight, it's got to be finished. This doesn't necessarily mean drastic or extreme. We're not looking for dead bodies strewn in the street, blood and guts, cries of extreme pain, or unconsciousness. But the fight must be a done deal. A completed fight is when either you or your attacker (hopefully him) quits, surrenders, stops fighting due to discomfort, or can't get back up. Then, and only then, is it over.

Someday, if you find it necessary to engage in some hard-core self-defense, you don't want to kick the bad guy in the testicles and then stand back with your hands on your hips, thinking, "There! That'll show you!" The bad guy is a class-A, number-one poor sport. He is never going to wave the white flag or offer you the congratulatory handshake. Quite the contrary, if this guy can muster the energy to get back up again, he's going to come after you harder and more brutally than ever. Now he's really ticked off. His pride is wounded, along with a few of his other parts.

In the martial arts, a self-defense technique ends with what is called the finish. This is the crowning blow. You may have gotten him good a few seconds ago, but now you're really going to put an end to this problem. The finish can be a series of final punches. It can be three or four kicks in a forward direction to push him back and away from you so that you can run. Other times, it will be a massive, final power punch while he's still on the ground. Often it will be a move to push the enemy away from you as you gain distance, preparing to escape and run.

We see the problem of the unfinished fight depicted in movies all the time. In the last scenes of the film, there seems to be an obvious winner. The hero gives the bad guy some awesome slammer that we assume has finally rid the world of this horrible character. The bad guy crashes and burns. Everyone thinks he's a goner. The hero wipes the blood from his face. He is exhausted. He staggers to his feet, studying the motionless body of his enemy on the ground. And then the hero makes his big mistake. He turns his back on his opponent, thinking the time has come for him to walk into the sunset. But to everyone's surprise, the bad guy is back. And this time with his most horrific attempt yet at total destruction of our hero.

I watched this play out in real life many years ago in Santa Monica.

Some intoxicated nitwit was standing in the middle of a busy street, kicking the doors of passing cars. Traffic was heavy, so the cars were either traveling very slowly or stuck in major gridlock. This guy was going car to car, kicking at the doors. People were too frightened to get out of their cars to stop him. He was obviously out of his mind on drugs or alcohol.

Then suddenly here came this other guy, who attempted to be somewhat of a Good Samaritan. He exited his car and actually tried to reason with the drunk and get him off the street. But, after a while, the two of them started arguing. That soon escalated into a pushing and shoving match.

Finally, each man pushed one last time. Then they backed off from each other with their hands up as if to say, "Okay, dude, that's it." Suddenly, right before my eyes, I watched it all unfold. The Good Samaritan made his big mistake. He turned his head, looked over at his car, pivoted his hips, and started to leave, thinking it was time to head off into the sunset. Through his drunken stupor, the car-kicking fool recognized his only opportunity for a crowning blow. He transitioned forward with incredible speed, coldcocking the Good Samaritan for all he was worth.

This time the nice guy went down. With a broken nose. And blood all over the place.

Never turn your back. Not before, during, or after. In fact, don't turn your head, your face, or change your vision or your focus. Unless you have multiple attackers and they're still coming at you from other directions, you must never look away from your attacker and from what you thought was the end of a fight. Remember the way a cat fights? With her eyes. The same goes for us.

The fight is over when he's sucking the dust off the ground. That's when you stop fighting and start running as fast as your legs can carry you.

Defense Dos and Don'ts

- Don't leave any unfinished business in a fight.
- Do make sure he's down-and-out, and not coming back for more.
- Don't look away until you get away.

▶ *Power Point!* ◀

Before you head for the sunset, finish up the job.

◄ 33 ►

DECIDE WHAT TO DO ABOUT GUNS AND KNIVES

Nothing in life is so exhilarating as to be shot at without result.

WINSTON CHURCHILL

You've just been caught empty-handed.

The bad guy's packing heat. Or he's got cutlery you've only seen hanging from the belt of the chef at Benihana's Japanese restaurant. This is right where your most serious decision turns into a guessing game. Our choices are more crucial than ever, with consequences so life-altering, they must be pondered with the utmost care. Unfortunately, from this vantage point, we will never fully understand all the ramifications right now. Nor will we ever be completely prepared. But if, God forbid, we ever face an assailant who's waving a knife in our face or pointing a gun at our chest, we will have a few things settled.

Fighting like a girl has just hit its highest elevation—that of life and death.

It's also hit rock bottom.

Security experts say that most of the time, people will do what they're told to do at gunpoint. The U.S. Department of Justice calculated that weapons were used in 24 percent of violent crimes in 2005. Nine percent of the time these criminals used a firearm, and 6 percent of cases involved a knife.

When considering bad guys and guns and knives, it all comes down to one thing: control.

One karate instructor–deputy sheriff explained it like this: "To the criminal, these weapons are power tools. The bad guy thinks that if he can wave a gun around or put a knife to your rib cage, he's going to have all the power and control in the situation. He thinks he'll be in charge."

The criminal uses the power tool to achieve the goal he has in mind. His goal might be to take all your money, to steal your car, to rape or sexually assault you, to take your purse and beat you in the head with it, whatever. You may or may not figure out his goal. However, if you do, and his goal is some inanimate object, you're probably going to hand it over and try to escape. If his goal involves a human being, you'll have to decide to either fight for your life or submit to his control.

With the bad guy's power tool in mind and the possibility of his crimes, a woman needs to ask herself two questions:

1. Did the bad guy pick up the power tool that day and say to himself, "Today I'm going to commit a heinous criminal act. And here's how I'll do it. With this power tool. And if the woman I choose to target tries to stop me, I'm perfectly willing to use this power tool to seriously hurt or even kill her. I'll take my chances of being tracked down by the police like the dirty dog I am. I'll risk being incarcerated for the rest of my life. I'll even go to death row. That's how important this goal is for me."

2. Or did the bad guy pick up the power tool that day and say to himself, "Today I'm going to commit a heinous criminal act. And here's how I'll do it. With this power tool. But if the woman I choose to target tries to stop me, I can always leave. I can get out of there. I don't need cops. I don't need to go to prison. I could always go find somebody else someday."

Granted, we're giving this bad guy a lot of credit for thinking. There's a good chance he doesn't do a heck of a lot of that. There's also a great possibility that he's hyped up on drugs or alcohol, so he's incapable of rational thinking. But even a half-baked, drugged-out loser knows whether he's a killer or not. He knows if and why he'll murder someone. He knows whether he'd fight to the death for that goal. He knows how much attention he's willing to stir up. He's held that gun or knife in his hand long enough, and he's wondered.

Now comes your decision. If a bad guy with a gun or a knife is trying to commit a serious crime against you, someone you love, or against your physical body, how will you react?

Let's reexamine one of our earliest questions on this journey: are you a fighter?

Better yet, are you a gambler?

Are you willing to bet that this pathetic piece of slime is just trying to threaten you or control you with that power tool? Do you think that fighting back or running away would be enough of a crimp in his plan that he'd just give up and look elsewhere for an easier victim? Or are you betting that if you don't comply with his wishes, he will use the power tool to deliberately kill you? Is this guy pointing that gun in your face in order to take something from you or make you do something? Or is he going to pull the trigger and watch you die?

This is a situation where there are no sure bets. You must make your decision as well as your own luck.

A videotape from a convenience store robbery was recently on a news broadcast. The thief pointed a gun at the store cashier, who stood behind the counter, and demanded all the money in the till. He shouted, "I've got a gun! I'll kill you, man!"

But the cashier refused. He started poking at the thief and even throwing out his fist at the bad guy.

"I'll shoot you. I'll shoot you, man." The robber must have said this half a dozen times.

Then the cashier leaped over the counter and there they were on the floor in an all-out brawl. The bad guy still had the gun, but nothing new to say other than, "I'm gonna shoot you. I swear, I'll shoot you right now."

But he never did. It sounded as if he was counting on his power tool to negotiate the transaction for him, but he knew he didn't want to take it far enough to close the deal with a bullet.

Time and again, the experts say if your attacker has a gun and you are not under his control, always run! It's estimated that only four times out of a hundred these guys actually hit someone with a bullet. Even then, it's usually not a vital organ. They also recommend that when you run, do so in a zigzag pattern—then it's even more difficult for the shooter to actually hit you. The attacker who's armed with a knife is going to have to be up close and personal in order to be a serious threat to you. If there's any kind of distance between the two of you, run with all your might.

If the attacker has the gun or knife pressed right up to your body, you have more decisions to make. Think back to chapter 9 to what you decided you'd be willing to fight for. If the bad guy is telling you what his goal is or making it clear with his actions, such as dragging you over to his car or pulling your pants down, you should know already whether you're fighting or not, regardless of the weapon he's holding. Remember, this is the decision that compelled you to think about what you were willing to die for. If he wants your car keys, throw them across the street and make him go after them as you take off running. If you have a gun or a knife pressed against you, you always have the choice of waiting for that window of opportunity that provides an escape. But don't wait too long, and never allow him to transport you in his or your vehicle. Don't ever get into the situation of being taken to that second location, scary weapon or not.

With knives there's always the chance you'll be cut. You can live with cuts to the skin. You just don't want any major arteries slashed.

With guns and knives you may think, in the words of my karate instructor, "You're screwed." But you do still have choices that will allow you to claim a certain amount of power and control in the situation.

In the following accounts, women made their choices while facing attackers with weapons. One ran. One fought. One complied. One did a combination of complying, fighting, and running. All four took their chances and survived gruesome attacks with significant success. They placed their bets and made their luck.

Sylvia encountered a knife-wielding attacker while walking to lunch one day. When this man approached her on the street, he pulled out his power tool—a knife—from under his jacket and started coming after her. She decided to run as fast as she could to get away from him. But he chased her into the street. Sylvia screamed and kept running for dear life. She wondered how long she'd be able to run at that fast pace and how she would ever get away from him entirely. The man with the knife continued fast on her heels.

Out of the blue, a motorcycle policeman came around the corner. He heard all the screaming, spotted Sylvia on the run, and saw the man chasing her with a knife. He sped to the rescue, jumped off the bike, tackled the bad guy, and arrested him.

To this day, Sylvia knows just how lucky she was to get some major backup in the middle of that serious attack. But she was quite effective at helping herself. After all, she took off running with absolutely no hesitation, and she screamed loudly enough to attract the officer's attention. In doing so, she managed to buy herself some time, create a window of opportunity, and land in the middle of some incredible good fortune.

Joan also made some courageous decisions and lucked out against an attacker with a knife.

One night, Joan pulled into her garage with no idea that a man was waiting near her condo complex. This predator had been lurking about for a while, knowing that sooner or later a lone woman would return home. As soon as Joan got out of the car, he struck. With a knife in his hand, he used it in a jabbing motion at her until she ended up back inside her car in an attempt to get away from him. He climbed on top of her. Knowing that she could be raped, stabbed, and killed, Joan went nuts and began using every ounce of strength to battle this young man. She made herself ignore the fact that he had a power tool and concentrated on getting him off her. She screamed, punched his chest, scratched his arms and face, gouged his eyes, and finally kicked him off her. A neighbor who heard the commotion went outside to investigate and saw the assailant running away.

Joan ended up with minor cuts and bruises all over her body, but she was never actually stabbed. The man got away, but police eventually found him.

Those two women were successful against assailants with power tools. They made brave choices that caused them to break through their fears with immediate movement. Our next victim's story is quite different, involving multiple attackers and multiple victims.

One night Vicki was closing the upscale restaurant in Beverly Hills where she was the assistant manager. The patrons had all left. Several other employees were still cleaning up the dining room. The front doors were locked, but the back door to the alley was propped open to allow some cool air to blow in as the dishwashers finished for the evening. Vicki was counting the money and going through the receipts when three men with guns came in through the alley.

The gunmen took everyone in the place hostage, forcing them onto the floor. Vicki found herself facedown on the dirty carpet. She thought of her young daughter at home, but she remained alert to the situation at hand. The robbers took all the money and every bit of cash and jewelry from each employee. The hostages cooperated. At one point, one of the robbers put his gun inside Vicki's mouth. Again she visualized her daughter at home, wondering if this image in her mind would be her last. She also realized she was the only woman among the captives and wondered if she would be raped. Still, she didn't move. The gunman traced her head and back with the gun, then he finally left her alone.

The gunmen took all the material goods they wanted, including food, then departed, leaving all the hostages unharmed. After waiting a few minutes, the restaurant employees finally got up from the floor and called police. The trio of criminals was never apprehended.

These guys didn't go in there to hurt, rape, or kill anybody. They went in there with power tools intended to scare everyone as they hunted for cash and other inanimate objects. This group of hostages stuck together, stayed quiet, complied with their attackers, and got very lucky as a result.

Vicki gave up a ring that had been a family heirloom, as well as other jewelry and some money. She also suffered from post-traumatic stress disorder for several months. But she was able to go home to her daughter that night.

Vicki had the advantage of having other people nearby during the ordeal. Our next victim was alone when danger struck, but still managed to keep safe.

Lesley was walking to her car in the grocery store parking lot when a man with a gun came into her life. He rushed up and put a gun one foot away from her chest and demanded her keys.

She'd already gotten her keys out in the store, so she was able to move quickly. "Sure, there you go," she said, dropping her groceries right below her on the ground and tossing the keys ten feet away. Then she took off running in the opposite direction. The man stood there for a second, took a step toward her, then went the other way to follow the keys.

Lesley ran back into the market and called 911. Police found the carjacker within two hours.

Here's another great example of a woman who was thinking on her feet. Lesley conquered her fear with movement, and because she appeared to be heading in all directions at once, she did a decent job of getting this bad guy into reactive mode. After her assertive verbal response, a surprise dumping of her groceries, a quick toss of her keys, and a sprint in another direction, he paused before going after the keys. He seemed to wonder what to do. By then she was already on the other side of the parking lot.

Even when staring at the blade of a knife or the barrel of a gun, these women managed to accomplish the number one goal in any attack—to escape.

Perhaps you're interested in power tools for your own use. If you want to incorporate such weapons into your personal security plan, here are a few things to consider.

When it comes to knives, you're probably already armed and dangerous. You've most likely got dozens in the kitchen drawers. If you're looking for something fancier, you can usually purchase some sophisticated knives at a sporting goods store.

With guns, there are some major concerns for home use. First of all, consider the children residing there with you before bringing firearms into your home. Their curiosity leads to many of the gun accidents at home. And according to the Violence Policy Center's analysis of FBI data, a woman has a better chance of dying from a handgun than using one to protect herself. It's been estimated that for every woman in the United States using a handgun to kill in self-defense, another one hundred women die in handgun homicides.

But if you do wish to purchase a gun, it's best to thoroughly research the various types available beforehand. Put in some time at a local shooting gallery or range to see which type of firearm is best suited to you and to really learn how to use it. Be sure to check with local law enforcement authorities on the gun laws in your immediate area. Regulations and restrictions vary throughout the country, from state to state, and even from city to city. You'll also need local authorities to explain exactly how you're allowed to transport a gun in your car. And don't forget to keep it in a safe place at home, especially if there are children around.

Maybe you'd prefer something with less kick. If so, there are energy weapons such as Air Tasers and stun guns. These items deliver various watts of electrical charges that affect the nervous system while shocking and jolting the person. The results can be quite physically debilitating, and except for some rare cases, not deadly.

With energy weapons, it is again necessary to check with local authorities to discuss the legalities of using them in your state and city. In some states, it's illegal to own energy weapons, and certain cities have laws against their possession and use.

Defense sprays (such as pepper spray) are common personal security weapons that many women use. When blasted into a bad guy's face, the combination of substances such as tear gas, ultraviolet dye, and hot cayenne peppers causes breathing problems, pain, teary eyes, and a runny nose. Sometimes it takes a few seconds for the effects to kick in. On rare occasions, the impact is diminished due to alcohol or drugs used by the person sprayed. Most often, though, it does the trick. It causes the bad guy enough discomfort and disability to allow the victim's escape.

Some states even have restrictions on defense sprays, so before you buy a canister, call your local police or sheriff's department and ask for the specific guidelines in your area.

Sophia always kept her pepper spray close by. Her husband, a police officer, had purchased the canister for her and attached it to her key ring. He instructed her on its use and advised her never to hesitate spraying it if she felt it was necessary.

A year and a half later, a very suspicious man with a crazed look in his eyes spotted Sophia walking in a parking lot. He stalked her, followed her into a grocery store, and came at her in a threatening manner down one of the aisles, blocking her passage, then suddenly making a move toward her.

Sophia shouted a warning that she would use her pepper spray if he came any closer. But he kept coming.

Sophia held her key ring with the pepper spray, readied herself, took aim, and fired. She nailed him, too. He stopped in his tracks and was immediately overcome by the chemicals. He went down to his knees, rubbing at his eyes, and then he stumbled to his feet and ran out the door.

When it comes down to you and an armed attacker, remember that power tools are often used only to control people. Your best bet is to escape and run, go nuts and fight, or cooperate and comply until your opportunity to fight or flee arrives. This is where your intuition and gut feelings need to kick in. Only then will you instinctively know what to do and how far your attacker plans to go with that power tool.

Defense Dos and Don'ts

- Don't think a weapon means an automatic surrender.
- Do know that his power tool might be intended as his means to control you.
- Do realize what you're willing to take a bullet or a knife slice for.

➤ *Power Point!* ◄

Evade the blade. Run from the gun.

Linda's Story

It was the day Linda's life changed forever.

She'd just been grocery shopping with her fifteen-month-old son. Afterward, while walking to her van, she noticed a man seated behind the steering wheel of a vehicle parked on the passenger side of her car. He remained there while she loaded the groceries and her baby into the van. Then he jumped out of his car and into Linda's backseat. He put a semiautomatic gun to her child's head and demanded that Linda drive.

"I instantly knew it was an Uzi," Linda later said. "I also knew that my life's purpose had just narrowed down to one thing: saving my son from whatever this guy had in mind."

Linda began to drive. The carjacker demanded her money, and Linda gave him everything in her purse.

"That's not enough," he told her. "Let's go to the ATM."

Linda didn't have her ATM card with her that day. "I know a place nearby that cashes checks," she offered. "I'll take you there." Linda actually worked at the check cashing business, and she hoped her sudden arrival with this stranger would cause her fellow employees to summon help.

Linda's son was left in the car as she and her attacker went inside.

"I walked in with this unknown man, totally acting as if I was a new customer. My coworkers immediately sensed that something was wrong, and they played along quite well. One of them even slipped into the back room to call the police. They stalled for as long as they could by having me fill out several forms."

But Linda's carjacker got nervous, because the process took so long, "We're outta here," he suddenly announced, forcing Linda to leave before the police arrived.

She made a desperate try to get into the van ahead of her armed attacker, and to lock the doors before he could climb into the vehicle. But he beat the lock and jumped in beside her in the passenger's seat.

"Got any credit cards?" he asked, forcing her to resume driving. Linda nodded, feeling the pressure of the Uzi against the side of her head.

"That's when I started driving erratically," Linda later recalled. "I was cutting people off and doing crazy things.

I tried so hard to draw attention to myself and to this horrible man. I even made a left turn right into oncoming traffic, but no one seemed to notice or care."

The carjacker forced her to pull into a large mall parking lot and demanded that she drive toward a secluded area. When he placed his hand on her thigh, Linda promptly backfisted him in the face. By now her son, still fastened into his car seat, was screaming at the top of his lungs. All of Linda's groceries had spilled onto the floor and were rolling around the car.

"At this point, I'd had it. I was feeling desperate, crazy, more aggressive, and definitely experiencing that maternal thing. I decided I was going to get my son out of this alive, even if I died in the process. I refused to back down to this criminal. He made several attempts to touch me, and I punched him every time. I didn't even care that he had a gun."

The carjacker, already upset with Linda's noncompliance and wild driving, decided to move to the backseat with her son again. But in his attempt, he slipped on some of the vegetables scattered on the floor and lost his balance. The magazine fell out of the bottom of the Uzi. He dove to the floorboards to retrieve it.

Linda recognized her sudden luck and seized the opportunity to escape. She braked, jumped out of the car, darted around to the van's sliding side door, yanked her little boy out of his car seat, and ran into a department store as fast as she could. Screaming for help, she raced straight for the fine jewelry counter where she knew heightened security measures would be in place.

The police arrived within minutes, but Linda's ordeal was far from over. Outside, the carjacker had sped off in her van with all her possessions and extensive knowledge *of her personal information from the driver's license in her purse. He knew who she was and where she lived. When Linda gave vital clues for a composite drawing of her abductor, police instantly recognized their suspect. They wanted this maniacal criminal something bad. In each of his prior cases of horrendous violence, his victim was carjacked, raped, sodomized, and mutilated. He used a knife to carve up one victim's stomach. He bit off an eyebrow of another victim. Police were now aggressively hunting for an absolute monster.*

Officers guarded Linda's home and family around the clock. Two weeks later, they finally apprehended her abductor, but by then he'd tortured a sixth victim, a police officer's wife.

In the end, this man was stopped for a traffic violation, and the police officer noticed that his appearance matched the composite. The first day of his pretrial, he pleaded guilty to his entire string of violent crimes. He was imprisoned for several life sentences for rape, sodomy, assault with a deadly weapon, theft, and carjacking. He remains behind bars, ineligible for parole for seventy years.

After the incident, Linda took various precautions to increase her personal security, including self-defense classes and carrying Mace.

◄ 34 ►

DECIDE TIMING IS EVERYTHING

Sir, how can you be so fast?
In what?
I mean, how can I get my kick fast?
Kick faster.

BRUCE LEE,
JEET KUNE DO: BRUCE LEE'S COMMENTARIES
ON THE MARTIAL WAY

Y ou just ran out of time.

We have established that fights are "quick and dirty." It's estimated that most of them are over in less than twenty seconds. By the time the bad guy pounces at you from behind, knocks you to one side, snatches your purse, and takes off running, it's over. He's gone. You're skinned-up. He's got your credit cards. You're broke. All of this in only four or five seconds.

The bottom line—time is up. Way up.

In more ways than one, really, because here we are, making our final decision and preparing to conclude our journey together. It's now that we find ourselves coming full circle, back to the very beginning of our path, and the main reason that we began making all of these decisions in the first place. Because we've got a serious time crunch on our hands! In any attack, time is always the lost commodity. In fact, at that point, there's not a bit of it left.

It's high time we did something about it, too.

This isn't necessarily the worst news for someone who's been fighting like a girl as long as you have. First of all, by making all of your decisions, you are now prepared. That constant state of readiness will save you a great deal of time should the bad guy ever show up. The fact that you are so aware will probably keep the bad guy away from you anyway. Not to mention the fact that your weapons, props, and moves are all systems set to go.

Here's the good news about attacks going down so fast. Could you imagine surviving such ordeals if they didn't?

Years ago, when my karate instructor informed us that most fights were usually over within ten to twenty seconds, I was dumbfounded. I'd obviously seen far too many movies with fight scenes that went on forever. Some of them lasted forty-five minutes. Well, no wonder women think they can't fight! Who could keep up that level of activity? Never mind the fight scenes with superpowers, the ones with regular people have characters doing things no one on earth could ever be capable of. For example, the guy who takes sixteen punches to the head but keeps getting right back up. Or the woman who runs a mile to get away from the bad guy, jumps onto a moving freight train, fights the guy on top of one of the cars (being careful to duck the tunnel at the right time), then jumps off, rolls in the dirt, swims across the river, has an underwater fight with some new energetic guy, fights the sleazy guard at the secret underground warehouse, then manages to crack the computer code to dismantle a nuclear bomb, all while simultaneously fighting four more bad guys who are trying to nuke the world!

Fighting is hard. Deathly, horrifically hard. It is, without a doubt, one of the hardest things a woman will ever have to do in her life. But it's not as hard as Hollywood's been making us believe. And not nearly as time-consuming.

Most of us could probably keep fighting for twenty seconds. High energy, lethal counterattack moves, optimum force exploding from our ki, proper weapon usage to targets on the opponent's body. All that followed by a brisk run for the hills. It might be tough to keep that going for twenty minutes, but twenty seconds? Absolutely.

So what does the female do when she's being attacked and finds herself desperate for more time? She simply buys some.

Here are some nifty ways to buy time in a fight.

- *Put a lock on it.* Yes, a bad guy can break the window of your car or bust his way into the front door of your house if he really wants to. But if you keep things locked up tight, it's going to take him a while. He'll be tiring himself out a bit in the meantime, too. This means more time on your hands to weigh your options. While he's busy with the locked door, you'll be grabbing your cell phone and your pepper spray and heading out the other exit. Or you'll be grabbing a weapon you have stashed in your car or already sliding out the other door.

- *Toss it out.* When somebody is attempting to rob you of an inanimate object, throw it several feet away and start running in the opposite direction. You'll end up with more time and distance as a result.

- *Space out.* Space equals time. The bigger the space between you and the bad guy, the more time you have to carry out your own plans of escape. Even if it's just a few feet or a couple of yards, this additional distance between you and the bad guy buys precious seconds and brings you closer to survival. Always be willing to go after more space—move, shift positions, or change locations in order to gain time. Do it quickly.

- *Expect it.* If some guy is following you through the parking lot, guess what? Something's up! Because some guy is following you through the parking lot! Go ahead and anticipate danger. Don't wait to get hit by a sledgehammer with the news! Never delay in your efforts to help or prepare yourself. Run. Sprint all the way to safety.

  I spoke with a young woman who is ready for the worst every time she walks at night alone or through a parking lot. Because of this, she carries her cell phone with 911 already dialed and her finger ready to push Send. She figures she's saving at least five to ten seconds of fumbling around with her phone pad in the dark. (If you choose to do the same, remember the dispatcher who answers your cell call could be either with your state's highway patrol or one of the police or sheriff's agencies in your area. That person will have no idea where you are, so make that the first thing you say into the phone. Some cellular phone companies are making headway in this area and beginning to trace the location of the 911 caller down to a smaller radius. Soon the technology will be able to pinpoint the location exactly.)

- *Spit it out.* Talking is another way to stretch the time. Let all that verbal self-defense kick in with major lip service. If you can talk and get him talking, you'll be buying yourself some time. If you have the gift of nonstop chitchat that drives your family and friends crazy, this may be just the ticket for you in a self-defense situation. Keep in mind, however, he might despise small talk and become even more violent, forcing you to kick his butt some other way.

So what do you do with all that extra time you just purchased? You look for opportunity elsewhere. You find your way out. You run and hide. You do anything and everything to beat him at his own game. And to beat the clock, too.

Those few seconds you gained may be your only shot for an escape.

We no longer have a sliding glass door with a screen, but when we did, I always practiced using a time trick.

The men in my family continually made their little cracks about it, because I always kept the screen door of the slider locked in the summertime. The only way I could relax and watch television on the couch at night in the heat of the summer was if the screen door was in the locked position.

"This is definitely not keeping any bad guys out," my husband would say, exasperated when he'd have to wait for me to get up off the couch and unlock the screen door so that he could come inside.

I received similar comments from my two sons.

"Mom, this little lock is pretty much worthless, you know," Ty would say.

"Yeah, Mom, anybody could just slice the screen door with a knife, unlock it, and get in here," Luke would add.

"Perhaps," I'd answer them, "but, by then, I will have gained just enough time."

They'd stare at me.

"You see, first the bad guy would try opening it, but it wouldn't open. That would take at least two or three seconds. Plus, I'd hear him messing with the screen door. Then he'd get his knife and begin to cut. Okay, another four or five seconds. Then he'd finally yank the screen open. I figure I'd have at least ten extra seconds by the time he finally got in here."

"So?"

"So that gives me my most valuable commodity in a situation with a bad guy. Time. I hear him trying the door, I'm up. I go from the couch to the fireplace in less than three seconds. I know this. I've timed it."

I watched my sons frown at each other.

"I grab the poker off the hearth and get into position. Two more seconds, tops."

Their eyebrows shoot up as they begin contemplating which of their friends' mothers would actually have timed out the emergency fireplace poker grab.

"Five seconds, and I'm armed."

There is a pause, and then I suddenly see it. This look in both of my sons' eyes. It's the one I used to have myself so many years ago when my dad took his stance in the hallway and forced me to punch him in the stomach with all my might.

"You're so weird, Mom."

"Yeah, maybe so, but I think I've got the timing down."

When it's time to fight like a girl, the timing will be everything. That's why we already put in time on this journey together to heighten our personal security and improve our overall awareness. It's the reason our decisions have been contemplated and settled, once and for all.

Because when the time comes to fight like a girl, there'll be no time left.

Defense Dos and Don'ts

- Do act quickly when an attacker strikes.
- Do plan on using time tricks to save seconds in fights.
- Don't waste a speck of time that you could be using by moving, defending, or running.

→ *Power Point!* ←

The time is now. The decisions are yours.

CONCLUSION
The Final Round

There was a woman whose life touched and inspired others so deeply that they encouraged me to begin writing this book. Her name was Roberta Happe, and though she and I never met, I feel uniquely connected to her. I've spent time with her friends. I've taught self-defense to the women who knew her. I've talked with her sweet mother and listened to fond memories.

Edie Happe said it was her daughter's fun-loving spirit that set her apart from the other kids. Roberta was beautiful, energetic, and full of life. She could play both soccer and the violin. She loved to travel. She was fascinated with weddings, brides, and bridal magazines ever since the age of four, when she first glimpsed a bride in her flowing white gown. And just as Roberta's last name would suggest (it's pronounced "happy"), her lighthearted attitude gave her every reason to look forward to life ahead. After graduating from USC, she successfully moved on to a position at a nonprofit organization that assisted the developmentally disabled. Best of all, she and a wonderful young man had made plans to become engaged.

But on the evening of February 22, 2001, after Roberta left her Los Angeles office and walked through a parking structure, she was brutally assaulted by the man who would ultimately take her life. His name was Jason Thompson, and police now believe that he'd loitered near her office building throughout the day and possibly stalked Roberta hours earlier.

No one but the killer knows exactly how it all went down. Police speculate that he approached Roberta as she sat in her car, and that somehow he was able to force his way into the passenger seat. The parking lot's security guard remembers seeing the odd presence of an unfamiliar man in Roberta's car. He even noticed the solemn look on her normally cheerful face. But these observances went unreported at the time. In a short while, Thompson's picture was recorded on an ATM surveillance video standing behind Roberta as she withdrew hundreds of dollars from her bank account. About two hours later, her body was discovered by joggers in a park in nearby Culver City. Roberta had been raped, tortured, strangled, and stabbed repeatedly with a ballpoint pen.

Police arrested Jason Thompson a week later in Michigan. He eventually entered a guilty plea and was sentenced to life in prison without the possibility of parole.

Hers was a life full of promise—cut short at just twenty-three years. This lovely young lady should've been a bride and a wife someday, a working professional, a contributor to society, a mom, a neighbor, and a friend. She should have traveled the world and grown into a wise and spirited old woman. But instead, her family was brought to its knees and an entire community was shaken with horror due to the acts resulting from one man's psychotic urge to attack, hurt, and kill.

This is why we've come all this way.

And this is why you and I must decide.

In order to honor Roberta and the countless others like her, we have to make our personal security choices. And then we have to *live* by these defense decisions. We must decide for our daughters' sakes. For our mothers, grandmothers, and sisters. We'll do it for our best friends and the girls in the office. For the women in our lives who teach us what's really important in this world. And for the ones who keep us smiling and laughing all day long.

And yes, most of all, we'll do it for ourselves.

It's time to get going, to start moving, to step it up a bit, and to mix things around some. Actually, it's time to change the world, but we realize our only chance of that is to change us—from the inside out.

Now you know exactly what to do. You understand what it means to fight like a girl with everything you've got. Your body knows how to protect itself to the final round, and your mind is leading the way. You've learned the dangers of indecisiveness. You've discovered who's out there and what they want from you. You know what you're made of and what you're willing to fight for. Your confidence is visually apparent to everyone. Your awareness skills have begun to empower you with new strength. Your fighter within has been called up for active duty, and this time she's got ki. You're determined to move, to mad-dog, to make rules and draw lines. You're committed to your intuitions and to improving your verbal self-defense. You're getting in shape. You're getting ready. You're staying *active* and in the game. You're relying on yourself as your own private bodyguard, but when necessary you won't hesitate to swing a baseball bat or a cast-iron frying pan, either. You're prepared to "go nuts," to be quick and dirty about it, and to engage in some audacious behavior in order to take full control of your personal security.

Why on earth would you want to do this any other way?

Someday, before the fight breaks out, you'll smell trouble when it hasn't even started brewing. Prior to any flying punches, you'll spot impending danger as it's coming from a mile away. On that day, you'll thank your decisions for working on your behalf. Then you'll know you've been fighting like a girl, and that this is a fight that will save your life.

Resources

Government Agencies

U.S. Department of Justice
950 Pennsylvania Avenue, NW
Washington, D.C. 20530-0001
(202) 514-2000
www.usdoj.gov
e-mails: AskDOJ@usdoj.gov

Includes the Office on Violence Against Women, (202) 307-6026, and the Office for Victims of Crime, (202) 307-5983.

Federal Bureau of Investigation (FBI)
J. Edgar Hoover Building
935 Pennsylvania Avenue, NW
Washington, D.C. 20535-0001
(202) 324-3000
www.fbi.gov

See the list of field offices nationwide for local addresses and phone numbers.

Public and Victim Assistance

National Center for Victims of Crime (NCVC)

2000 M Street, NW

Suite 480

Washington, D.C. 20036

(202) 467-8700

www.ncvc.org

> *Download the Stalking Fact Sheet, the Campus Dating Fact Sheet, and the Teen Dating Violence Fact Sheet*

Help Line: 1(800) FYI-CALL

Victims can also e-mail: gethelp@ncvc.org

> *Includes the Stalking Resource Center, the Dating Violence Resource Center, and the Teen Victim Project.*

Information and Assistance with Rape and Sexual Assault

Rape, Abuse and Incest National Network (RAINN)

2000 L Street, NW

Suite 406

Washington, D.C. 20036

(202) 544-1034

www.rainn.org

National Sexual Assault Hot Line: 1 (800) 656-HOPE (4673)

e-mail: info@rainn.org

> *Check out the statistics.*

Rape Treatment Center

Santa Monica—UCLA Medical Center

1250 Sixteenth Street

Santa Monica, California 90404

(310) 319-4000

www.911rape.org

National Sexual Violence Resource Center (NSVRC)

123 North Enola Drive

Enola, Pennsylvania 17025

1 (877) 739-3895

www.nsvrc.org

resources@nsvrc.org

Missing or Victimized Children

National Center for Missing and Exploited Children

Charles B. Wang International Children's Building

699 Prince Street

Alexandria, Virginia 22314-3175

(703) 274-3900

www.ncmec.org

Hot Line: 1 (800) THE-LOST (1 [800] 843-5678)

Domestic Abuse

National Domestic Violence Hotline

P.O. Box 161810

Austin, Texas 78716

24-Hour Hot Line: 1 (800) 799-SAFE (7233)

Car and Highway Safety

California Highway Patrol (CHP)

CHP Headquarters

P.O. Box 942898

Sacramento, California 94298-0001

(916) 657-7261

www.chp.ca.gov

For nonemergency questions: 1 (800) TELL-CHP

Home Safety

Neighborhood Watch Program
National Sheriffs' Association
1450 Duke Street
Alexandria, Virginia 22314-3490
(703) 836-7827
www.usaonwatch.org
e-mail: Info@usaonwatch.org

Firearms Training

American Defense Enterprises
12021 Wilshire Boulevard
Suite 774 (mailing address only)
Los Angeles, California 90025
(310) 514-1020
www.AmericanDefenseEnterprises.com
> *Extensive firearms training for members of the military, law enforcement,
> and special forces, as well as ordinary civilians and women.*

Airline, Travel, and Hotel Security

Federal Aviation Administration (FAA)
800 Independence Avenue, SW
Washington, D.C. 20591
FAA Safety Hot Line: 1 (800) 255-1111
www.faa.gov

Transportation Security Administration (TSA)
U.S. Department of Homeland Security
Arlington, Virginia 22202
Consumer Response Center: 1 (866) 289-9673
www.tsa.gov

TSA-ContactCenter@dhs.gov

Download the Permitted and Prohibited Items List for air travel.

Gutsy Women Travel, LLC
101 Limekiln Pike
Glenside, Pennsylvania 19038
1 (866) IM-GUTSY (1 [866] 464-8879)
www.gutsywomentravel.com

See the Serious Safety Tips for Women Travelers.

SafePlace Corporation
3518 Silverside Road
22 The Commons
Wilmington, Delaware 19810
Customer Relations: (302) 479-9000
www.safeplace.com
info@safeplace.com

This company tests and certifies hotels for safety.

Martial Arts, American Karate, and Self-Defense Information

Upland Martial Arts Center
Sensei Chris Pellitteri
1386 East Foothill Boulevard
Suite L
Upland, California 91786
(909) 931-4623
www.uplandmacenter.com

Look for "The Martial Arts Info Guide," Total Nunchaku training DVDs, and various printouts.

Impact Bay Area
146 East 12th Street
Oakland, California 94606

(510) 208-0474

www.impactbayarea.org

info@impactbayarea.org

> *This is the group whose members train by pounding on a man in fully padded armor.*

Defense Weapons (including pepper spray, Mace, stun guns, batons, personal alarms, and spy gear)

www.defendingwomen.com

www.urbansafetysupplies.com

www.encomsafety.com

> *Order defense gear online.*

For information on Roberta Happe or to make a donation, please contact:

The Roberta Happe Memorial Fund

c/o Vista Federal Credit Union

500 South Buena Vista Street

Burbank, California 91521-7370

The Roberta Happe Memorial Internship

Frank D. Lanterman Regional Center

3303 Wilshire Boulevard, Suite 700

Los Angeles, California 90010

www.lanterman.org

Crescenta Valley High School Scholarship/Roberta Happe

Crescenta Valley High School

2900 Community Avenue

La Crescenta, California 91214

www.cvfalcons.com

Additional Reading

Kathleen Baty, *A Girl's Gotta Do What a Girl's Gotta Do: The Ultimate Guide to Living Safe & Smart*. Emmaus, PA: Rodale, 2003.

Gavin de Becker, *Fear Less: Real Truth About Risk, Safety, and Security in a Time of Terrorism*. New York: Little, Brown and Company, 2002.

Gavin de Becker, *The Gift of Fear: Survival Signals That Protect Us from Violence*. New York: Dell Publishing, 1997.

Gavin de Becker, *Protecting the Gift: Keeping Children and Teenagers Safe (and Parents Sane)*. New York: The Dial Press, 1999.

John Corcoran and John Graden, *The Ultimate Martial Arts Q & A Book: 750 Expert Answers to Your Essential Questions*. New York: Contemporary Books, 2001.

Simon Harrison, *Kung Fu for Girls: Self-Defense with Style*. Philadelphia: Quirk Books, 2004.

Joe Hyams, *Zen in the Martial Arts*. New York: A Jeremy P. Tarcher/Putnam Book, 1979.

Jeet Kune Do: Bruce Lee's Commentaries on the Martial Way, John Little, ed. Boston: Tuttle Publishing, 1997.

Chuck Norris, *The Secret Power Within: Zen Solutions to Real Problems.* New York: Broadway Books, 1996.

Sun Tzu, *The Art of War: Complete Texts and Commentaries.* Trans. by Thomas Cleary. Boston: Shambhala Publications, Inc., 2000.

Notes

Introduction

2 *statistics indicate that every two and a half minutes, someone is raped or sexually assaulted . . .* "Statistics: Key Facts," Rape, Abuse, and Incest National Network (RAINN), www.rainn.org/statistics/index.html (accessed February 2, 2007). Data from Shannan M. Catalano. "National Crime Victimization Survey: Criminal Victimization, 2005" (U.S. Department of Justice, Bureau of Justice Statistics).

3 *Webster's describes self-defense as "the right to defend oneself with whatever force is reasonably necessary . . ."* Webster's New World College Dictionary, s.v. "self-defense."

6 *With almost 2.5 million women victimized in personal crimes . . .* Cathy Maston and Patsy Klaus, "Criminal Victimization in the United States," 2005 Statistical Tables, table 2 (U.S. Department of Justice, Bureau of Justice Statistics), www.ojp.usdoj.gov/bjs/pub/pdf/cvus05.pdf (accessed February 2, 2007).

3. Know Your Enemy: The Statistics

20 *In 2005, most violence occurred during the day . . .* U.S. Department of Justice, Bureau of Justice Statistics, "Crime Characteris-

tics, 2005," www.ojp.usdoj.gov/bjs/cvict_c.htm (accessed February 2, 2007).

20 *but two-thirds of rapes and sexual assaults took place* . . .   DOJ, BJS, "Crime Characteristics, 2005," www.ojp.usdoj.gov/bjs/cvict_c.htm (accessed February 2, 2007).

21 *the highest percentage of rapes occurring in the months of* . . .   U.S. Department of Justice, Federal Bureau of Investigation, "Forcible Rape-Crime in the United States, 2004," www.fbi.gov/ucr/cius_04/offenses_ reported/violent_crime/forcible_rape.html (accessed February 2, 2007).

21 *The FBI reports more than two million unlawful entries to commit a felony or theft annually* . . .   U.S. Department of Justice, Federal Bureau of Investigation, "Burglary-Crime in the United States, 2004," www.fbi.gov/ucr/cius_04/offenses_reported/property_crime/burglary .html (accessed February 2, 2007).

21 *Violent attackers often hit close to home* . . .   Maston and Klaus, "Criminal Victimization in the United States," 2005 Statistical Tables, table 61 (DOJ, BJS), www.ojp.usdoj.gov/bjs/pub/pdf/cvus05.pdf (accessed February 2, 2007).

21 *Other common sites were streets, schools* . . .   Maston and Klaus, "Criminal Victimization in the United States," 2005 Statistical Tables, table 61 (DOJ, BJS), www.ojp.usdoj.gov/bjs/pub/pdf/cvus05.pdf (accessed February 2, 2007).

22 *When it comes to rape and sexual assault, more than 36 percent take place* . . .   Maston and Klaus, "Criminal Victimization in the United States," 2005 Statistical Tables, table 61 (DOJ, BJS), www.ojp.usdoj .gov/bjs/pub/pdf/cvus05.pdf (accessed February 2, 2007).

22 *while almost 24 percent take place in the home of a friend, neighbor, or relative* . . .   Maston and Klaus, "Criminal Victimization in the United States," 2005 Statistical Tables, table 61 (DOJ, BJS), www.ojp .usdoj.gov/bjs/pub/pdf/cvus05.pdf (accessed February 2, 2007).

22 *Rapes by intimates* . . . *often take place at or near the victim's home* . . .   Maston and Klaus, "Criminal Victimization in the United States," 2005 Statistical Tables, table 63 (DOJ, BJS), www.ojp.usdoj.gov/ bjs/pub/pdf/cvus05.pdf (accessed February 2, 2007).

22 *Rapes by strangers often occur . . .*   Maston and Klaus, "Criminal Victimization in the United States," 2005 Statistical Tables, table 63 (DOJ, BJS), www.ojp.usdoj.gov/bjs/pub/pdf/cvus05.pdf (accessed February 2, 2007).

22 *In 2005, more than 16 percent of violent crimes in the United States occurred on the job . . .*   Maston and Klaus, "Criminal Victimization in the United States," 2005 Statistical Tables, table 64 (DOJ, BJS), www.ojp .usdoj.gov/bjs/pub/pdf/cvus05.pdf (accessed February 2, 2007).

22 *the occupations most vulnerable to attacks are . . .*   Detis T. Duhart, "Violence in the Workplace, 1993–99" (U.S. Department of Justice, Bureau of Justice Statistics), www.ojp.usdoj.gov/bjs/pub/pdf/vw99.pdf (accessed February 2007).

23 *Leisure activity by victims away from home accounted for 22 percent of violent attacks and 29 percent . . .*   Maston and Klaus, "Criminal Victimization in the United States," 2005 Statistical Tables, table 64 (DOJ, BJS), www.ojp.usdoj.gov/bjs/pub/pdf/cvus05.pdf (accessed February 2, 2007).

23 *Activities at home brought about more than 21 percent of violent attacks and almost 25 percent . . .*   Maston and Klaus, "Criminal Victimization in the United States," 2005 Statistical Tables, table 64 (DOJ, BJS), www.ojp.usdoj.gov/bjs/pub/pdf/cvus05.pdf (accessed February 2, 2007).

24 *African-American women are murdered at a rate almost three times higher . . .*   Marty Langley, "When Men Murder Women: An Analysis of 2004 Homicide Data" (Violence Policy Center), www.vpc.org/studies/ wmmw2006.pdf (accessed February 2, 2007).

24 *More than 48 percent of the rape and sexual assault offenders in 2005 were black men . . .*   Maston and Klaus, "Criminal Victimization in the United States," 2005 Statistical Tables, table 40 (DOJ, BJS), www.ojp.usdoj.gov/bjs/pub/pdf/cvus05.pdf (accessed February 2, 2007).

24 *and almost 33 percent were white . . .*   Maston and Klaus, "Criminal Victimization in the United States," 2005 Statistical Tables, table 40 (DOJ, BJS), www.ojp.usdoj.gov/bjs/pub/pdf/cvus05.pdf (accessed February 2, 2007).

24 *American Indian and Alaskan Native women are more likely to report* . . . Patricia Tjaden and Nancy Thoennes, "Full Report of the Prevalence, Incidence, and Consequences of Violence Against Women," from the National Violence Against Women Survey, 2000 (U.S. Department of Justice, National Institutes of Justice), www.ncjrs.gov/pdffiles1/nij/183781 .pdf (accessed February 2, 2007).

24 *Hispanic women are less likely than non-Hispanics to report a rape* . . . Tjaden and Thoennes, "Full Report of the Prevalence, Incidence, and Consequences of Violence Against Women," from the National Violence Against Women Survey, 2000 (DOJ, NIJ), www.ncjrs.gov/ pdffiles1/nij/183781.pdf (accessed February 2, 2007).

24 *reports thirty-eight thousand carjackings per year* . . . Patsy Klaus, "National Crime Victimization Survey: Carjacking, 1993–2002" (U.S. Department of Justice, Bureau of Justice Statistics), www.ojp.usdoj.gov/ bjs/pub/pdf/c02.pdf (accessed February 2, 2007).

24 *Ninety-three percent take place in cities and suburbs* . . . Klaus, "National Crime Victimization Survey: Carjacking, 1993–2002" (DOJ, BJS), www.ojp.usdoj.gov/bjs/pub/pdf/c02.pdf (accessed February 2, 2007).

24 *68 percent happen at night* . . . Klaus, "National Crime Victimization Survey: Carjacking, 1993–2002" (DOJ, BJS), www.ojp.usdoj.gov/bjs/pub/ pdf/c02.pdf (accessed February 2, 2007).

24 *74 percent of the time weapons are used* . . . Klaus, "National Crime Victimization Survey: Carjacking, 1993–2002" (DOJ, BJS), www.ojp.usdoj .gov/bjs/pub/pdf/c02.pdf (accessed February 2, 2007).

24 *and more than half the time* . . . Klaus, "National Crime Victimization Survey: Carjacking, 1993–2002" (DOJ, BJS), www.ojp.usdoj.gov/bjs/ pub/pdf/c02.pdf (accessed February 2, 2007).

25 *one in twelve women will be stalked* . . . "Stalking Fact Sheet" (NCVC, Stalking Resource Center), www.ncvc.org/src/AGP.Net/components/ DocumentViewer/Download.aspxnz?DocumentID=40616 (accessed February 2, 2007). Data from Patricia Tjaden and Nancy Thoennes, "Stalking in America, 1998" (U.S. Department of Justice, National Institutes of Justice).

25 *77 percent know their stalkers . . .* "Stalking Fact Sheet" (NCVC, Stalking Resource Center), www.ncvc.org/src/AGP.Net/components/ DocumentViewer/Download.aspxnz?DocumentID=40616 (accessed February 2, 2007). Data from Tjaden and Thoennes, "Stalking in America, 1998" (DOJ, NIJ).

25 *13 percent of female students report being stalked at school . . .* "Stalking Fact Sheet" (NCVC, Stalking Resource Center), www.ncvc .org/src/AGP.Net/components/DocumentViewer/Download.aspxnz? DocumentID=40616 (accessed February 2, 2007). Data from Bonnie S. Fisher, Francis T. Cullen, and Michael G. Turner, "The Sexual Victimization of College Women, 2000" (U.S. Department of Justice, National Institutes of Justice).

25 *Eighty percent of the victims know their stalkers . . .* "Stalking Fact Sheet" (NCVC, Stalking Resource Center), www.ncvc.org/src/AGP.Net/ components/DocumentViewer/Download.aspxnz?DocumentID=40616 (accessed February 2, 2007). Data from Fisher, Cullen, and Turner, "The Sexual Victimization of College Women, 2000" (DOJ, NIJ).

25 *Fifty-nine percent of stalked females are victimized by an intimate partner . . .* "Stalking Fact Sheet" (NCVC, Stalking Resource Center), www.ncvc.org/src/AGP.Net/components/DocumentViewer/Download .aspxnz?DocumentID=40616 (accessed February 2, 2007). Data from Tjaden and Thoennes, "Stalking in America, 1998" (DOJ, NIJ).

25 *The FBI reports a forcible rape in this country every five minutes . . .* U.S. Department of Justice, Federal Bureau of Investigation, "Crime Clock—Crime in the United States, 2004," www.fbi.gov/ucr/cius_04/ summary/crime_clock/ (accessed February 2, 2007).

25 *For more than two decades, experts have either quoted or debated a Ms. magazine study . . .* Christina Hoff Sommers, "Researching the 'Rape Culture' of America." Analysis of the one-in-four figure and data from a 1985 *Ms.* magazine report by Mary Koss, www.leaderu.com/ real/ri9502/sommers.html (accessed February 2, 2007).

25 *Current statistics estimate that one in six American women . . .* Rape, Abuse, and Incest National Network (RAINN), "Statistics: The

Victims of Sexual Assault (2004)," www.rainn.org/statistics/victims-of-sexual-assault.html (accessed February 2, 2007).

26 *54 percent of rape and attempted rape victims are under eight-een* . . . Tjaden and Thoennes, "Full Report of the Prevalence, Inci-dence, and Consequences of Violence Against Women," from the National Violence Against Women Survey, 2000 (DOJ, NIJ), www.ncjrs .gov/pdffiles1/nij/183781.pdf (accessed February 2, 2007).

26 *almost 22 percent of those are under the age of twelve* . . . Tjaden and Thoennes, "Full Report of the Prevalence, Incidence, and Conse-quences of Violence Against Women," from the National Violence Against Women Survey, 2000 (DOJ, NIJ), www.ncjrs.gov/pdffiles1/nij/ 183781.pdf (accessed February 2, 2007).

26 *More than five million cases of intimate partner violence are carried out* . . . "Intimate Partner Violence: Fact Sheet" (Centers for Disease Control and Prevention, National Center for Injury Prevention and Con-trol), www.cdc.gov/ncipc/factsheets/ipvfacts.htm (accessed February 2, 2007). Data from Patricia Tjaden and Nancy Thoennes, "Extent, Nature, and Consequences of Intimate Partner Violence: Findings," from the Na-tional Violence Against Women Survey, 2000 (U.S. Department of Justice, National Institutes of Justice).

26 *Seventy-three percent of rape and sexual assault victims are at-tacked by non-strangers* . . . Shannan M. Catalano, "Criminal Victim-ization, 2005," National Crime Victimization Survey (U.S. Department of Justice: Bureau of Justice Statistics), www.ojp.usdoj.gov/bjs/pub/pdf/ cv05.pdf (accessed February 2, 2007).

26 *In 38 percent of those, the offender is described as a friend* . . . Catalano, "Criminal Victimization, 2005," National Crime Victimization Survey (DOJ, BJS), www.ojp.usdoj.gov/bjs/pub/pdf/cv05.pdf (accessed February 2, 2007).

26 *while in 28 percent of those cases it is an intimate* . . . Catalano, "Criminal Victimization, 2005," National Crime Victimization Survey (DOJ, BJS), www.ojp.usdoj.gov/bjs/pub/pdf/cv05.pdf (accessed Febru-ary 2, 2007).

26 *Of rapes that occur on college campuses, nine out of ten are*

committed by an individual known ... Bonnie S. Fisher, Francis T. Cullen, and Michael G. Turner, "The Sexual Victimization of College Women, 2000" (U.S. Department of Justice, National Institutes of Justice), www.ncjrs.gov/pdffiles1/nij/182369.pdf (accessed February 2, 2007).

27 *Victims were able to help themselves by using protective measures ...* Maston and Klaus, "Criminal Victimization in the United States," 2005 Statistical Tables, table 72 (DOJ, BJS), www.ojp.usdoj.gov/bjs/pub/pdf/cvus05.pdf (accessed February 2, 2007).

27 *Victims of rape and sexual assault fought back and avoided injury ...* Maston and Klaus, "Criminal Victimization in the United States," 2005 Statistical Tables, table 73 (DOJ, BJS), www.ojp.usdoj.gov/bjs/pub/pdf/cvus05.pdf (accessed February 2, 2007).

27 *They managed to scare off their attackers ...* Maston and Klaus, "Criminal Victimization in the United States," 2005 Statistical Tables, table 73 (DOJ, BJS), www.ojp.usdoj.gov/bjs/pub/pdf/cvus05.pdf (accessed February 2, 2007).

27 *they escaped in 23 percent of cases ...* Maston and Klaus, "Criminal Victimization in the United States," 2005 Statistical Tables, table 73 (DOJ, BJS), www.ojp.usdoj.gov/bjs/pub/pdf/cv05.pdf (accessed February 2, 2007).

27 *Firearms are used in 70 percent of murders ...* Catalano, "Criminal Victimization, 2005," National Crime Victimization Survey (DOJ, BJS), www.ojp.usdoj.gov/bjs/pub/pdf/cv05.pdf (accessed February 2, 2007). Data from the Federal Bureau of Investigation, "Murder-Crime in the United States, 2004."

27 *In 2005, rape and sexual assault victims were confronted by unarmed attackers ...* Catalano, "Criminal Victimization, 2005," National Crime Victimization Survey (DOJ, BJS), www.ojp.usdoj.gov/bjs/pub/pdf/cv05.pdf (accessed February 2, 2007).

27 *Knives and firearms were each used 3 percent of the time ...* Catalano, "Criminal Victimization, 2005," National Crime Victimization Survey (DOJ, BJS), www.ojp.usdoj.gov/bjs/pub/pdf/cv05.pdf (accessed February 2, 2007).

5. The Big Fears

45 *It is illegal in all fifty states and a felony on the first offense in fifteen of them . . .* "Stalking Fact Sheet" (NCVC, Stalking Resource Center), www.ncvc.org/src/AGP.Net/components/DocumentViewer/Download.a spxnz?DocumentID=40616 (accessed February 2, 2007).

45 *Most stalkers are men and most women know who their stalkers are . . .* "Stalking Fact Sheet" (NCVC, Stalking Resource Center), www.ncvc.org/src/AGP.Net/components/DocumentViewer/Download.a spxnz?DocumentID=40616 (accessed February 2, 2007). Data based on Patricia Tjaden and Nancy Thoennes, "Stalking in America, 1998" (U.S. Department of Justice, National Institutes of Justice,).

47 *For example, robbery victims often find themselves face-to-face . . .* Catalano, "Criminal Victimization, 2005," National Crime Victimization Survey (DOJ, BJS), www.ojp.usdoj.gov/bjs/pub/pdf/cv05.pdf (accessed February 2, 2007).

47 *rape and sexual assault victims are less likely . . .* Catalano, "Criminal Victimization, 2005," National Crime Victimization Survey (DOJ, BJS), www.ojp.usdoj.gov/bjs/pub/pdf/cv05.pdf (accessed February 2, 2007).

48 *shocking increases in the popularity of some hazardous club drugs . . .* National Institute on Drug Abuse, "Community Drug Alert Bulletin—Club Drugs," www.drugabuse.gov/ClubAlert/ClubDrugAlert.html (accessed February 2, 2007). Data from a 2003 Monitoring the Future study.

49 *almost 62 percent of rapes and sexual assaults never being recounted . . .* Maston and Klaus. "Criminal Victimization in the United States," 2005 Statistical Tables, table 91 (DOJ, BJS), www.ojp.usdoj.gov/bjs/pub/pdf/cvus05.pdf (accessed February 2, 2007).

49 *women with childhood histories that include sexual abuse . . .* Statistics from the Pennsylvania Coalition Against Rape, www.pcar.org/about_sa/stats.html (accessed February 2, 2007). Data from L. L. Merrill, et al., "Childhood Abuse and Sexual Revictimization in a Female Navy Recruit Sample" (Naval Health Research Center, 1997).

7. Levels of Force

63 *"The punches will not wait for you . . ."* *Jeet Kune Do: Bruce Lee's Commentaries on the Martial Way,* ed. by John Little (Boston: Tuttle Publishing, 1997), p. 165.

14. Decide to Live Life in a State of Awareness

113 *"on one's guard, vigilant, knowing or realizing, conscious and informed . . ."* *Webster's New World College Dictionary,* 4th ed., s.v. "aware."

33. Decide What to Do About Guns and Knives

245 *weapons were used in 24 percent of violent crimes in 2005 . . .* Shannan M. Catalano, "Criminal Victimization, 2005," National Crime Victimization Survey (DOJ, BJS), www.ojp.usdoj.gov/bjs/pub/pdf/cv05.pdf (accessed February 2, 2007).

245 *Nine percent of the time, these criminals used a firearm and 6 percent of cases involved a knife . . .* Catalano, "Criminal Victimization, 2005," National Crime Victimization Survey (DOJ, BJS), www.ojp.usdoj .gov/bjs/pub/pdf/cv05.pdf (accessed February 2, 2007).

252 *using a handgun to kill in self-defense, another one hundred women die . . .* Karen Brock, "A Deadly Myth: Women, Handguns, and Self-Defense, 1998" (Violence Policy Center), www.vpc.org/studies/myth.htm (accessed February 2, 2007).